Philosophy of Mind in Sixth-Century China

Diana Y. Paul

Philosophy of Mind in Sixth-Century China

Paramārtha's 'Evolution of Consciousness'

Stanford University Press, Stanford, California
1984

Stanford University Press
Stanford, California

Printed in the United States of America
ISBN 0-8047-1187-9
LC 82-42862

Acknowledgments

I SHOULD LIKE to acknowledge all the colleagues who have helped toward the completion of this book. The principal scholars who have influenced my own work and continue to provide intellectual support for another proposed study of Paramārtha are my Japanese colleagues, all currently working on their own manuscripts on Paramārtha, whom I had the good fortune to consult and to discuss my ideas with while in Japan. Professor Jikido Takasaki kindly shared his own research with me during many discussions at Tokyo University. Professor Gadjin Nagao, who is completing a translation of the first two chapters of the *Mahāyāna-saṃgraha*, the culmination of a ten-year research project, spent many long hours going through my work and making helpful suggestions. Professor Masaaki Hattori, whose book on Yogācāra is the clearest exposition of Yogācāra I know, carefully went through my entire manuscript while I was staying near Kyoto University.

To my many other colleagues—Yuichi Kajiyama, Lewis Lancaster, Al Dien, Douglas Daye, Julius Moravcsik, Whalen Lai, Alan Sponberg, Noriaki Hakamaya, and many, many others—I wish to extend my thanks for assistance, critical comments, and support through the long years of this project. I owe my deepest gratitude to George Hart, my colleague and former Sanskrit instructor, for the many, many days he read Sanskrit with me and for opening my world to the marvels of computer technology.

He is my very special friend and colleague, and working with him continues to be a delight.

My research assistants Graeme Johnson, Kenneth Tanaka, and most especially, Elizabeth Kenney, who worked many long hours poring through the various drafts of this book, were responsible for allowing me to meet my deadlines. Gigi Wang and Jon Atkin were my computer assistants whose meticulous attention to detail on the computer made preparing this book an easier task. My editor, Shirley Taylor, labored over the final draft with skill and care.

Early versions of parts of this work appeared in the *Journal of Indian Philosophy*, the *Journal of the International Association of Buddhist Studies*, and *Philosophy East and West*. I am grateful to the journals, and to the University Press of Hawaii, publisher of *Philosophy East and West*, for permission to incorporate this material.

The Translations Program of the National Endowment for the Humanities sponsored my research in the summer of 1977 and during my sabbatical leave in 1981-82. I am particularly grateful to the program's director, Susan A. Mango, for her assistance. The Center for East Asian Studies at Stanford University awarded a travel grant to Japan and provided research assistant funds to assist in the final stages of my project. The Department of Religious Studies, Stanford University, also provided funds for preparation of the manuscript, and the Office of the Dean, Humanities and Sciences, provided computer funds. Without their generous support, the publication of this work would have been virtually impossible.

D.Y.P.

Contents

Philosophy of Mind in Sixth-Century China

Introduction

BY THE SIXTH century A.D., Buddhism had been in existence for over one thousand years in India, its land of origin, and had been transplanted in China for six hundred years or more. In both north and south China, Buddhism had permeated intellectual thought, institutions, and the arts. Much of the Buddhist canon had been translated from Indian and Central Asian languages into Chinese, and written commentaries by Chinese monks were well established as part of the emergence of distinctly Chinese interpretations of Indian Buddhist ideas. By the time Paramārtha arrived as a missionary-monk, in 546, south China had become immersed in theories of Buddha-nature, of the perfectability of human existence, and was beginning to develop its own schools: San-lun or the Three Treatises School (of Mādhyamika); Nieh-pan or the Nirvāṇa school; and Ch'eng-shih or the Satya-siddhi school centered on Abhidharma doctrine. But Indian *sūtras* and *śāstras* were still regarded as dogma that could not be tampered with, and intentional innovations in Buddhist philosophy by the Chinese were rare.

Of the many translators who carried the Buddhist doctrine to China, Paramārtha ranks as the translator par excellence of the sixth century, on a level with Kumārajīva, the brilliant translator who preceded him in the fifth century in north China, and with Hsüan-tsang who succeeded him in the seventh century. Although Paramārtha, unlike these other two great translators, did not enjoy the sustained imperial patronage that would have allowed him the security and stability to translate the huge number of manuscripts he brought with him to China, he nonetheless, in spite of his circumstances, succeeded in translating some of the most difficult texts in the Buddhist corpus.

Paramārtha is a key figure in the introduction of philosophical ideas that would subsequently excite the Chinese imagination to develop the great Buddhist philosophical systems compatible with Chinese culture. He paved the way for the creative explosion of the glorious schools of Sui and T'ang Buddhism: Hua-yen, T'ien-t'ai, Fa-hsiang, and Ch'an. T'ien-t'ai and Hua-yen developed on the basis of Paramārtha's translations and as a response to his She-lun school. Their principal masters (Chih-i of T'ien-t'ai school and Fa-tsang of Hua-yen school) had thoroughly studied Paramārtha's main works, and these texts inspired their creation of systematic and distinctively Chinese versions of the ideas that Paramārtha transmitted. Ch'an Buddhism, too, used Paramārtha's corpus as a foundation for its attempts to reform Buddhism during the T'ang dynasty.

Hsüan-tsang, who in many ways eclipsed Paramārtha, was nonetheless greatly influenced by him and was instructed by some of Paramārtha's disciples. In order to evaluate the quality of Paramārtha's translations, he was obliged to travel to India to obtain Sanskrit manuscripts. On the basis of his evaluations and retranslations of many of these Yogācāra texts, Hsüan-tsang established the Fa-hsiang school of Yogācāra during the T'ang dynasty.

These great schools of Chinese Buddhism no longer merely imitated Indian Buddhist thought and approaches. They became formidable intellectual forces in the Sui and T'ang dynasties on the basis of the work of Chinese thinkers. Fa-hsiang was indebted to Paramārtha's translations of important Yogācāra tenets; and the literature of other schools also was influenced to some extent by Paramārtha's pioneering work.

The translations that earned Paramārtha his status as a preeminent translator are almost exclusively Yogācāra. His most renowned translations essential to the traditions of Chinese Buddhism were of the works of the two great fourth-century Indian Yogācārin philosophers, the brothers Asaṅga and Vasubandhu: the *Abhidharma-kośa*, *Madhyānta-vibhāga*, *Viṃśatikā*, and *Triṃśikā* by Vasubandhu; and the *Mahāyāna-saṃgraha* and portions of the *Yogācārabhūmi* by Asaṅga. In addition, Paramārtha's most complex and undoubtedly most significant work was his translation of Vasubandhu's *Mahāyāna-saṃgraha-bhāṣya* (*She ta-sheng lun shih*), a commentary on Asaṅga's compendium of Yogācāra doctrine. It was this text that served as the foundation for the She-lun school.

Asaṅga and Vasubandhu's major treatises were systematized in the Indian school of Buddhism known as Yogācāra or Vijñānavāda. Their writings were interpretations of the teaching of Emptiness, the doctrine central to all Mahāyāna, which denies the self-existence or substantiality of all phenomena. According to this doctrine of Emptiness, nothing exists independently by its own nature or power nor does anything have unchanging characteristics. Yogācāra or Vijñānavāda, while adhering to this central doctrine of Emptiness, more extensively explores the question of the nature of subjectivity, that is, the constituents of mental processes that deceive the perceiver into thinking that self-existent entities do indeed exist. For Yogācāra or Vijñānavāda, to assert that all phenomena are Empty means that they are mentally constructed—that all interactions upon what we consider reality were mental only. Mind and its world are a closed system of purely mental operations. What exists are only images or symbols evolved from consciousness, and it is these constructs that we misconstrue as an external world of objects. The mental constructs are themselves signs that indicate to us that consciousness is functioning, and our world of experience is essentially composed of images created by our own minds. Consciousness diversifies into many modes that have an apparent externality but are really modes of consciousness: one idea generates another idea, not an external object. Objects, then, are hypostasized ideas. Consciousness assumes many different, ever changing, and pluralistic forms. But consciousness is to be interpreted not as distinct and static modes but as phases in the evolutionary process in which experience unfolds. The phases are interacting, and none has absolute or ultimate status. The process is described in terms of a logical structure, not in terms of a chronological or temporal one. Each phase involves the creation of a panorama of sense data that we construe as an objective world. "The only reality recognized in this school is the reality of thought. And by thought is meant, not the objective content of thought, nor the subjective thinker, but a mere thinking."[1] In other words, perception is not an event of a relational kind between an external or ontological object and a name, concept, or epistemological object, but is simply the activity or process of a mind.

When Yogācāra literature was first introduced into China in the first half of the fifth century, the difficulties of translating Yogācāra texts must have seemed formidable indeed. The two translations of the *Bodhisattva-bhūmi* by Dharmarakṣa (385-433) and Guṇavarman (367-431) were apparently the first texts of the Yogācārin corpus translated into Chinese. Guṇabhadra (394-460) translated both Yogācāra and Tathāgatagarbha *sūtras*, most notably the *Śrīmālādevī-sūtra*, the *Laṅkāvatāra-sūtra*, and the *Saṃdhinirmocana-sūtra*. During the North-South dynastic period, the transmission of Yogācāra literature was greatly accelerated through the efforts of Bodhiruci of Northern Wei, Ratnamati, and Buddhaśanti, who translated the *Daśabhūmika*, the *Ratnagotra-vibhāga* (a Tathāgatagarbhan treatise), and the *Mahāyāna-saṃgraha*. These texts more extensively introduced Vasubandhu's and Asaṅga's corpus. In the Ratnamati/Bodhiruci recension of the *Daśabhūmika*, the theory of the *ālaya-vijñāna*, the subconscious reservoir of an individual's sum total of experience, began to have an impact on Chinese Buddhism. By the time Paramārtha arrived in China, two forms of Yogācāra had been established, Northern Ti-lun and Southern Ti-lun.

In addition to translating Yogācāra treatises, Indian and Central Asian monks also translated literature concerned with Tathāgatagarbha, another important strain of Indian Buddhist thought. Guṇabhadra had translated the *Śrīmālādevī-sūtra*, and Ratnamati had translated the *Ratnagotra-vibhāga*; the latter, heavily dependent upon the *Śrīmālādevī-sūtra*, is the only commentary now extant in Sanskrit that focuses exclusively on Tathāgatagarbha. Since Tathāgatagarbha literature was translated at the same time as Yogācāra and by the same masters, these two types of thought became closely linked in the minds of their Chinese audience. This association of Tathāgatagarbha with Yogācāra carried over into some of Paramārtha's interpretations as well. Moreover, interpreting and expanding on Paramārtha's translations, the later Buddhist schools of the Sui and T'ang placed much emphasis on the fusion of these two systems. Doctrinally, Tathāgatagarbha focuses on the belief that all sentient beings possess the potentiality of becoming enlightened or a Tathāgata. Metaphorically represented as an embryo or seed, the neophyte mind is said to develop and mature in the womb of itself until eventual Buddhahood. The enlightened aspect of the mind, "the intrinsically pure nature of mind," is indestructible. The Tathāgatagarbha theory reinterprets the doctrine of Emptiness, attributing positive qualities to this concept. In Indian literature, the synthesis between Yogācāra and Tathāgatagarbha often consisted of a blend of the more devotional Tathāgatagarbha belief in the immaculate purity of the mind and the more philosophical Yogācārin analysis of mental processes. Paramārtha's ideas, particularly his concept of *amala-vijñāna* or "pure consciousness," have often been regarded as an amalgam of Yogācāra and Tathāgatagarbha, because of the philosophical interfusion begun in India and the historical association of the two doctrines from the onset in China. The attention drawn to the purity of the *amala* was compatible with Tathāgatagarbha, and the philosophical analysis of mental processes culminating in the *amala-vijñāna* was borrowed from Yogācāra. Certainly the later schools of Sui and T'ang Buddhism interpreted much of Paramārtha's corpus in light of Tathāgatagarbha; their own sectarian developments represent such a synthesis.

Many of the most characteristic tenets of Yogācāra are discussed in the *Chuan shih lun* (CSL), the text that reveals the outline of Paramārtha's Yogācāra thought. In addition, this short text also includes an explanation of Paramārtha's important innovation, the concept of the *amala-vijñāna,* which is not found in his much longer works. This text is a translation of the *Triṃśikā-kārikās* by Vasubandhu, along with lengthy exegesis by Paramārtha. The *Triṃśikā* explains in abbreviated form the fundamental tenets of Yogācāra, the mature synopsis of the philosophical foundation for Yogācāra. The CSL, then, is a crucial text for understanding the most central teachings of Yogācāra as formulated by Vasubandhu and interpreted by Paramārtha. It is an extremely significant document not only for interpreting Paramārtha's own ideas but also for demonstrating essential differences between Indian and Chinese Yogācāra. Finally, the CSL indicates the proclivities of subsequent Chinese schools of Buddhism.

The CSL is a complete text, not fragmented as are some of Paramārtha's other translations. As a synopsis, it provides an entrance into the philosophical system Paramārtha transmitted. At the same time, it presents a number of sophisticated arguments without the details and intricacies encountered, for example, in the *She ta-sheng lun*. The text presents a "systems" approach to cognitive functions, a series of stimulus-response patterns that reinforce certain modes of behavior and attitudes. This view of the mind makes the text fascinating not only for humanists in Asian studies but also for those in comparative philosophy and psychology. The evolution-of-consciousness processes presented in the CSL assume a subconscious "clearinghouse" (*ālaya-vijñāna*), which stores, collates, and programs mental states in a way somewhat like that of a computer. The Yogācāra Buddhists, like many cognitive psychologists of today, initiated an extremely ambitious undertaking: to create a single uniform theoretical framework to represent such diverse cognitive functions as language, processing memory, perception, reasoning, and emotions. The analysis of mind delineated in Paramārtha's exegetical writings accounts for the diversity of modes of perception and concept-formation. He approaches the philosophy of mind phenomenologically, that is, in a step-by-step analysis from the most primitive layers of consciousness to the level of linguistic discourse in accordance with Yogācāra doctrine. For the comparative philosopher, what is new in Yogācāra Buddhism is the psychological underpinnings of its thesis: language evokes psychological attitudes and emotions; emotions distort perceptions; meditation serves as therapy besides being a practice essential for the system to make sense.

Although there are philosophical inconsistencies from one text to another, for Paramārtha, at least, Yogācāra is a system in which the world we experience evolves from acts of cognition continually in operation, and no other world is ours to *experience* (which is not the same thing as saying that no other world *exists*).

Paramārtha was a prolific translator and commentator who apparently created controversy in his own time, leading to the rather sudden disappearance of some of his works and to the fragmentation of others. Very likely, too, some works attributed to Paramārtha are apocryphal texts not translated by him.

Though there are many difficulties in translating Paramārtha's texts, they are somewhat alleviated by the fact that the Sanskrit original of the *Triṃśikā* and its commentary by Sthiramati are available for comparison. Moreover, Hsüan-tsang's version of the *Triṃśikā*, published as the *Wei-shih san-shih sung* and incorporated in his *Ch'eng wei-shih lun*, provides valuable information on major differences between his and Paramārtha's interpretations of Vasubandhu's ideas.

Scholarship on Paramārtha reached its zenith in the 1930's and 1940's when the major studies on Paramārtha and Yogācāra were released in French and Japanese. Many translations of classical works of Yogācāra such as the Sanskrit recensions of the *Viṃśatikā*, *Triṃśikā*, and Hsüan-tsang's recension of the *Mahāyānasaṃgraha* were also completed at this time. However, the attention Paramārtha deserves has not often been granted. Too often his innovative contribution to Chinese Buddhism has been ignored in favor of studying his translations from Sanskrit sources. Comparison with the Indian tradition is of course important for discovering divergences and interpolations, but Paramārtha's main contribution is his almost singlehanded transmission of Yogācāra to China. The *Chuan shih lun* is the earliest Chinese translation of the *Triṃśikā* and thus represents the initial presentation of this Indian philosophy of mind to a Chinese intellectual audience.

The present study begins with a discussion of Paramārtha's official biography and hagiographical elements and presents the general historical and political context of the time in both India and south China. In that turbulent era in China, the scholar Paramārtha, while working zealously at his philosophical and religious enterprise, was obliged to be constantly alert to political danger, and those circumstances are certainly responsible for some of the textual inconsistencies and fragmentations of Paramārtha's work. Chapter 2 continues the subject of Paramārtha's work, showing the roles of his key disciples and presenting some of the important doctrinal disputes between Northern and Southern Ti-lun.

The two following chapters are devoted to an introduction to Paramārtha's philosophical treatment of Yogācārin views on language and the process of cognition, both central to this system of thought. The structures of consciousness are delineated and key arguments are paraphrased.

Chapter 5 places the *Chuan shih lun* within the context of a larger document of which it almost certainly was a part at one time. In the analysis of the text, Hsüan-tsang's translation and the Sanskrit original are used as additional sources to illuminate Paramārtha's contribution to Chinese Buddhism and his originality. This chapter of analysis is followed by the translation of the text. Appendix A is a chronology of the major events in Paramārtha's life and Appendix B is a list of works allegedly translated by Paramārtha. Appendix C is a lineage of major disciples of Ti-lun and She-lun Buddhism. Many of the notes (following the Appendixes), especially those to the translation, deal with technical Buddhological issues.

I

The Life and Times of Paramārtha

IN RELIGIOUS biographies or hagiographies, the selection of biographical facts is especially critical to the emergence of an image of the religious personality.[1] The sixth century *Kao seng chuan* (KSC) (Biographies of Eminent Monks) offers a combination, in most instances, of common human experiences that show the Buddhist monks as sharing the emotions, ambitions, and weaknesses of ordinary men and also events that characterize monks as uniquely religious and spiritually eminent. In other words, the KSC and its sequel, the *Hsü kao seng chuan* (HKSC) (Continued Biographies of Eminent Monks), chronicle the lives of those who were recognized to have exemplified the religious ideals of the Chinese Buddhist monastic community.[2] The biography of Paramārtha in the HKSC portrays a saintly scholarly figure against the background of the emotionally and politically turbulent times of the sixth century A.D.

During this period marking the close of the North-South dynastic period in China, philosophical schools of Buddhism emerged and flourished together with Indian missionary-monks who had gained the patronage of the various Chinese courts. It is not an exaggeration to say that intellectual Buddhism in China was in great measure shaped by the interpretations of translators. Naturally when the imperial hegemony was a stable one, translation work was far more productive and scholarship won greater recognition than in troubled periods of political and social upheaval. The most significant translations and scholarship were usually carried out only with the financial support of highly influential state officials. In fact it is legitimate to claim that the direction of Chinese intellectual Buddhism was controlled in many ways by the interpretations of the major translators who settled in China from India and Central Asia.

Of course, Buddhist "schools" in China were not educational institutions with organizational hierarchies and an absolute doctrinal authority based upon codified dogma. The historical, political, geographical, and economic realities of the time were critical to the survival of any scholastic endeavor, religious or secular. For the period at the end of the North-South dynasties, in particular, our knowledge is necessarily colored by the personalities and influences of the great Indian masters who served as the teachers and translators of innovative religious doctrines to their Chinese Buddhist disciples. These Indian Buddhist pioneers were not content to translate the scriptural texts for mere scholastic purposes; they wanted to interpret texts in a way that would enable their Chinese followers to analyze the work by writing their own commentaries, thereby transforming Buddhism into a religion that could be assimilated into the Chinese culture. These Indian Buddhist monks also had to adjust to the political and economic challenges of the time in order to achieve their aspirations.

It was during the chaotic times of the Liang and Ch'en dynasties that Paramārtha transmitted the philosophical ideas of Yogācāra Buddhism to the elite classes of south China. Paramārtha, an Indian Buddhist monk, was the first to disseminate, to any great extent, Yogācārin philosophical and religious tenets in China. His work marked the beginning of a period of active interpretation and discussion of some of the most significant texts of the Yogācārin or "Consciousness-Only" tradition. Paramārtha was recognized as a major philosopher and exegete of Yogācārin Buddhism, and an important influence on the development of Chinese Buddhist thought from the Liang dynasty up through the middle of the T'ang. By providing a systematic and representative collection of core texts for his loyal followers, Paramārtha enabled the Chinese Buddhist monks to prepare the foundation for the two great classical T'ang Buddhist schools: Hua-yen, whose most notable proponents were Chih-yen (602-68) and Fa-tsang (643-712); and Fa-hsiang, whose primary proponents were Hsüan-tsang (600-664) and his disciple, K'uei-chi (632-82), also known as Tzu-en.[3]

Largely as a result of Paramārtha's extensive translations and exegeses, Yogācārin Buddhism was to affect Chinese thought for over three hundred years. Not only the Ch'an and Hua-yen Buddhists but also the later neo-Confucians, who were greatly influenced by them, owed much to Paramārtha's systematic thought. Paramārtha's works were to be the turning point in a long-standing debate among Buddhist scholars concerning the phenomenology of mind and the essential character of human nature. Paramārtha was primarily interested in analyzing the structures of conscious acts and their relationship to spiritual enlightenment. If human nature is intrinsically good and destined for enlightenment, he asked why do human beings refuse to believe and to act like the enlightened beings they fundamentally are? This question, lying at the heart of Mahāyāna, is the focus of all of Paramārtha's major tracts of writing.

During his lifetime, Paramārtha saw his work variously received: he enjoyed a period of eminence and recognition of his brilliant and innovative analyses of Buddhist doctrine but also suffered when his patrons were overthrown or had reversals. A preliminary investigation of the personality and political life of Paramārtha will assist in understanding his place in the history and development of Buddhist thought. He was a religious and philosophical advocate of previously unknown Buddhist theories. He was a political survivor who, though ostracized for the views he cherished and hoped to disseminate, managed to continue his work in the midst of the turmoil. Not only did he survive jealous Buddhist court monks who plotted his banishment from the central sphere of political and religious influence, but he did so mostly on his own, without the help of highly placed patrons that might have been possible in more economically stable times.

The specifically religious dimension of Paramārtha's life, in accordance with the overall hagiographical intent of the HKSC, stands out sharply from the sparse historical details of his life before his arrival in China. Lacking specific details, we must place Paramārtha briefly within the political and religious context of sixth-century India and its colony Funan where Paramārtha resided for some time, and then look at the unsettled political and economic nature of southern China on the eve of Paramārtha's departure for Canton.

India and Funan

Paramārtha was born in A.D. 499, approximately one hundred fifty years after the Yogācārin philosopher Vasubandhu, the single most important influence on Paramārtha's intellectual development. By the end of the fifth century Ujjain, in the present north central state of Madhya Pradesh, was no longer part of a unified north India under the Guptas, who had ruled since the first half of the fourth century. The final collapse of the Guptas did not occur until the middle of the sixth century, but the glory of the empire had already faded greatly. With the demise of the dynasty, north India reverted into feudal kingdoms. In the Kathiawar Peninsula, Valabhī separated from Magadha so that Paramārtha's family, in Ujjain, was part of an autonomous kingdom, the province of Malwa.

There is no evidence that the Guptan empire exercised anything but nominal control over western Malwa, including Ujjain, except perhaps in theory.[4] In western Malwa, north of Ujjain, there were several feudal lords during the early life of Paramārtha. The most important was King Yaśodharman, whose heroic deeds in battling the Hūṇa king Mihirakula, son of Toramāṇa, are of legendary dimensions.[5] We know that Mihirakula was an adherent of a Śaivite sect of the Brahmanical tradition and was alleged to have fiercely persecuted the Buddhists.[6] Mihirakula and his troops met with fierce resistance, having been defeated by Yaśodharman of Malwa some time between 527 and 533.[7] There is some disagreement on whether or not Mihirakula pressed on to Magadha to be defeated by Narasiṃhagupta Bālāditya II.[8]

Even under Mihirakula and the Maitrakas, the provincial rulers were allowed to continue their reign over the people.[9] Paramārtha's contemporaries, then, during his youth were Mihirakula in Ujjain and Narasiṃhagupta Bālāditya II, a Later Guptan king, of Magadha. Yaśodharman of Malwa, who captured Mihirakula in approximately A.D. 532, would have been the reigning power in Ujjain about the time of Paramārtha's departure for foreign lands. One can only assume that Paramārtha enjoyed the patronage of both Yaśodharman and Bālāditya II, at least to the extent of receiving financial support for his missionary effort. Since we are not certain of the precise date when Paramārtha left for China—it was probably around 545—he may have had the patronage of either Bālāditya II or, more likely, his son, Kumāragupta III, both of whom, like most of the Later Guptans, were patrons of Buddhism. The Maukhari ruler Dhruvasena I of Valabhī, the monastic center for Yogācāra Buddhism of the type that Paramārtha advocated, reigned approximately A.D. 525-45 and may have supported Paramārtha's missionary efforts as well.

According to the HKSC, Paramārtha set sail at some unknown date for distant lands to propagate the Buddhist teaching. The only country named in the HKSC besides China as a place of missionary activity is Funan.[10] Funan had been in India's possession since the first century A.D. and in Paramārtha's time was the center of the busy India-China trade zone that encompassed much of the Indochinese subcontinent (Cambodia, parts of Thailand, and the lower part of the Mekong delta in Vietnam). As an Indian colony, Funan was predominantly Hindu, but Buddhist missionary activity during the sixth century must have intensified since it is said that the Buddhists also had a strong following.

It is known that Buddhist monks had already been sent to China from Funan to translate texts during the imperial reign of Wu of Liang. Saṃghapāla (or Saṃghabhara) (460-524) resided in China from 506 until 522. Mandra (or Mandrasena) collaborated with him.[11] The king, Rudravarman, son of Jayavarman, had commissioned at least six emissaries to China, from 517 until 539, and had sent various lavish presents to the imperial court, including a sandalwood image of the Buddha, pearls, a live rhinoceros, saffron, and a relic of the Buddha (purportedly a twelve-foot-long strand of hair).[12]

Two facts can be documented with regard to the state of Buddhism in this region at the time of Paramārtha. First, government support of Buddhism was an important element in trade relations between Funan and China, and Buddhist missionary envoys to China from this area had been relatively frequent for some time before Paramārtha went to Canton; Paramārtha was not by any means the first of the line. Second, Rudravarman must have been the sovereign at the time Paramārtha was engaged in missionary activity in Funan and apparently had some interest in Buddhism, if not for personal reasons, at least for reasons of political strategy. His reign was to come to an abrupt end about the time that Paramārtha left Funan.

Although Hinduism was the state religion of Funan, the fact that Emperor Wu selected this geographical area as a resource center for recruiting eminent Buddhist monks suggests that there was a good deal of missionary activity by Buddhist monks in Funan during the sixth century. But by the beginning of the seventh century, Buddhism had virtually disappeared from Funan. Paramārtha may have already suspected that Buddhism was beginning to lose its support in Funan when he accepted the invitation to go to China.

Southern China during the Late Liang and Early Ch'en

The Ta-t'ung reign period (535-46) marked the beginning of the fourth decade of the reign of Emperor Wu of Liang. It is well known that Emperor Wu of the Liang dynasty (reigned 502-49) was the most fervent supporter of Buddhism to occupy the throne in China. This fact is reiterated in Paramārtha's biography in the HKSC: ". . . the virtue of Emperor Wu of Liang extended over all parts of the land, causing the Three Jewels [of Buddhism] to flourish. . . . The emperor wished to transmit and translate the teachings of the *sūtras*, no less than during the Ch'in dynasty [Former Ch'in: 351-94; Later Ch'in: 384-417]. In addition, he [wished to have] published materials surpassing in number those of the days of the Ch'i dynasty [479-502]."[13]

Emperor Wu, the founder of the Liang dynasty in south China, had originally been of Taoist persuasion, and he maintained his ties to Taoism even after being converted to Buddhism in 504, and in spite of his subsequent decrees exerting pressure on Taoists to return to the laity.[14] Wu began his reign in a period of great prosperity and economic stability but grew more and more indifferent to affairs of government as the years went by. Envisioning himself as an exemplary Buddhist sovereign, he had many Buddhist temples constructed, the most famous being the T'ung-t'ai temple (built 521-27), thus draining the state treasuries of enormous sums of money and increasing the burden on the economy.

At the age of sixty-three, in the year of T'ung-t'ai's completion, Wu retired for a brief time as a monk, and it was at the T'ung-t'ai temple that he engaged in some of his most noteworthy and controversial Buddhist practices, including "dharma assemblies" where the subtleties of *sūtras* would be discussed at length and where he granted amnesty to criminals or made pronouncements. On four occasions—two times shortly before Paramārtha arrived in Chien-k'ang (Nanking)—Wu "abandoned his body" and surrendered himself as a temple servant in order to raise donations for the temple from wealthy aristocratic families.[15] The Inexhaustible Treasuries that he encouraged were vast collections of capital, estimated to be worth 10,960,000 pieces of gold in 533.[16] All these pious acts represented Wu's attempts to save himself and others from unfortunate states of rebirth. This religious zeal earned Wu praise as *p'u-sa t'ien-tzu,* "The Bodhisattva and Son of Heaven," but also the criticism of Confucian historians, who called him a spendthrift who allowed corrupt Buddhist practices to continue unchecked. The historians also criticized him for not observing the penal code and for being overly lenient toward prisoners in accordance with his interpretation of the Buddhist practice of compassion.

For all his financial excesses in the name of Buddhism, Emperor Wu of Liang, particularly in the early period of his almost fifty-year reign over south China, did carry out important social and economic reforms, and he also managed to stabilize governmental organizations by maintaining tight control over the Southern Dynastic aristocracy.[17] However, from the end of the Eastern Chin the firmly established aristocratic families had lost much of their monopolization of government posts with the concomitant rise of the "cold men" (*han-jen*) who were ambitious commoners, currying favor with local lords.

The history of the shifts in power during the Southern Dynasties must always take into account the history by which the great landowning regional lords made alliances with the "cold men" for business, profit, and capital. The aristocratic families who had emigrated from the north, taking flight from the Hsien-pei invaders for the safe regions of the south along the Yangtze delta, gained high-status administrative positions but often possessed no real power. And the provincial governors, who were princes of the imperial family, always had to be mindful of the needs of the native southern Chinese clans surrounding them, which meant that they were usually in a weak position with regard to controlling their own garrisons, since the military recruits came from those same families.

Politically, the centralized government was a system in which each prince moved from one garrison to another, with a metropolitan headquarters in the capital city of Chien-k'ang (same as Chien-yeh referred to in the HKSC and known today as Nanking). Militarily, the Liang dynasty was vulnerable not only to attack from the foreign rulers of the Toba-Wei house in north China but also to rebellions within their own ranks. By the end of the Liang, although the threat from north China had temporarily declined owing to the division into Eastern and Western Wei, the domestic threat was greater than ever, as a result of the oppression of the peasants and farmers by their landlords. The Liang sought to take advantage of this division by increasing military intervention. Emperor Wu, late in his career, turned to the "cold families" (*han-men*) in hopes of using their power to gain north China. These trusted men had been excellent government servants, usually in low positions that belied their true power, and they had not antagonized the aristocratic émigrés, though they were looked down on by them because of their plebian origins.

Working against Emperor Wu's ambitions were the competitive and ambitious intentions of some of the powerful southern Chinese clans along with émigrés from the north who wished to appropriate for themselves the throne of south China. In addition, a weakened Liang dynasty was no longer able to spend vast sums on both war expenditures and Buddhist practices. The shortage of copper cash had been a general problem since the time of Liu Sung.[18] The weakened currency and inflated prices of grain during the latter part of the Liang dynasty caused many of the "cold families" who were merchants to prosper while forcing peasants and farmers to become soldiers for powerful native regional lords.

The rise of the notorious rebel Hou Ching and the marshaling of forces against Emperor Wu is a long, complicated web of intrigue that remains controversial among historians.[19] Hou Ching began as a powerful general of the Eastern Wei dynasty in north China. He was one of Kao Huan's principal military aides who forced Emperor Hsiao-wu to flee west to Ch'ang-an, where he was assassinated by Yü-wen T'ai in 534. Kao Huan then set up a puppet emperor, Emperor Hsiao Ching, in Loyang in 535, establishing Eastern Wei. In 547, almost thirteen years after the inauguration of the Eastern Wei dynasty, Kao Huan died. His eldest son, Kao Ch'eng (d. 549), the de facto ruler, did not look so favorably upon his father's cohort, Hou Ching, but Kao Ch'eng was assassinated in 549 by a Liang prisoner of war.[20] Kao Ch'eng's younger brother, Kao Yang (529-59), then succeeded as the military power behind the throne, proclaiming himself emperor (Wen-hsüan) in 550 and establishing the Northern Ch'i. After a quarrel with Kao Yang, Hou Ching plotted another military campaign, this time allying himself with Yü-wen T'ai of the Western Wei, Kao Ch'eng's old rival and the Hsien-pei power behind the throne in 547. Although Yü-wen T'ai was uneasy about the alliance with Hou Ching, he commanded Hou Ching to seize the Eastern Wei capital of Loyang. Hou Ching felt trapped between the two rival forces and in 548 decided to ally himself with Emperor Wu in order to gain his assistance in this crisis.

By this time Emperor Wu was well into his dotage and had delegated the bulk of administrative responsibilities to his competent officials as well as to numerous incompetent relatives. Against the will of some of his most trusted advisers, Emperor Wu enfeoffed Hou Ching as Prince of Honan to cause trouble for both the Eastern and the Western Wei. Throughout the ensuing military hostilities precipitated by Hou Ching, Emperor Wu was ineffectual in rallying forces to defend the capital and the entire empire from the duplicitous Hou Ching. Assisted by one of Emperor Wu's own sons, Hou Ching seized the capital city of Nanking on April 24, 549, after a six-month insurrection in which there was almost no resistance from the troops under imperial command. Hou Ching consolidated his position virtually unopposed. With dignity befitting an imperial authority, Emperor Wu received Hou Ching at court when the rebel stormed the palace gates.[21] Emperor Wu died of starvation on June 12, 549, while under house arrest.

Hsiao Kang, son and heir to Emperor Wu, was placed on the

throne by Hou Ching.[22] Meanwhile, Hsiao I, seventh son of Emperor Wu and Prince of Hsiang-tung, attempted to build his forces and take over the throne. When his nephews, Hsiao Yü and Hsiao Ch'a, refused to send him aid, although they were under his command, Hsiao I sent an army to attack Hsiao Ch'a who then called in Western Wei to defend him. Since the Western Wei was superior militarily to the Liang, Hsiao I agreed to a northern boundary after Western Wei's advance in 550. By the early part of 551, Hsiao I was moving his troops up the Yangtze while Hou Ching was moving down river.

After two and a half years of nominally supporting the rightful heir to the throne, Hou Ching had the puppet emperor Chien-wen (Hsiao Kang) intoxicated and then assassinated by suffocation in the seventh month of 551 and, at the same time, murdered many of his children. Then, following a brief three-month interim reign of Hsiao Tung, Emperor Chien-wen's successor, Hou Ching proclaimed himself emperor of Han on January 1, 552, and imprisoned Hsiao Tung.[23] Only three months after Hou Ching ascended the throne, however, he was forced to flee Nanking (April 28, 552) under pressure from troops commanded by the powerful generals Wang Seng-pien (d. 555) and Ch'en Pa-hsien (503-59), acting on the orders of Hsiao I.[24] On May 26, 552, General Wang Seng-pien received the body of Hou Ching who had been killed by Yang Kun, and put it on public display in Nanking. The corpse was savagely torn to pieces by the people and eaten, and the bones set afire. The head was taken to Chiang-ling where Hsiao I had it suspended in the marketplace, then cooked, lacquered, and deposited in the armory.[25]

Hsiao I, who had originally been enfeoffed as Prince of Hsiang-tung and had been living in Chiang-ling, approximately 450 miles southwest of Nanking, proclaimed himself emperor of the Liang in Chiang-ling on December 13, 552, and moved the capital there.[26] Hsiao's general Wang Seng-pien, who had overthrown Emperor Wu's assassin, Hou Ching, was the power behind the restoration of the Liang, and was still in Nanking. Perhaps suspicious of Wang Seng-pien's own political ambitions, the new emperor wisely chose to stay in Chiang-ling but sent both generals to Nanking. Nearly all the aristocratic émigrés who had survived the fall of Nanking sought refuge where Hsiao I resided.[27] Fearing also that he might be overthrown by his younger brother,

Hsiao Chi, in Szechuan, Hsiao I (Emperor Yüan) had him assassinated by the Western Wei in August 553.[28] The regions of Szechuan, however, were then seized by the Western Wei under the forces of Yü-wen T'ai.

Western Wei began to expand its territories, encroaching upon the northwestern Liang borders. This military campaign eventually removed most of Liang's power, and at the close of 554 Chiang-ling was easily taken by the Western Wei, allegedly by the order of Hsiao I's nephew, Hsiao Ch'a. Western Wei plotted the death of Hsiao I.[29] Hsiao I was crushed to death while a captive of Western Wei, and on February 7, 555, Hsiao Ch'a became the puppet emperor (posthumously known as the Prince of Yüchang), in the shadow of the military rule of the Western Wei.

Meanwhile, in the capital of Nanking Emperor Yüan's two generals, Wang Seng-pien and Ch'en Pa-hsien, were busy trying to outmaneuver each other for the ultimate power behind the throne, at the same time constantly under the threat of both Western Wei and Northern Ch'i, successor to Eastern Wei. Because of the interruption in the normal line of succession, the question of who should sit on the throne of Liang was complicated. Hsiao Fang-chih, son of Hsiao I, was originally proclaimed heir-apparent by both generals, but later, Hsiao Yüan-ming, nephew of the late Emperor Wu, a repatriated heir to the throne living in Northern Ch'i where he had been in exile, was sent with troops to gain control of eastern Liang territory. Wang Seng-pien then acceded to Northern Ch'i demands, switching his allegiance to Hsiao Yüan-ming in order to please them. On July 1, 555, Hsiao Yüan-ming became the puppet emperor under Northern Ch'i, and Hsiao Fang-chih was designated heir, a virtual demotion. The Northern Ch'i now had Nanking securely in their possession. This situation lasted a mere five months before a conflict between the troops of Ch'en Pa-hsien and Wang Seng-pien left Wang Seng-pien (the general who defeated Hou Ching) dead. Hsiao Yüan-ming, who had been sponsored by Wang Seng-pien, was deposed, and the fifteen-year-old Hsiao Fang-chih, Prince of Chin-an, ascended the throne as emperor (posthumously known as Emperor Ching), with the sponsorship of Ch'en Pa-hsien.[30] A treaty was reached between the Northern Ch'i and the Liang; after an appropriate waiting period of two years, Ch'en Pa-hsien ousted Hsiao Fang-chih as a puppet emperor and proclaimed himself emperor on November 16, 557, beginning the Ch'en dynasty.

Paramārtha

A standard account of Paramārtha's family background and place of birth is given in the HKSC, said to be based upon a biography by Ts'ao P'i, a nephew of Paramārtha's favorite disciple, Hui-k'ai.[31] This biography not only establishes his foreign origins but also gives credence to the fact that an Indian Buddhist missionary-monk was as refined and as intellectually well trained a man as those of upper class Chinese society. We are told that Paramārtha's personal name was Kulanātha, which means "savior of the family"; Paramārtha, his religious name, means "absolute truth." Paramārtha's birthplace, Ujjain (Ujjayinī), was one of the seven sacred cities in Hindu tradition, and his parents were Brahmans belonging to the prominent Bhāradvāja caste or clan (*gotra*).[32] Paramārtha is praised for the usual virtues of a Buddhist monk: for his impeccable morals, his calm and dignified demeanor, and his proficiency in scripture, literary arts, magic, fine arts, and crafts. A truly gifted man intellectually whose knowledge went beyond Buddhist doctrine, he also seems to have been well suited temperamentally for a missionary career, having undertaken long and arduous journeys without fear of foreign people's "treachery."[33] It is also said that his beneficent presence was compatible with the dispositions of the native people he encountered. These are, of course, prerequisites for the ideal missionary-monk which Paramārtha represents.

Very little is known of Paramārtha's life in India. He was a monk (*śrāmaṇa*) who had gained a considerable religious reputation for scholarship and for his travels. The biographical record in the HKSC mentions that Emperor Wu of Liang devoutly yearned to extend Buddhism throughout China, and to that end, during the Ta-t'ung era (535-45) he commanded his Palace Rear Guard Chang Fan and a contingent to accompany the ambassador from Funan (Cambodia) back to his own country.[34] Emperor Wu wished to invite eminent scholars in Mahāyāna Buddhism to bring significant *sūtras* and *śāstras* to China. At this time Paramārtha's reputation as a scholar and missionary living in Funan presumably was brought to the ambassador's attention, for the ambassador sent Paramārtha to Emperor Wu's court in compliance with the imperial order.

Aside from these facts, nothing is known of Paramārtha's adulthood up until his early forties, when he arrived in Canton, China. It is possible that he lived as a missionary in Funan for some length of time, since he had evidently gained the favor of the ambassador and, presumably, the government in general.

The first of many documentary discrepancies in the account of Paramārtha's mission to China concerns the circumstances of his departure from Funan. According to his official biography in HKSC, he was sent to China from Funan and brought many texts with him.[35] It is clear from historical records, both Buddhist and dynastic, that Emperor Wu of Liang exerted tremendous effort and donated large sums of money to make Buddhism prosper and to seek out Buddhist missionaries. The account in the HKSC is based upon Pao-kuei's introduction to the "new" *Suvarṇaprabhāsa-sūtra* (*Hsin-ho chin kuang-ming ching*), eighth *chüan*, preserved in the *Li-tai san-pao chi* (LTSPC):

> Emperor Wu of Liang felt pity for beings who would be reborn in the three [unfortunate] destinies and grieved over their fall into the four kinds of gestation [womb, egg, moisture, or spontaneously generated]. He [wished to] set sail to rescue the drowning, holding on to the torch of wisdom, in order to enlighten [others'] delusion. During the Ta-t'ung period the emperor sent a rear guard Chang Szu to Funan to send back to China eminent monks and Mahāyāna *śāstras* and *sūtras* of various kinds. This country [Funan] then yielded in turning over the western Indian Dharma Master from Ujjain, namely Paramārtha, who in Liang was called Chen-ti, and many *sūtras* and *śāstras* in order to honor the emperor.
>
> After the Dharma Master Paramārtha had traveled to many kingdoms he had settled in Funan. His manner was lively and intelligent and he relished details in scriptural texts and profound texts, all of which he had studied. In the first year of T'ai-ch'ing (547) he went to the capital and had a visit with the emperor who himself bowed down to him in the Jeweled Cloud (Pao-yün) quarters of the palace in reverence to him, wishing for him to translate *sūtras* and *śāstras*. The law made it difficult for foreigners to be given official titles.[36]

This account may be reliable, since the Pao-kuei introduction was written in 597, only about fifty years after Paramārtha was summoned from Funan in approximately 545, and only twenty-eight years after Paramārtha's death in 569. Furthermore, Pao-kuei's teacher, Tao-an, who had been one of Paramārtha's followers, died in 581 at the end of the Northern Chou dynasty, only twelve years after the death of Paramārtha in 569.[37] Thus Pao-kuei's record, dealing as it does with a relatively recent period, may be more accurate in details than those of later writers. Some of these later accounts of Paramārtha's journey to south China say that Emperor Wu of Liang commissioned an envoy to go to Magadha, not Funan, to acquire *sūtras* and Dharma masters; at Magadha the envoy met the Tripiṭaka Master Kūlanātha who at first adamantly refused to go to China but eventually boarded a ship with his attendant Gautama and many others, bearing a rosewood statue of the Buddha to be presented at the imperial court.[38] The *K'ai-yüan shih chiao mu-lu* (KYL) combines parts of both versions of the journey, namely, that the Rear Guard Chang Fan (or Chang Szu) accompanied the Funan ambassador to his own country and then went to Magadha.[39] This account given in KYL of first going to Funan and then to Magadha is the most questionable of all the sources, since passages are cited verbatim from both the HKSC and the colophon to the *Ta-sheng ch'i-hsin lun* but are synthesized into a composite.

Of the four historical documents that mention the imperial envoy, the *Ch'i hsin lun* is allegedly apocryphal and the KYL incorporated portions of the *Ch'i hsin lun*. If one excludes these two records because they are unreliable historical sources, then there can be no doubt that Paramārtha was in Funan engaging in missionary activity some time during the Ta-t'ung era of the Liang dynasty.

Besides the conflicting textual evidence about Funan, there is uncertainty about the year of Paramārtha's departure. None of the historical records gives an exact date. The official biography in the HKSC says only that during the Ta-t'ung era (which lasted slightly more than ten years) the mission led by Rear Guard Chang Fan was sent to seek out Buddhist monks and scriptural texts. All other documents that indicate a time of departure follow the HKSC.

It is known, however, that Paramārtha reached Nanhai (modern Canton) on September 25, 546, the last year of the Ta-t'ung era. Allowing ample travel time, we may assume that he left Funan toward the latter half of the Ta-t'ung era. Stopping at various places along the coast, he reached the capital city, Chien-yeh (south of modern Nanking), two years later, in the intercalary month of the second year of T'ai-ch'ing (August 20-September 17, 548).[40] When he arrived at court, the eighty-five-year-old Emperor Wu prostrated himself before Paramārtha in an extraordinary act of reverence and received him in audience at the Pao-yün temple.[41]

At the time of this audience with the sovereign, Paramārtha was almost fifty years of age and an experienced world traveler as well as missionary-monk. The patronage of the Liang court promised an opportunity for more translation work. But Hou Ching's plotting of the overthrow of the regime was probably already under way even as Paramārtha began his new venture. Only two months after Paramārtha arrived in Nanking, the rebellion commenced, and in June 549, only eight months after that, Emperor Wu died of starvation while under house arrest.

The next recorded event is Paramārtha's arrival in Fu-ch'ün, Chekiang, in the Fu-yang district, approximately 150 miles southeast of Nanking, near Mount Hsiao, during the tenth month of the fourth year, T'ai-ch'ing (October 26-November 25, 550). There, under the sponsorship of Lu Yüan-che, the regional governor of Fu-ch'un, Paramārtha resumed his translation activities. With a staff of twenty accomplished monks, including Pao-ch'iung (504-84),[42] Paramārtha translated the *Shih-ch'i-ti-lun* (Treatise on the Seventeen Bodhisattva Stages) in five *chüan* during the fourth year of T'ai-ch'ing (550). This text is now lost.[43] Lu Yüan-che was a recent convert to Buddhism and had expected that the illustrious Paramārtha would instruct him in the scriptures while in his residence. According to the KYL, the monks apparently had some difficulties in translating this text and therefore discontinued the effort.[44] The HKSC states that "although [the political and military situation of] the country had not yet been settled, he [Paramārtha] transmitted the text with an appendix [or glossary]."[45] However, "transmitted" (*chuan*) does not necessarily indicate that the text was completely committed to writing, so there need not be any contradiction between the sources, HKSC and KYL. Both the older catalogue, the LTSPC, and the more recent *Ta t'ang nei tien lu* (NTL) omit any mention of an interruption in the translation, but both catalogues give the same date and place of translation as found in the HKSC and KYL.[46]

After presumably beginning the translation of the *Treatise on the Seventeen Bodhisattva Stages*, Paramārtha returned to the capital city in the third year of T'ien-pao (552) by invitation of none other than Hou Ching himself.[47] Undoubtedly Hou Ching knew of Paramārtha's activities at Governor Lu Yüan-che's since he summoned him to court. The HKSC laments: "At this time there was continuous warfare and famine; the Dharma was close to ruin."[48] In the interim period of two and one-half years at Governor Lu Yüan-che's estate, Paramārtha may have had the solitude to begin the translation work that had been his chief purpose in traveling to China, but he was at the same time undoubtedly distressed about political affairs at court where the murderer of Emperor Wu now dictated national policy. His monastic assistants must have been especially dispirited at the starvation, devastation, and barbarisms in their homeland.[49] Although none of the records gives any explanation of why the translation of the *Treatise on the Seventeen Bodhisattva Stages* was interrupted, psychological reasons as well as scholarly difficulties must have been compelling to the monks assisting Paramārtha in rendering the original text into Chinese.

The HKSC is noncommittal on Paramārtha's feelings about Hou Ching's summons. Paramārtha, who had unfortunately found himself in the midst of insurrection, was now being brought back to Nanking by the murderer of his former patron, four years after he first entered the palace gates as a new arrival from Funan. It is intriguing to speculate on the motives behind Hou Ching's invitation to Paramārtha. He evidently desired Buddhist support, indicated by his immediate orders for the construction of new Buddhist temples even though he had burned countless temples before he seized Nanking.[50] Perhaps the learned monk was to be used as a symbol of Hou Ching's purported zeal for the Buddhist path. Hou Ching probably wanted to exploit the prestige of a foreign monk as a way of improving his reputation after usurping the throne and ravaging the south. What better way to keep watch on Paramārtha and any possible political maneuvers by his wealthy provincial patrons than by keeping him under surveillance in the palace quarters on the pretense of interest in his scholarly activities? In any event, Paramārtha was not in a position to refuse Hou Ching's summons, so he left for the capital from Governor Lu Yüan-che's residence in Fu-ch'un and was duly honored by the rebel.

How long Paramārtha was in Fu-ch'un is impossible to calculate with certainty, but we can surmise that he left Nanking immediately before or after Emperor Wu's death in June 549, moving to Fu-ch'un the following year. Assuming that either Paramārtha or his supporters realized that his life was in danger, he escaped an ignominious death at the hands of Hou Ching by moving to Fu-ch'un. Approximately two and a half years later, in 552, he had his audience with Hou Ching. The monk must have realized that he was in a politically sensitive situation and must conduct himself in the rebel's presence with the subtlest diplomacy. Paramārtha did not have to endure the tensions of such circumstances for very long, however. Since it is known that Hou Ching's reign lasted one hundred twenty days, we can estimate that Paramārtha lived amidst the unchanneled violence of life in Hou Ching's palace for no more than four months.[51]

During the three years of Emperor Yüan's reign, beginning with the Ch'eng-sheng era on December 13, 552, Paramārtha settled at the Cheng-kuan temple in Nanking. One can infer from this that Paramārtha, instead of being in Chiang-ling with the imperial court of Emperor Yüan, decided to stay in Nanking where the real powers, the generals Wang Seng-pien and Ch'en Pa-hsien, were aligning their forces. There, with more than twenty monks, including Yüan-ch'an, Paramārtha translated the *Suvarṇaprabhāsa-sūtra* (*Chin kuang-ming ching*).

Again, the records show some points of disagreement. First of all, the HKSC does not mention any specific date for translating the *Suvarṇaprabhāsa*, only mentioning that Paramārtha translated the text at the Cheng-kuan temple in Nanking during Emperor Yüan's reign, that is, during the Ch'eng-sheng period (552-55). Some of the other sources give different dates. LTSPC gives the date of the first year, Ch'eng-sheng, namely 552, and the place of translation at the Cheng-kuan temple and at Yang Hsiung's residence in the Ch'ang-fan region of Nanking.[52] Both NTL and KYL agree on this, giving the identical time and place of translation.[53] The KC gives the third year of Ch'eng-sheng (554).[54] The Tunhuang manuscript of the introduction to the first *chüan* of the composite *Suvarṇaprabhāsa* translation, undertaken by Pao-kuei, states that the earlier redaction by Paramārtha was translated from the second month, twenty-fifth day, of the second year Ch'eng-sheng (March 25, 553) until the third month, twentieth day, of that same year (April 18).[55] Thus, the LTSPC, NTL, KYL, and KC records would be in error unless we assume that the period delineated in the Tunhuang manuscript is much too short for translating a *sūtra* seven *chüan* in length. Indeed, not only would Paramārtha's rate of translating probably not permit such an extraordinary feat, but also the uprising of Hou Ching was not a very conducive environment for scholarly pursuits. It is therefore more reasonable to assume that Paramārtha and his staff began the translation during the first year of Ch'eng-sheng (552) and continued to revise and refine the work until about April 18 of the following year. The KC, which is the only record to give third year Ch'eng-sheng (554), may be regarded as either an error or, perhaps, an indication that further revisions of the translation were made in 554. Documentary evidence of two translation sites for the *Suvarṇaprabhāsa-sūtra* indicates that the translation staff most likely worked on the text first at the Cheng-kuan temple in 552 and then moved to Yang Hsiung's residence in the Ch'ang-fan region of Nanking from March 25, 553, until at least April 18, 553.[56]

From Nanking Paramārtha traveled approximately three hundred miles southwest to Yüchang, in the second month, third year, of Ch'eng-sheng (March 19-April 17, 554). The HKSC mentions that this is a return visit to Yüchang, though since none of the existing documents mentions a first visit to that city, the HKSC may be in error on this point: Paramārtha may have been paying his first visit to Yüchang. The KC would seem to support this view in stating that Paramārtha "went" to Yüchang, not that he returned there. (The KYL, which is in part based on the HKSC, follows the HKSC text exactly.) On the other hand, since Hsiao I (Emperor Yüan) assumed the throne in Chiang-ling in December 552, Paramārtha may possibly have visited him at his earlier residence at Yüchang, presumably while on his way to the Cheng-kuan temple in Nanking, in order to pay his respects. At any rate, Paramārtha's journey to Yüchang in 554 would have taken some time. At Yüchang he is said to have met the eminent monk Ching-shao (508-83).[57] His visits to temples in the immediate vicinity, namely Shih-hsing and probably Hsin-wu, most likely occurred at that time.

Ui hypothesizes that the first time Paramārtha went to Yüchang was on his way to Nanking from Nanhai (modern Canton).[58] That is, when Paramārtha first disembarked from his ship in Canton on September 25, 546, he stopped at various places while traveling about the Kwangtung region for two years prior to his arrival in Nanking, some time between August 20 and September 17, 548. One of the places between Canton and Nanking along the possible water routes is Yüchang, about midway between the two great urban centers. T'ang Yung-t'ung gives the same hypothesis for Paramārtha's first purported visit to Yüchang.[59] In any event, Yüchang became a refuge for Paramārtha on several occasions, for it reappears in the biography later on.

At the Pao-t'ien temple in Yüchang in the year 554, Paramārtha, aided by Hui-hsien and ten other monks, completed translation of the *Mi-lo hsia sheng ching* (Sūtra of Maitreya's Descent [from Heaven]) and the *Jen wang po-jo ching* (Sūtra of the Perfection of Wisdom of the Benevolent King).[60] There he met the famous scholar Ching-shao, who was forty-six years of age; Paramārtha was fifty-five years old. According to Ching-shao's biography in the HKSC, Paramārtha said of Ching-shao that "it is rare to meet with such an [eminent] person."[61] It should be noted that, according to the LTSPC and NTL, *Jen-wang po-jo ching shu*, a commentary on the *Sūtra of the Perfection of Wisdom of the Benevolent King*, was composed five years earlier, in 549, but this is highly improbable since Hou Ching was mounting his rebellion at that time; indeed, it seems unlikely that such a commentary ever existed.[62]

After completing these translations, Paramārtha moved to Hsin-wu where he resided at the Mei-yeh temple and may have translated the *Chiu shih i-chi* (Commentary on the Theory of Nine Consciousnesses) in two *chüan*, a text no longer extant.[63] From there he moved to Shih-hsing where he is said to have translated the *Ta-sheng ch'i hsin lun* (Awakening of Faith in Mahāyāna), in the second year of Ch'eng-sheng (553). Both the authorship of the text and the translation date are highly problematic, however.

From Shih-hsing, Paramārtha moved northward, across the

Nan-ling mountain range to Nan-k'ang (near modern Kiangsi, district of Kan). The Grand Guardian Hsiao Po escorted him across the mountains and through the territory of Ouyang Wei, the imperial representative of Shih-hsing (called Tung Heng-chou under Emperor Yüan) and honorary marquis of the area.[64] Since Hsiao Po had made many trips to oversee the region around Shih-hsing, on several occasions explicitly to outmaneuver Ouyang Wei, he was experienced in crossing the Nan-ling mountains and could conveniently accompany Paramārtha to Nan-k'ang at the same time that he supervised the area under the guise of assisting a Buddhist monk in his travels.[65] This journey across the mountains must have taken place between the closing months of 554 and the third month of 557 (April 15-May 13) when Hsiao Po was killed.[66] In the second month of 557, one month before his death, Hsiao Po, having raised his army in rebellion against the emperor, crossed the Nan-ling mountains to Nan-k'ang. It was probably at this time that Paramārtha was escorted to Nan-k'ang, having spent a good part of the years 555 and 556 in Shih-hsing. During this period, Paramārtha "translated in these various places in a hurried manner without a patron."[67] At Shih-hsing Paramārtha is said to have translated the *Sui-hsiang lun chung shih-liu ti shu* (A Commentary on the Sixteen Truths from the Lakṣaṇānusāra-śāstra), a commentary on the *Abhidharma-kośa* attributed to Guṇamati.[68]

In the third year of Chao-t'ai (557), at the very close of the Liang dynasty, Paramārtha completed the translation of the *Wu-shang i ching* (*Anuttarāśraya-sūtra*) (Supreme Foundation Sūtra) in the ninth month, eighth day (October 16), at the request of Liu Wen-t'o, secretary of Nan-k'ang, P'ing-ku district.[69] This date is found in the colophon to the *Wu-shang i ching* preserved in the KYL, which criticizes the LTSPC for cataloging this text as a Ch'en dynasty period translation.[70]

For at least a second time, Paramārtha returned to Yüchang, in the seventh month of the second year of Yung-ting (July 31-August 29, 558). He also visited Lin-ch'uan (in Kiangsi, directly south, approximately forty miles from Yüchang) and Chin-an (in Fukien, a port city along the coast, three hundred fifty miles southeast of Yüchang). First, he stopped at Lin-ch'uan, the closer of the two places, where he translated two treatises by Vasubandhu, *Chung-pien fen-pieh lun* (*Madhyānta-vibhāga*) (Discernment between the Extremes and the Middle Way) and the *Wei-shih lun* (Treatise on Consciousness-Only).[71]

At Chin-an Paramārtha apparently had an audience with several important monks, Seng-tsung, Fa-chun, Chih-wen (509-99), Hui-jen, Hui-k'ai, Fa-jen, Hui-kuang, and Fa-t'ai, who had crossed to the Ling-nan region especially for that purpose. According to Fa-t'ai's biography, Paramārtha had been traveling in China for more than ten years when he desired to go back to his homeland, but he was detained by Ouyang Wei in Kwangchow.[72] In the same source it is recorded that Fa-t'ai, Seng-tsung, Hui-k'ai, and others desired to be instructed and went to the Chih-chih temple in Kwangchow to receive Paramārtha's teachings. Hui-kuang's biography also mentions that he was being instructed at the same time as Seng-tsung, Hui-k'ai, and Fa-chun, but it omits any mention of traveling across to the Ling-nan region.[73] According to Chih-wen's biography, Chih-wen, Seng-tsung, Fa-chun, and other eminent monks stopped at Chin-an with Paramārtha. It is not clear from the text when this meeting took place, nor if the meeting was the first one with Paramārtha or a subsequent visit.[74] The only clear indication of a visit to Chin-an is at this time. Liang-an, which has been tentatively identified by Ui as meaning Chin-an, was one of the places of residence for Paramārtha in 563, some five years later. Hence, we can say that these monks who sought the missionary's new Buddhist teachings met him in either 558 at Chin-an or in 563, if we accept Ui's identification of Liang-an with Chin-an.[75] Only one translation is associated with Chin-an, *Ch'eng lun shih i* (An Explanation of Correct Doctrines), cited in the LTSPC and NTL, as translated at the Fo-li temple during the Ch'en dynasty.[76]

Paramārtha, now in his late fifties, was beginning to tire of moving from place to place. His biography says:

> Although Paramārtha transmitted *sūtras* and *śāstras*, the practice of [the Buddhist] religion was deficient, and he was depressed, for his original objective had not been realized. Furthermore, observing the vicissitudes of the times [for disseminating Buddhism], he desired to sail to *Laṅkāsukha* [Malaysia]. Monks and laity earnestly begged him to promise to stay. He could not shrug off public appeals, and so he stayed in the southeastern regions (*nan-yüeh*) [of China]. Together with his old friends from the preceding Liang dynasty, he reviewed his translations. Whenever the words and the meaning conflicted, these would all be

recast and organized in order to make them consistent throughout [the text], from beginning to end.[77]

Despite his state of mind, it was while Paramārtha was in southeastern regions of Fukien and Kiangsi that he commenced translation work on what were to be some of his most important works, many of which are collected in the *Taishō*. The Korean Yogācārin master Wŏnch'ŭk, in his commentary on the *Saṃdhinirmocana, Chieh-shen-mi-ching shu,* places the translation of the *Saṃdhinirmocana* (*Chieh-chieh ching*) by Paramārtha within the Pao-ting era of the Northern Chou (561-65), while he was at the Ssu-t'ien-wang temple. Wŏnch'ŭk cites an index of Paramārtha's works that dates the text in the second year T'ien-chia (561) in Chien-tsao temple.[78] In all the *sūtra* catalogues, however, no date or place of translation is specified other than the general dating of the text as a Ch'en dynasty translation.

According to Ui, Hui-k'ai gives the dates of translation of the *Wei-shih lun* (Treatise on Consciousness-Only) as from the fourth month, sixteenth day, in the fourth year T'ien-chia (May 23, 563) until the third month, fifth day, in the fifth year of T'ien-chia (April 1, 564). In Ui's opinion, the *Mahāyāna-saṃgraha* (Acceptance of Mahāyāna) (*She ta-sheng lun*) was translated immediately after the *Wei-shih lun,* although this disagrees with the HKSC, which reverses the order, placing the translation of the *Saṃgraha* before the *Wei-shih lun.*[79] Fa-t'ai's biography—though it is not entirely clear on the exact sequence of events—suggests that the *Saṃgraha* was translated at Ouyang Wei's residence in Kwangchow.[80] Since Ouyang Wei died in 563, his patronage of the *Saṃgraha* translation project could have taken place only up through that year, the fourth year of T'ien-chia. The *Saṃgraha* was therefore probably translated before the *Wei-shih lun,* in agreement with the accounts in the HKSC, NTL, LTSPC, and KYL.[81] The translation may have been initiated in 561 at the Chien-tsao temple, under the sponsorship of Governor Wang Fang-she, and then continued at the Ssu-t'ien-wang temple and either completed in Ouyang Wei's residence in 563 or continued after his death when his son, Ouyang Ho, became Paramārtha's financial sponsor.

By the fourth year of T'ien-chia (563) Paramārtha had won prominence throughout southern China and had acquired an ardent group of disciples, many of whom, like Hui-k'ai, Seng-tsung, Ching-shao, Fa-k'an, and Fa-t'ai, traveled great distances to listen to his teachings, particularly those based on the *Saṃgraha*:

All prominent monks in Chien-yeh [Nanking]—Seng-tsung from Chien-yüan temple in Yang-tu, Fa-chun, Seng-jen, and others—had been impressed by what they heard about the new teaching. Therefore, they traveled far south of the Yangtze in order personally to receive Paramārtha's excellent answers [to their questions] about the new teaching. Paramārtha was delighted that they had desired to come to him, and translated the *Mahāyāna-saṃgraha* and other *śāstras* for them, which took a total of two years. He again commented on the doctrinal meanings [of texts], roaming from one place to another, without peace of mind.[82]

Some time before or in the midst of translating the *Saṃgraha*, Paramārtha must have grown disheartened at his circumstances, even though he had a following of earnest disciples and Governor Wang Fang-she attempting to boost his morale. On the twenty-fifth day, ninth month, of the third year T'ien-chia (November 7, 562), according to Ui, or during the ninth month of that same year (September 17-October 16), Paramārtha vowed to leave China, and in fact set sail for India in a small boat from Liang-an. But strong winds and his "fate" drove him back to Canton in the twelfth month (January 10-February 9, 563) after three months at sea. Following this ill-fated departure, he was invited by Ouyang Wei to live at the Chih-chih temple in Canton and work on the translations of the *Saṃgraha* and *Wei-shih lun*. Although we do not know the exact month of Ouyang Wei's death in 563, the HKSC makes it clear that Paramārtha had the financial backing of Ouyang Wei's son, Ho, after the father died. Ouyang Ho (538-70) apparently was intellectually gifted and contributed to or actively observed the translation proceedings. "Paramārtha considered these conditions, realizing that it was impossible to return west,"[83] and for a period, under a fairly stable rule in China, proceeded with his translation work at a rapid pace.

In the HKSC a bit of hagiography follows the description of Ouyang Ho's patronage of Paramārtha and his staff. Paramārtha's moral character is brought out in a series of anecdotes that, like many others in the histories of Buddhist monks, describe contacts with supernatural powers as if they were actual experiences. These tales are difficult to analyze, but their contribution to the forming of a tradition is significant to the historian. The Indian missionary apparently had an island retreat in the delta of the Pearl River off Canton. The waters were turbulent, and the cliffs on the water's edge were very steep. Paramārtha, however, was believed to be able to cross the waters effortlessly while Ouyang Ho dared not cross the treacherous waters. On one occasion Paramārtha went to visit Ho. The HKSC says: "Paramārtha spread out his sitting mat on the water and sat cross-legged on it, as if he were riding a boat. He floated over the waters to the shore. When he climbed ashore to greet him [Ouyang Ho], the sitting mat was not wet, and he spread it out as usual [to sit on]. Other times he would use a lotus leaf as a boat to ride across. There are many examples of such marvels [pertaining to Paramārtha]."[84]

Active and intense translation activity (of texts such as the *Vajracchedikā*, *Kuang-i fa-men ching*, and *Abhidharma-kośa*), made possible through the generosity of the Ouyang family, continued for some five years. But during the sixth month of the second year Kuang-t'ai or Kuang-ta (July 10-August 8, 568), Paramārtha came to a decision:

> Paramārtha had grown weary of the world and felt extremely fatigued. It seemed better to him to prepare for an early rebirth in a better world. So he went into the mountains north of Nanhai [Canton] to commit suicide. At that time, Chih-k'ai [Hui-k'ai] was lecturing on the *Abhidharma-kośa*. On hearing what had happened, he hurried to him [Paramārtha]. Monks and laity ran after one another into the countryside [toward the mountains]. The governor [Ouyang Ho] also dispatched envoys and guardsmen to restrain him. He [the governor] personally prostrated himself [in front of Paramārtha]. Only after detaining him for three days did he [Paramārtha] return to his normal state.[85]

After the attempted suicide, Paramārtha stopped at the Wang-yüan temple with his closest disciples, Seng-tsung and Hui-k'ai, who had requested that Paramārtha be invited to the capital by Emperor Wen. Monks at court "who were in prestigious positions and had great reputations were afraid of losing [status] and so memorialized, saying 'Those groups of works translated beyond the mountains [in the Kwangtung and Kwangsi regions] mainly expound 'Consciousness-Only' without sense objects (*wu-ch'en wei-shih*). Their words are antagonistic to government policy and damaging to the national morale. He should not be allowed in China proper but relegated to the hinterlands.' The emperor agreed. Therefore, the innovative writings from Nanhai remained hidden throughout the Ch'en Dynasty."[86]

Two months later, on the twelfth day, eighth month, of the second year of Kuang-t'ai (September 18, 568), Paramārtha's favorite disciple, Hui-k'ai, died. Paramārtha grieved deeply for him and, with the rest of his disciples, burned candles and incense in Fa-chun's room. He continued to translate the *Abhidharma-kośa*, no longer assisted by Hui-k'ai, but he soon became very sick himself. On February 12, 569, at noon, five months after Hui-k'ai's death, Paramārtha died at the age of seventy. The next day his body was cremated and a stūpa was erected at Ch'ao-ting (near Canton). On the thirteenth day (February 15) Seng-tsung, Fa-chun, and others returned to Mount Lu in Kiangsi to carry on the work of Paramārtha.

When one considers the prodigious amount of translation activity that Paramārtha undertook in spite of the political upheavals around him, one realizes how dedicated a scholar he was. He stuck to his close and difficult textual study with amazing tenacity and endurance. The biography of Paramārtha in the HKSC clearly reiterates the theme of survival in undertaking perilous work, doomed to be potentially threatening not only to the heads of state but also to other Buddhist monks who were aspiring power brokers in the capital city: "Now during Paramārtha's time in the Liang dynasty, there was chaos and anarchy. The response [to crisis] was defeatist and fatalistic. The roads and river ways were seldom traveled. He roamed about as a missionary; in accordance with regional affinities he pursued his course. This resulted in the fragmentation of collections of texts and frequent separation from some of his translators."[87]

This would hold true, in Paramārtha's case, not only for the Liang but also for the Ch'en dynasty. Paramārtha's biographer portrays him as a patient, assiduous monk in a hostile society, and also as a saint, honored as the Master of the Bodhisattva Precepts,[88] and as one who could perform miracles. This may even hint at the wonder with which the biographer esteemed Paramārtha's many translations, for would it not be something of a miracle and a demonstration of a highly disciplined nature to translate extremely difficult philosophical texts while being forced to move from place to place? The biography holds one's interest in another way as well. The mental dejection of a monk who was compelled to be not just a reclusive missionary scholar but a political survivor is poignant and realistic. Not accustomed to the political arena of southern Chinese society, Paramārtha was so frustrated by the continual confrontation with various officials that he tried to take his own life. But his case was the rule rather than the exception among the Buddhist clergy in southern China, where a pragmatic alliance between various provincial military men such as Ouyang Wei and his son Ho was necessary both economically and politically.

The wise and stoic Paramārtha comes to life as a missionary-monk first and foremost, as a politically astute foreigner second, and yet also as one whose human relationships reinforced the image of the brilliant, culturally adaptable man of spartan and restrained manner. Two interesting anecdotes from his biography are worth quoting in full:

> Once when the weather was bitterly cold, Paramārtha was wearing only thin clothing, and he endured it without mentioning it all night. Some of his students were seated by his side. Hui-k'ai and others stood quietly by him in attendance throughout the night. They debated and conversed for a long time until their voices had become quite loud. At one point when Paramārtha fell asleep, [Hui-]k'ai quietly covered him with a garment, but Paramārtha was secretly aware of it and let it fall to the ground. His stoicism and contentment with little was like that. [Hui-]k'ai continued to serve Paramārtha, becoming increasingly closer to him as time passed.
>
> Another time Paramārtha sighed three times from frustration. Hui-k'ai asked the reason for this, and Paramārtha replied: "You and the others are sincere about the True Dharma and it is fitting that you should assist in its transmission. Only it grieves me that these are not the times for disseminating the Dharma. My purpose in coming here has been obstructed." [Hui-]k'ai heard this and was saddened. For a long time he wept. Kneeling before Paramārtha he said: "The Great Dharma is cut off from the world, but you have come all this way to China. The people have no responses [to meet these times]. Can anything be done to remedy this?"
>
> Paramārtha pointed his finger to the northwest and said: "In that direction there will be a great kingdom, neither too near nor too far. After we all have died, it [the Dharma] shall be greatly prosperous, but we shall not see its ascendance. That is why I sighed deeply."[89]

These anecdotes illustrate the affection that Paramārtha's devoted disciples had for him as well as the disposition and character of the man. This missionary-monk's reputation and stature as a scholar made him sought after by politicians and by renowned Chinese Buddhist monks who became his disciples. But it is his brilliance as a translator and philosopher that preserved his status as one of the geniuses in Chinese Buddhist history. As the inspiration prefiguring the distinctively Chinese Buddhist schools formulated during the Sui dynasty, Paramārtha was one of the key figures in constructing and systematizing a psychological analysis of mind. An examination of Paramārtha's particular interpretation of Yogācārin Buddhism and his impact on Chinese Buddhism will bring to light his original contributions to the development of Chinese Buddhist thought during the subsequent period of Buddhism's zenith in Sui and T'ang.

II

The Dissemination of Paramārtha's Ideas

IN ASSESSING Paramārtha's contributions to later developments in Chinese Buddhist thought, one encounters many textual and historical difficulties. It is generally recognized that Paramārtha ranks with Kumārajīva and Hsüan-tsang as one of the greatest and most prolific translators of Buddhist scripture and commentaries; unfortunately, only a small portion of his original corpus is preserved in the Chinese Buddhist canon.[1] The quality of his translations from the Sanskrit has been the subject of much controversy; his Korean critic Wŏnch'ŭk and the Chinese Buddhist K'uei-chi, as well as modern Japanese Buddhologists, have debated the issue.[2]

To compound the problems of an incomplete corpus and scholarly conflicts over the accuracy of Paramārtha's translations, we lack adequate documentation on two of the most significant schools of Buddhist thought during the North-South dynastic period, namely, the She-lun and Ti-lun schools and their subsequent offshoots. These two schools inherited Paramārtha's transmission of Yogācārin and Tathāgatagarbhan ideas, and they developed their own exegeses on his writings. By the time of the T'ang dynasty, both the She-lun and Ti-lun schools had been eclipsed by other schools, most notably the Hua-yen and the Fa-hsiang systems of scholastic Chinese Buddhism.[3] A subsequent loss of many of the texts and historical accounts of She-lun and Ti-lun's major proponents has made reconstruction of the two schools' lineages virtually impossible.[4] Yet these two systems of Buddhism represent the repository of Paramārtha's philosophical and religious views. Before tentatively indicating the more prominent figures in these two sectarian branches, based upon available primary source materials, we must look at the circumstances of Paramārtha's most important disciples immediately after their great teacher's death on February 12, 569.

The propagation of Paramārtha's works was, it appears, abruptly terminated in the south after the deaths of his direct disciples. During the Liang and Ch'en dynasties the Buddhist scholarly community at the southern court was interested in the *Nirvāṇa-sūtra, Larger Prajñāpāramitā*, and *Ch'eng-shih* systems of thought, and Paramārtha's treatises were put aside. After the Northern Chou persecution in 574, well-known Ti-lun scholars fled to the south and later brought Paramārtha's texts to north China. Ironically, while Paramārtha's views were virtually suppressed in the south, they became the dominant philosophy in the scholarly world of the northern provinces.

Paramārtha's Disciples and Lineage

SENG-TSUNG, FA-CHUN, AND CHIH-HSIU

Before Paramārtha died, he made a last request to his disciples that they zealously transmit and copy his works. We may assume that his closest disciples, those who had assisted him for a long period of time, fervently attempted to carry out his wishes.[5] In Paramārtha's biography, his disciples Seng-tsung, Fa-chun, and others who remain unnamed, returned to Mount Lu in Kiangsi on February 14, 569, the day after Paramārtha's body had been cremated and a stūpa erected at Ch'ao-ting, outside Canton.[6] There are no individual biographies for Seng-tsung and Fa-chun that would provide us with information to trace the dissemination of texts on their return trip to Mount Lu; thus it is difficult to determine whether they were successful in their mission. Paramārtha's writings were said to be entrusted to his disciple Chih-hsiu,[7] although Seng-tsung, Fa-chun, and other monks carried his translations and commentaries with them to Kiangsi. Seng-tsung arranged the commentaries, adding some comments without altering the main lines of Paramārtha's ideas. He helped in the important revisions to the *Mahāyāna-saṃgraha* and was the first to make notes on the text, but these notes are now lost. He also wrote a biography of the Indian missionary that was widely circulated at the time of the composition of the HKSC. This biography is now lost. Perhaps Chih-hsiu was entrusted with copies of Paramārtha's commentaries after Seng-tsung had arranged and annotated them. We have no information or separate biographical documentation on the monk Chih-hsiu and only one mention of him after the master's death. We do know that Chih-hsiu, Tao-ni, and twenty other monks bound the *Saṃgraha* and its commentary together and were known for their lectures on this material. No other monks are named in Paramārtha's biography in connection with the posthumous transmission of his ideas.

FA-T'AI, CHING-SUNG, CHIH-NING, AND SENG-PIEN

Much valuable information is available on the monk Fa-t'ai (d. 601), who appears to have been one of the most influential and active disseminators of Paramārtha's teachings.[8] Surviving his teacher by thirty-two years, Fa-t'ai had a long career of transmitting the new doctrines of the Indian missionary-monk. According to his HKSC biography, Fa-t'ai met Paramārtha at the Chih-chih temple in Canton, then under the patronage of Governor Ouyang Wei. Fa-t'ai was in Yang-tu, studying at the Chien-yuan temple with Hui-k'ai, Seng-tsung, Fa-jen, Fa-chun, Chih-wen (509-99),[9] and Hui-k'uang (534-613).[10] They all decided to travel together across the Yangtze, over one thousand miles south-westward to Canton. Since Fa-t'ai stayed with Paramārtha as one of his scribes in Canton, we may speculate that he and the other monks met Paramārtha no earlier than 562 when Paramārtha moved to Ouyang Wei's temple headquarters. In the third year of T'ai-chien (571), two years after Paramārtha's death, Fa-t'ai returned to Nanking with Paramārtha's writings, commented on them, and lectured on the *Mahāyāna-saṃgraha* and the *Abhidharma-kośa*.[11] Because of the emperor's preference for the teachings in the San-lun and in the *Larger Prajñāpāramitā-sūtra* (*Pañcaviṃśatisāhasrikā-prajñāpāramitā-sūtra*), Fa-t'ai's lectures were said to have been poorly attended.

In Fa-t'ai's biography we also find mention of his most famous disciple, Ching-sung (537-614), who had fled to Nanking during the Northern Chou persecution as did so many other Buddhist monks from north China.[12] Ching-sung had been a student of

Hui-shun,[13] a direct disciple of Hui-k'uang (467-536?) of Southern Ti-lun.[14] Having heard the new teaching of Paramārtha's views from Fa-t'ai, Ching-sung avidly studied Paramārtha's works. By 590 Ching-sung had returned to P'eng-ch'eng to lecture on Paramārtha's philosophical treatises and to write a commentary on nine consciousnesses.[15] Ching-sung may have been the first northern Chinese monk to disseminate Paramārtha's theories on Yogācāra in north China, but we have insufficient evidence to confirm this. Among his disciples were Fa-hu (576-643),[16] Chih-ning (562?-609?),[17] Tao-chi (577-637),[18] and Shan-hui (587-635),[19] all of whom were important members of the She-lun school. Of Ching-sung's disciples, Chih-ning is the most noteworthy. Chih-ning's disciples Seng-pien (568-642)[20] and Chih-tse[21] later are said to have become disciples of Hsüan-tsang. There is also evidence to suggest that Seng-pien was one of the early teachers of Chih-yen (602-68),[22] the second patriarch of the Hua-yen tradition. The biographies of these She-lun masters reveal the importance of two temple centers in the northern part of China, the P'eng-ch'eng temple and the Ta-ch'an-ting temple in Ch'ang-an.[23] While She-lun thought, emphasizing the *Mahāyāna-saṃgraha*, was on the ascendency in northern China, the south remained a bastion of Mādhyamika and Prajñaparamitā scholarship.

TS'AO P'I, HUI-K'AI, AND FA-K'AN

Another group of disciples stemming directly from Paramārtha can be tentatively reconstructed through Ts'ao P'i, nephew of Paramārtha's favorite disciple, Hui-k'ai (518-68), and biographer of Paramārtha. Ts'ao P'i's biography served as the textual basis for the HKSC. Probably Ts'ao P'i studied together with his uncle, Hui-k'ai, under Paramārtha, for almost fifteen years. What we know of Ts'ao P'i and Hui-k'ai is recorded in the HKSC, incorporated under biographical data for Fa-t'ai. Paramārtha said of Hui-k'ai: "If I had met you earlier to collect *sūtras* and *śāstras* before translating, I would not be lacking in anything [with regard to translation activities]. Now I have translated these two *śāstras* [the *Abhidharma-kośa* and the *Mahāyāna-saṃgraha*] and the words and phrasing are perfect. I have no regrets."[24] Hui-k'ai had been the principal scribe for both the *Abhidharma-kośa* and the *Mahāyāna-saṃgraha*. He apparently wrote his own commentaries on these two *śāstras*, one in eight *chüan* on the *Saṃgraha* and one in fifty-three *chüan* on the *Kośa*; both of these works have been lost. As Paramārtha's assistant and scribe, Hui-k'ai did not leave his mentor's side until the time of his own death in 568 at the age of fifty-one, an event that grieved Paramārtha deeply. The only fragments of Hui-k'ai's writings that are preserved are a colophon to the *Wei-shih lun* written in 563, a preface to the *Saṃgraha* written in 564, and an introduction to the *Kośa* written in 567.[25]

Ts'ao P'i, Hui-k'ai's nephew, was not a monk but a gentleman scholar who nonetheless became an instructor for Chinese Buddhist monks seeking assistance in understanding Paramārtha's philosophy. In Fa-t'ai's biography, Ts'ao P'i is described in the following manner:

> He was extremely intelligent, erudite, and refined. He traveled a great distance, hardly carrying anything [in the way of supplies] until he reached the south [Kwangchow] where he learned of the *Mahāyāna-saṃgraha*. He became informed in various sections [of the text] and was highly accomplished in all of them. In the third year of T'ai-chien (571) Ts'ao P'i was invited by the illustrious monk Ming-yung of the Chien-hsing temple to lecture on the *Saṃgraha* in front of more than fifty learned and eminent monks. Later he went to Chiang-tu to evaluate his previous work, remaining in the Pai-t'a temple to analyze treatises. His clothes were worn in the same style as a gentleman scholar. Rising from his seat, he discussed every complex point with all the renowned scholars around him. Seng-jung of the Ch'an-ting temple and Fa-k'an of the Jih-yen temple, among others, sought his instruction.[26]

From the biography of Fa-k'an (551-623), preserved in the HKSC, we know that the temple where Ts'ao P'i composed and assessed his own work was called the An-le temple.[27] Fa-k'an, in studying under Ts'ao P'i, became a praiseworthy student. Later he left Ts'ao P'i to spread Paramārtha's teaching at the Jih-yen temple, but we do not know the date of this departure. We do know that Ts'ao P'i was at the An-le temple at the close of the Ch'en dynasty, approximately 586 or 587, so that Fa-k'an had to have set out for the Jih-yen temple some time during the very beginning of the Sui dynasty, approximately in 589, and not earlier. None of the extant historical documents yields records of Fa-k'an's disciples, except for Hui-k'an (524-605),[28] nor is there any other mention of Ts'ao P'i's disciple, Seng-jung.

CHIH-CHI

Chih-chi (d. 601), another monk who played an important role in transmitting the Indian master's teachings, is not specifically mentioned by name in Paramārtha's biography, nor does he have a separate biography in the HKSC. Most of the biographical data we have on Chih-chi has been incorporated in Fa-t'ai's biography.[29] As a young monk, Chih-chi was primarily influenced by the Ch'eng-shih school of Buddhism. Later on he met the monk Fa-ming, and together they became interested in the literature on the *Vajracchedikā-prajñāpāramitā-sūtra*. Chih-chi also studied the doctrines of the *Vibhāṣa* and Mādhyamika before meeting Paramārtha at Ouyang Wei's temple residence. There, in collaboration with Hui-k'ai and Tao-ni, he assisted Paramārtha in the translation of both the *Saṃgraha* and *Kośa* and compiled a commentary on the *Kośa* with the assistance of twenty other monks. After Hui-k'ai and Paramārtha died, the task of disseminating Paramārtha's scholarship fell to Tao-ni and Chih-chi.

In the ninth year of T'ai-chien (577), Chih-chi continued his lectures on the *Kośa*, faithfully transmitting Paramārtha's teachings. By this time, only a few of the monks who had had direct contact with Paramārtha were still living or of an eminent stature.[30] Chih-chi was one of the few who became famous not only for his lectures on the *Kośa* but for his erudition on the *Nirvāṇa-sūtra*. However, during the persecution of 592 (the twelfth year of K'ai-huang), all Buddhist commentaries and temples were burned in the region governed by Wang Chung-hsüan in Kwangchow.[31] In the first year of Jen-shou (601) Fa-t'ai died and Tao-ni returned to Chiu-chiang. Chih-chi compiled a chronology of Paramārtha's translations and commentaries, in wide circulation during the time of the HKSC but now no longer available.[32] Chih-chi's line of transmission is truncated since we do not know the complete names of his disciples.

TAO-NI AND TAO-YÜEH

Tao-ni, the monk often associated with Chih-chi and Hui-k'ai, had become an expert on the philosophy of the *Mahāyāna-saṃgraha* by the beginning of the Sui.[33] We can piece together some of his biographical facts by looking at the biographies of other She-lun disciples. Accompanied by his disciple Chih-kuang, Tao-ni left Nanking in the tenth year of K'ai-huang (590) to go to the capital city of Ch'ang-an.[34] The two monks resided at the Ta-hsing-shan temple to continue their promulgation of Paramārtha's ideas. Owing in part to Tao-ni's and Chih-kuang's departure from Nanking, Kiangsu and Anhwei provinces began to lose their influence as centers of She-lun learning. One monk who was to have great influence in the burgeoning school of She-lun was Tao-yüeh (568-636).[35] His biography tells us that at a young age he met Tao-ni, who had become quite renowned for his exegeses on She-lun thought; this was before Tao-ni left Chiu-chiang and moved to the capital. By the tenth year of K'ai-huang (590), Tao-ni and his disciples were ordered to Ch'ang-an by imperial decree and forbidden to lecture on the *Mahāyāna-saṃgraha* in south China.

At this time (590) Tao-yüeh was only twenty-two years old, eight years after his novitiate as a Buddhist cleric. Much later, Tao-yüeh was invited to the Hsien-ming temple in Kwangtung where he obtained a copy of Paramārtha's long commentary on the *Abhidharma-kośa*, his translation of the *Shih pa k'ung lun*[36] (a portion of the *Madhyānta-vibhāga*), and Hui-k'ai's annotations. The Hsien-ming temple was one of Paramārtha's temple residences as well as Hui-k'ai's main residence. In the year 612, Tao-yüeh went to the Ta-ch'an-ting temple, which by now had established a reputation as a center of She-lun learning and had over three hundred monks. Tao-yüeh was forty-four years old and was highly regarded as a scholar. Other eminent monks, such as Fa-ch'ang (576-645), Chih-shou (567-635), Seng-pien (568-642), and Hui-ming, engaged in debate with the self-effacing Tao-yüeh but were defeated.[37] On another occasion (627) the Indian monk Prabhākāramitra (translator of the *Mahāyāna-sūtrālaṃkara*) who resided in the capital met Tao-yüeh and praised him for his masterful knowledge of the *Abhidharma-kośa*.[38] Hsüan-tsang studied the *Kośa* under Tao-yüeh and the *Saṃgraha* under Hui-hsiu (548-645), another disciple of Tao-ni and T'an-ch'ien.[39] Tao-yüeh was a prolific writer but nothing remains of his work.

T'AN-CH'IEN

By far the most important single individual responsible for the diffusion of She-lun thought was the monk T'an-ch'ien (542-607). Like Paramārtha, T'an-ch'ien lived during a time of great political turbulence. When Emperor Wu of Northern Chou initiated his persecution of Buddhism, T'an-ch'ien fled to Nanking in 577.[40] He had already become quite knowledgeable in the doctrine of the *Avataṃsaka-sūtra* (Hua-yen ching), Ti-lun literature, as well as in the *Laṅkāvatāra, Vimalakīrti,* and the *Ta-sheng ch'i hsin lun* and had been a disciple of T'an-tsun, Hui-k'uang's student.[41] While residing at the Tao-ch'ang temple, T'an-ch'ien received a copy of the *Saṃgraha* from the governor in Kwei-chou (Kwangsi prefecture).[42] In 581, after the initial attempts to establish the Sui, T'an-ch'ien returned north to P'eng-ch'eng and began to lecture on the *Saṃgraha, Laṅkāvatāra,* and *Ch'i hsin lun,* among other texts. His was believed to be the very first transmission to the north.[43] In 587 T'an-ch'ien went to the capital city of Ch'ang-an, at the invitation of Emperor Wen, and established a lecture hall at court while residing at the Ta-hsing-shan temple. He may have preceded Ching-sung by three years or so in bringing the She-lun to northern China, though Ching-sung was preaching in the north at about the same time. It is not clear whether the two men ever met. All the eminent monks and scholars of the time—Hui-yüan (523-92), Hui-tsang (522-605),[44] Seng-hsiu, and T'an-yen (516-88)[45]—attended T'an-ch'ien's lectures. Among T'an-ch'ien's writings were commentaries on the *Saṃgraha, Laṅkāvatāra-sūtra, Ta-sheng ch'i hsin lun,* and *Wei-shih lun,* and a treatise on the "nine consciousnesses."[46] All these texts are now lost.

T'an-ch'ien was undoubtedly one of the most scholarly and gifted Buddhist monks of his time, responsible not only for disseminating Paramārtha's corpus but also for synthesizing the dominant trends of Ti-lun and She-lun doctrine. His brilliant lectures on the *Saṃgraha* and other masterpieces of the Consciousness-Only or Yogācārin tradition drew the attention of all the intellectuals in Buddhist circles at Ch'ang-an. Even one of Paramārtha's second-generation disciples, Hui-hsiu (disciple of Tao-ni), became T'an-ch'ien's follower, attesting to T'an-ch'ien's command of the literature Paramārtha had introduced to his direct disciples.

HUI-YÜAN OF CHING-YING TEMPLE

Among T'an-ch'ien's many disciples, Hui-yüan of Ching-ying temple is the most renowned.[47] Originally Hui-yüan was T'an-ch'ien's teacher in the early stages of the latter's career. Later,

Hui-yüan became so influenced by his disciple's own interpretations of Yogācāra commentaries that this senior monk became one of T'an-ch'ien's disciples. We are indebted to Hui-yüan for providing some of the most important historical materials for reconstructing the lineages and philosophies of both the She-lun and Ti-lun schools of Chinese Buddhism. T'an-ch'ien's biography and Hui-yüan's writings, particularly his *Ta-sheng i chang* (Compendium on the Principles of Mahāyāna), provide us with a pattern of development in which former Southern Ti-lun proponents such as Hui-yüan, Chih-yen, and T'an-ch'ien became heavily influenced by Paramārtha's philosophical writings.[48] This blurring of the ideological and conceptual boundaries between Southern Ti-lun (once isolated in north China) and the She-lun system introduced into south China by Paramārtha—actually a fusion of two geographically separate schools of Chinese Buddhism—was the result, in part, of the Northern Chou persecution of Buddhists in the 570's, which caused many Buddhist disciples to flee to south China.

Because of scattered and sometimes contradictory data regarding Northern Ti-lun, it is virtually impossible to reconstruct its beliefs. However, Hui-yüan's accounts of the general development of Ti-lun before the schism into northern and southern branches help us to establish the basic tenets of some forms of Ti-lun thought. Although sometimes in an adversarial relationship with She-lun thought, Ti-lun was to become the most important branch of Buddhism to complement and sometimes to challenge Paramārtha's philosophy of mind during the second half of the sixth century in China.

Ti-lun and She-lun Buddhist Thought

Many Tathāgatagarbha and Yogācāra texts were introduced to China in the first half of the fifth century. Two translations of the *Bodhisattvabhūmi, P'u-sa ti-ch'ih ching* by Dharmarakṣa (385-433) and *P'u-sa shan chieh ching* by Guṇavarman (367-431), seem to be among the first Yogācāra literature found in China.[49] By the beginning of the sixth century the two very important Yogācārin texts, *Daśabhūmika-sūtra*[50] and *Laṅkāvatāra-sūtra*,[51] had been transmitted throughout north and south China. In addition, the *Sheng-man ching* (*Śrīmālādevī-sūtra*) had been translated by Guṇabhadra (394-468) in 435 and had become immensely popular.[52] These textual sources enabled Chinese Buddhist scholars to incorporate both Yogācāra and Tathāgatagarbha into one integrated system of thought.

In 508 Ratnamati, Bodhiruci, and Buddhaśānta arrived in Loyang, capital of Northern Wei, and began a collaborative translation of the *Shih-ti ching lun*[53] (*Daśabhūmika-sūtra-śāstra*), Vasubhandu's commentary on the *Daśabhūmika-sūtra*. In 513 Bodhiruci undertook a new translation of the *Laṅkāvatāra*,[54] indicating that this *sūtra*, with its hybrid form of Yogācāra-Tathāgatagarbha teaching, was viewed by Buddhist clerics of the day as an essential text for understanding the thought of Yogācāra. The philosophical disagreements that developed between Ratnamati and Bodhiruci were responsible for the establishment of two forms of Yogācāra in north China, the Bodhiruci branch, known as the Northern Ti-lun because the school was located north of Hsiang-chou, and the Ratnamati branch, known as the Southern Ti-lun, located south of Hsiang-chou.[55] The lineages and controversies between these two factions have been fully treated elsewhere in Buddhological literature and will be discussed only in a general manner here.

The main controversy in the schism between Ratnamati and Bodhiruci was over the fundamental psychological nature of human existence. The translation of the *Daśabhūmika-sūtra* had first introduced the Chinese to the theory of a subconscious repository for all habitual impulses, known as the *ālaya-vijñāna*, and they responded eagerly. Their interest in the nature of this subconscious was to some degree a reflection of the political turmoil in both north and south China, but it also grew out of a historical scholarly concern with the perennial philosophical and religious question of whether human beings are fundamentally good or evil. The very early form of Ti-lun developed forty years before Paramārtha's arrival in China. Therefore, the earliest Ti-lun doctrines could not have been influenced by Paramārtha's own ideas, although many tenets are compatible with those of this Indian master. There is no historical evidence to suggest that Fa-shang (495-580),[56] the great Ti-lun master associated with the southern branch, ever had an occasion to meet with either Paramārtha or his disciples. And though many Southern Ti-lun masters who were Fa-shang's disciples in succeeding generations would become zealous students of Paramārtha's works, most notably Hui-yüan, some Buddhologists consider the short-lived Northern Ti-lun branch to have been closer to Paramārtha's system of thought.[57] Both branches are important intellectual milieus, however, for determining the affinity of current Buddhist dogma with the innovative theories Paramārtha was committed to introducing to monastic scholars.

Since Southern Ti-lun was to have a greater degree of currency and a longer period of duration in the sixth-century developments of philosophical Buddhism than its northern counterpart, their doctrinal schema will be discussed first. In addition, Southern Ti-lun can be reconstructed relatively more substantially than the Northern Ti-lun since writings by Fa-shang and Hui-yüan exist whereas we have no firsthand accounts of Northern Ti-lun masters except in Southern Ti-lun documents.[58]

SOUTHERN TI-LUN

The Southern Ti-lun branch of Chinese Buddhism was founded by Ratnamati, after the schism with his co-translator Bodhiruci. Ratnamati's direct and primary disciple was Hui-kuang, who had many disciples and a national reputation as a scholar. Hui-kuang's most famous disciple, Fa-shang, and Fa-shang's disciple Hui-yüan, who is even more significant to the historian, provide us with some of our richest material for determining the intellectual concerns of sixth-century Buddhists in south China with regard to philosophy of mind.

Fa-shang (495-580). From the extant literary fragments of Fa-shang's *Shih-ti lun i-shu*,[59] we can speculate about Southern Ti-lun's notions of Dharma Body, Dharma Nature, and the seven states of ordinary cognition. Material in the *Shih-ti lun i-shu* has not been thoroughly analyzed by contemporary Buddhologists in their reconstructions of the Southern Ti-lun branch of Buddhist doctrine. It has been established, however, that the school of Southern Ti-lun asserts that the support for all experiences of phenomena is reality as it is (*tathatā*), termed Suchness, and is based in part upon Guṇabhadra's translation of the *Laṅkāvatāra*. Fa-shang described seven kinds of "evolutions of consciousness" (*shih chuan*) suggesting a theory of seven consciousnesses in his commentary, *Shih-ti lun i-shu*:

The Dharma Body is the body of the Dharma Nature (*fa-hsing*). Mind (*hsin*) is [the name for] the seventh state or mind. Ideation (*i*) is the sixth state or ideation. Consciousness (*shih*) is [the name for] the five states of consciousness. Therefore, the *Laṅkāvatāra-sūtra* states: "Mind is the chief collator. Ideation broadly collates. The phenomenal, acting states of consciousness (*hsien-shih; khyāti?*) discriminate in five ways. Separate from these seven kinds, consciousness evolves into wisdom." Therefore, it is said: "Only wisdom is the ground (*i-chih*)." [60]

Fa-shang explains what he means by wisdom in terms of the three-natures theory (*trisvabhāva*):

There are three kinds of shared aspects to wisdom. First, it is conditioned (*yüan-ch'i*). Second, it is false conceptualization. Third, it is Suchness. The "conditioned" (*paratantra*) refers to the seventh state, the *ālaya-vijñāna*, which is the foundation (*pen*) for *saṃsāra*. "False conceptualization" (*parikalpita*) refers to the six states of consciousness (*shih*) and mind (*hsin*), falsely generating discriminations that become attached to six sorts of sense data (*ch'en*). "Suchness" refers to the absolute truth of the Buddha Nature, supreme Emptiness. These three are understood as having different names but the same aspect. [61]

From the above passages we see a clearer picture of Fa-shang's epistemological schema. Mind, the seventh state, is the *ālaya-vijñāna*, and corresponds to the "conditioned" aspect of wisdom, *paratantra-svabhāva* or the nature of dependence in Yogācāra Buddhism. Ideation, the sixth state, and the consciousnesses of sensation and perception are the "false conceptualization" as an aspect of wisdom, *parikalpita-svabhāva* or the nature of false discrimination. One other feature or aspect of wisdom remains, namely, reality as it is, Suchness, the absolute truth of the Buddha Nature identified with Emptiness, and *pariniṣpanna-svabhāva*. This feature of wisdom is not explicitly enumerated as an eighth state of consciousness.

The system is more complicated than it first appears. Suchness, the truly real, is the principle of wisdom untainted by false discrimination or by conditions, yet wisdom functions in ordinary cognitive states, participates in discriminative acts, and is conditioned by previous and concurrent events. What this schema seems to suggest is that all phenomenal reality—wisdom in its three aspects—is ultimately based upon the supreme Emptiness equated with Buddha Nature and with Suchness. Nonetheless, false conceptualization and the conditioned mind are temporarily based upon the *ālaya-vijñāna* as their support or foundation.

One very unusual statement in the *Shih-ti lun i-shu* does provide evidence that Suchness is interpreted by Fa-shang as an eighth mode of consciousness: "In the stage of the eighth cognitive mode (*shih*), the seven consciousnesses have no [real] essence (*t'i*) and are based upon the real (*chen*) even though they function (*yung*) differently."[62] What is this eighth *shih* or cognitive mode? This eighth cognitive mode is the truly existent, the Buddha Nature denoted as Tathāgatagarbha:

> The false [conceptualizing faculty] is based upon the truly existent (*chen-yu*). Therefore, we assert that the *ālaya-vijñāna* is generated as the foundation for thousands of delusions. Thus, the [*Śrīmālādevī*] *sūtra* states: "Because of the Tathāgatagarbha we can talk about *saṃsāra*." Therefore, the Tathāgatagarbha is the foundation for all phenomena (*dharmas*). Because there are these two kinds of foundations, we have explained these two cases.[63]

These views are consistent with those in the *Śrīmālādevī-sūtra* and in the *Laṅkāvatāra-sūtra,* two texts we know to have had some influence on Fa-shang's intellectual development, in which the absolute foundation for reality is the intrinsically pure state of mind identified with the Tathāgatagarbha. Here we have some evidence to postulate that Fa-shang adhered to a system of thought in which there were seven cognitive processes engaged in misconceptions of reality, with the seventh state being the basis for the six sensory and ideational faculties. These seven states functioned epistemically in a different way from the one who has acquired wisdom, for they have no real essence (*t'i*) or other ground from Suchness, that is, as manifested in the Tathāgatagarbha. Therefore, according to Fa-shang's interpretation of Southern Ti-lun, the support for all experience has to be the reality of the Buddha Nature or Tathāgatagarbha, which is viewed as an eighth consciousness. This support functions temporarily through its mode as the *ālaya-vijñāna* when delusions and misconceptions occur but the substantiality or permanent reality of the *ālaya* is denied.

However, Suchness also has a dimension totally devoid of the *ālaya-vijñāna,* namely, mind as the absolutely real state of wisdom. When discrimination is no longer generated, this is the essential state of mind, "the truly existent" (*chen-yu*) and irreducible foundation for all phenomena. Consequently, Suchness must be considered to be logically prior to the other seven cognitive states besides being their ultimate cause.

We cannot, as yet, determine whether Fa-shang intended this eighth mode or Buddha Nature to be completely coextensive with the principle of the Dharma Nature. In an earlier discussion of Suchness in the *Shih-ti lun i-shu,* the Dharma is described as the essential Suchness (*tzu-t'i chen-ju*); the Dharma Nature of Suchness is used by Fa-shang, but Dharma Nature per se is never equated with either Buddha Nature or wisdom.[64] Hence, it is not certain whether Fa-shang intended to qualify the term Suchness in two ways: one as the *wisdom* of supreme Emptiness identified with the Buddha Nature; the other as the Dharma Nature itself, the *principle* of conditioned co-arising on a theoretical level without any concrete instantiation in phenomenal events. Fa-shang maintained that when the Dharma and the Buddha have interacted with each other, one sees the Suchness-Dharma Body. The implication is that the Dharma and Buddha are two separate categories finding their point of intersection in the Suchness-Dharma Body,[65] another term referring undoubtedly to the Tathāgatagarbha. The nonduality of the principle of reality and the wisdom of that reality is a distinctive feature of Tathāgatagarbha thought, but it is difficult to determine whether Fa-shang viewed Dharma Nature and Buddha Nature as identical or not.[66]

To summarize Fa-shang's system of conscious processes, there is a taxonomy incorporating a substructure of seven ordinary deluded states with their functional support being the *ālaya-vijñāna* overlaid with an eighth state of consciousness representing the essentially enlightened state of mind, the wisdom of reality as it is, in its nature of being Empty. The *ālaya-vijñāna* is the seventh state, and Tathāgatagarbha, a dimension of Suchness, is the eighth, intrinsically pure state of mind. This theory has no notion of a defiled state corresponding to the *manas.*

Why does Fa-shang develop this system? His view may be derived from the chapter on "Buddha Nature" in Bodhiruci's translation of the *Laṅkāvatāra-sūtra,* which posits that "the Tathāgatagarbha does not reside in the *ālaya-vijñāna.*" Southern Ti-lun usually did not take Bodhiruci's works as authoritative. Guṇabhadra's recension of the *Laṅkāvatāra* considers the *ālaya-vijñāna* and the Tathāgatagarbha as synonymous.[67] The *Śrīmālādevī-sūtra* describes the true consciousness or Tathāgatagarbha as the foundation for the other six sensory and ideational states. Fa-shang could have gleaned from Bodhiruci, rather than from Ratnamati, a theory of seven defiled or deluded conscious states and a theory of an eighth, undefiled state of consciousness epistemologically distinct from the other seven.[68] The *Saṃdhinirmocana* also enumerates the seventh consciousness as the *ālaya*.

This sorting out of two typological schemas for one system of ideas may give us the key to the controversies between different factions of Buddhist scholars in the sixth and seventh centuries. The "numbering system" of conscious processes and modes of activity has been the subject of much controversy among Buddhologists who have failed to see a common pattern evident in all the Tathāgatagarbha-Yogācāra syntheses, represented by texts such as the *Laṅkāvatāra, Śrīmālādevī,*[69] Paramārtha's corpus, and the Northern and some Southern Ti-lun texts. The rationale for the numbering of different cognitive modes seems to be to use the enumeration as a conceptual tool to distinguish the deluded states of conscious existence from the enlightened state, the Tathāgatagarbha, which is always intrinsically pure and untainted by defilement. Since most early Yogācārins were concerned with analyzing the deluded state, the central focus is on the ordinary cognitive processes of everyday life, and a notion of intrinsically pure mind conditioning defilement was vehemently denied. Fa-shang's taxonomy of seven consciousnesses synthesizes Yogācāra and Tathāgatagarbha. The additional cognitive state of a totally enlightened mind is the absolute reality, while the reality of the *ālaya-vijñāna* is ultimately negated as false.

Hui-yüan (523-92). Fa-shang's most famous disciple, the one who wrote several highly significant historical documents, is Hui-yüan, who was greatly influenced by T'an-ch'ien and She-lun Buddhist scholarship as well as by the texts, *Ch'i hsin lun* and the *Śrīmālādevī-sūtra*. The philosophical resources found in three of Hui-yüan's works, a commentary on the *Awakening of Faith in Mahāyāna* (*Ch'i hsin lun*) entitled *Ta-sheng ch'i hsin lun i-shu,*[70] his commentary on the *Daśabhūmika-sūtra* entitled *Shih-ti ching lun i-chi*, and his *Compendium on the Principles of Mahāyāna*

(*Ta-sheng i chang*), provide a wealth of information on the schematization of conscious states at that time. Altogether, Hui-yüan gives us enough data to determine with reasonable accuracy the religious concerns of sixth-century Chinese Buddhist intellectuals in the southern provinces. Of the three commentaries, the earliest is the *Shih-ti ching lun i-chi*, a commentary upon which the Ti-lun school's influence on Hui-yüan is evident. This commentary preserves a schema of eight conscious states illustrating a close affinity to his Southern Ti-lun master, Fa-shang, and will be discussed first.

Hui-yüan's later works, *Ch'i hsin lun i-shu* and the *Ta-sheng i chang*, will be interpreted subsequently in order to delineate the transition in philosophical position from the earlier taxonomy of eight consciousnesses to the "newer" theory of nine, which illustrates Paramārtha's influence on his ideas. We shall also ask the question: Why did Hui-yüan make the conceptual shift from Fa-shang's position to an innovative typology of nine conscious states? The tentative answer must lie in the fact that Hui-yüan, originally a student of the Southern Ti-lun school who, very late in life, met T'an-ch'ien and studied Paramārtha's corpus, recognized a need to change the epistemological model of his own earlier writings.

In the *Shih-ti ching lun i-chi*, Hui-yüan reflects Fa-shang's characterization of ordinary conscious activity in seven modes, taking the *Laṅkāvatāra-sūtra* as his scriptural authority:

> Based upon the *Laṅkāvatāra-sūtra*[71] there are five consciousnesses, a sixth consciousness, and a seventh consciousness that are classified into three types. In that *sūtra*, the seventh or false consciousness is the foundation for accumulation [of misconceptions] and is called mind (*hsin*). The sixth or ideation (*i*) is always examining sense data and is explained as ideation [alternatively, *i-shih*]. The mind—the five consciousnesses—completely separates out apparent sense fields and is explained as consciousness (*shih*). Now this will be explained later. Except for this, there is no other mind. . . . Therefore, separate from all states of mind, ideation, and consciousness there is no other mind, etc. But wisdom is the function; true consciousness (*chen-shih*) is the essence. The true pervades the previously mentioned seven [consciousnesses] and combines with them to make eight consciousnesses.[72]

Here we see the same breakdown into seven kinds of evolutions of consciousness found in Fa-shang's *Shih-ti lun i-shu* cited above, these seven representing the functioning of consciousness in ordinary, deluded activities. As in Fa-shang's system, these seven states have no real essence and are based upon the really true state of consciousness even though the lower seven conscious processes function in deluded ways. This eighth truly enlightened state of mind is the ground that permeates the other seven and supports them. However, even at this stage in Hui-yüan's intellectual development he seems to differ from his master Fa-shang in identifying this eighth state not only with the Tathāgatagarbha as does Fa-shang but with the *ālaya-vijñāna*, which Fa-shang relegates to the seventh mode of conscious activity. This indicates that Hui-yüan followed Guṇabhadra's recension of the *Laṅkāvatāra*, rather than that of his school's opponent, Bodhiruci of the Northern Ti-lun branch.

The *ālaya*[-*vijñāna*] is translated as "the insubmersible" (*wu-mo*) [subconscious?] consciousness. This is the eighth [consciousness], the mind of the Tathāgatagarbha which, according to conditions, flows and evolves. Because its essence is not lost, it is called "insubmersible." This is the fundamental nature of *saṃsāra*. The false cannot be selective [in its functioning] and must be based upon the true. Consequently, it is said that name and form are generated together in the *ālaya*. . . . What is meant by "name and form are generated together" is that name and form are generated from the true consciousness (*chen-shih*).[73]

Like Fa-shang, Paramārtha argues that false conceptualizations ("name and form") are temporarily based upon the *ālaya-vijñāna* as their mode of operation. For Hui-yüan, this mode is the eighth, not the seventh. Both Fa-shang and Hui-yüan seem to be in agreement about the nature of the foundation of delusion, namely, the *ālaya-vijñāna*. They also agree that the true consciousness is the ultimate ground, the real essence, of all experiences, and equate this state of mind with the Tathāgatagarbha, which Fa-shang and Hui-yüan both identify with an eighth state of mind. The idea of the *ālaya-vijñāna* as a fundamental consciousness supporting phenomenal reality is found in both Northern and Southern Ti-lun. The relationship between the *ālaya* and Suchness as that of the functioning of consciousness to its essence is asserted in Southern Ti-lun, especially in Fa-shang's writings, but also in Northern Ti-lun, as we shall see below. Hui-yüan's point of departure focuses on the relationship between the *ālaya-vijñāna* and the Tathāgatagarbha, the former being a conditioned aspect of the latter, and consequently the function of true consciousness itself. In other words, the *ālaya-vijñāna* is not entirely separate from the Tathāgatagarbha for Hui-yüan, nor is its reality denied as in the case of his teacher, Fa-shang. Fa-shang prefers to separate the conditioned and unconditioned into two distinct levels, the *ālaya-vijñāna* and the Tathāgatagarbha. Hui-yüan later adds the notion of a seventh state of conscious activity, a defiled state no longer identified with the *ālaya-vijñāna* as it was in Fa-shang's *Shih-ti lun i-shu*. This seventh state corresponds to Paramārtha's *ādāna-vijñāna*.

If we look at Hui-yüan's two other commentaries that deal with philosophy of mind after his influence from T'an-ch'ien and She-lun thought, that is, after the year 587 when T'an-ch'ien was lecturing on the *Saṃgraha* in Ch'ang-an, we can discover some clues to his schematization of the philosophy he developed in these later years. The *Ta-sheng ch'i hsin lun i-shu*, a four *chüan* commentary on the *Awakening of Faith in Mahāyāna*, is representative of Hui-yüan's original taxonomy of consciousness, although this text may actually have been composed by one of his disciples. This commentary fuses Tathāgatagarbha thought found in the *Śrīmālādevī-sūtra* with the doctrines expounded by Paramārtha. The mind has the aspect of reality or Suchness (*chen-ju hsiang*), being equivalent to a ninth mode of consciousness imbued with the essence of all phenomena.[74] The text adds that the One Mind (*i-hsin*), which is cut off from language and conditioning variables, is the same as the ninth consciousness.[75] Citing from the *Śrīmālādevī-sūtra*, it supports the famous statement: "If there were no storehouse consciousness (*tsang-shih*), there would be no planting [the seeds of] suffering. The seven (*mental*) phenomena within consciousness (*fa*) do not continue even momentarily nor can there be a revulsion from suffering nor [the aspiration for] seeking Nirvāṇa."[76] The mind as Suchness is the ninth consciousness[77] and, by implication, is the stimulator for the drive to seek enlightenment. In contrast to the ninth mode, the true aspect of consciousness (*chen-hsiang shih*) is the eighth consciousness,[78] the *ālaya-vijñāna*, which is transformed into a religious state of mind that functions in a world of deluded sentient beings, not transcending language or conditioning processes.

The description of the seventh consciousness in both the *Ta-*

sheng ch'i hsin lun and the *Ch'i hsin lun i-shu* provides some interesting information that illustrates an influence from Paramārtha's *Chuan shih lun* and its related texts but with alterations in Paramārtha's system of consciousnesses. Though a comparison between the *Ch'i hsin lun i-shu* and Paramārtha's system is not the purpose of this study, it would be useful to note the description of the seventh consciousness given in the commentary attributed to Hui-yüan.

The arising of the unenlightened mind (*pu-chüeh hsin*) is the seventh consciousness, for that which has false concepts (*nien*) is equivalent to the defiled mind. We understand and express this as the false consciousness (*wang shih*). Alternatively, the unenlightened has its foundation in ignorance. The defiled mind is the karmic consciousness which includes the consciousness of continuity [into another existence].[79] . . . The seventh consciousness is not the same as the indestructible essence that is identical to the true mind (*chen hsin*). Question: If the seven consciousnesses are destroyed, who attains *bodhi* and who realizes Nirvāṇa? Interpretation: Although the aspects of the mind are terminated, the nature of mind is preserved and this nature of mind that is preserved is identical to true consciousness.[80]

From even these brief passages, we can see that many of the functions the *Ch'i hsin lun i-shu* attributes to the seventh consciousness—the defiled consciousness—are ascriptions Paramārtha applies in tandem to the *ālaya*, particularly with reference to being the foundation of ignorance or karmic consciousness requiring termination in order for enlightenment to take place. Moreover, the *Ch'i hsin lun i-shu* does not use the terms *amala-vijñāna* or *ādāna-vijñāna*.

What becomes evident in the above exegesis on the *Awakening of Faith in Mahāyāna* is a synthesis of earlier Ti-lun thought with the innovative ideas of T'an-ch'ien and She-lun. The mind has the aspect of Suchness, one of the three aspects of wisdom Fa-shang discussed, corresponding to *pariniṣpanna-svabhāva* or the ultimate nature of reality. This mind of Suchness is no longer enumerated as an eighth level, corresponding to Fa-shang's Buddha Nature or Tathāgatagarbha, but is the added level of a ninth consciousness, similar to Paramārtha's famous innovation of a ninth consciousness called the *amala-vijñāna*. This reality is the essence of all things and is identical to the One Mind described in the *Awakening of Faith in Mahāyāna*, the unconditioned state of mind cut off from language and all concept-formations. The true *aspect* of consciousness (*chen-hsiang shih*), in contrast to true consciousness per se (*chen-shih*), is the eighth consciousness or *ālaya-vijñāna*/Tathāgatagarbha, the active, dynamic consciousness engaged in a world of deluded beings and of language and concepts. Hence, the *ālaya* is, in fact, a combination of true and false consciousness. This becomes more explicit in the *Ta-sheng i chang*.

An elaborate model of eight consciousnesses is presented in the *Ta-sheng i chang* (Compendium on the Principles of Mahāyāna). Taking as his scriptural authority Guṇabhadra's recension of the *Laṅkāvatāra-sūtra*, the commentator brings out the following characteristics of the seventh and eighth conscious modes:

The *ādāna* should strictly be translated as "the unenlightened" (*wu chieh; nirmokṣa*?)[81] because its essence is ignorance which darkens the mind. More technically translated, there are eight different types. (1) It is the consciousness of ignorance because its essence is the stage of fundamental ignorance. (2) It is the consciousness of *karma* because, based upon the [previously mentioned] mind of ignorance, the false thoughts (*wang-nien*) that are of nonenlightenment suddenly become active. (3) It is the functional consciousnesses (*pravṛtti-vijñāna; chuan shih*) that are based upon the previous consciousness of *karma*. Its mental characteristics gradually evolve (*chuan*) into external characteristics that are falsely discriminated and grasped. (4) It is the consciousness of pure perception ("appearance")(*hsien-shih; khyāti-vijñāna*?) because an unreal object is produced, appearing in one's own mind like the appearance of forms and characteristics in a mirror. (5) It is the consciousness of knowledge that falsely discriminates between "pro and con" (*wei shun*), pure and impure, in relation to the appearance of objects in the previous consciousness of pure perception. This false discrimination [which evaluates and judges] is called knowledge, but it is not what we consider knowledge of enlightenment. (6) It is the consciousness of continuity because the false object attracts the mind, and the mind, following after its objective world, produces objects without end. It maintains the results of good and bad actions continuously. (7) It is the false consciousness because all the previous six types are not real. (8) It is the consciousness of appropriating because it appropriates and grasps an ego or it appropriates all false characteristics [of things as belonging to an ego].

The *ālaya-vijñāna* should strictly be translated as "the insubmersible" (*wu-mo*).[82] Although it is in *saṃsāra*, it is not lost or submerged in it. More technically translated, there are eight other names for it. (1) It is a storehouse consciousness (*tsang-shih*), the Tathāgatagarbha. As [the *Laṅkāvatāra*] *sūtra* says: "The Tathāgatagarbha is a storehouse consciousness." In this consciousness all Buddha-dharmas, more numerous than the sands of the Ganges, making up the real world of phenomena (*Dharma-dhātu*) are included. Thus it is called a storehouse. It is also called a storehouse because the meaning of Emptiness has concealed it. (2) It is the sage's consciousness because it generates the functions of the great sage. (3) It is the supreme consciousness because it is the highest excellence. Therefore, the *Laṅkāvatāra-sūtra* says it is to be considered the supreme mind (*paramārtha-citta*). (4) It is called pure consciousness and is also called the immaculate consciousness (*wu-kou*) because its essence is not defiled. Therefore, [the *Śrīmālādevī-*]*sūtra* says it is "the intrinsically pure mind" (*prabhāsvara-citta*). (5) It is true consciousness because its substance is not false. (6) It is the consciousness of Suchness (*chen-ju; tathatā*). The [*Ch'i hsin*] *lun* explains this: "Because the essential nature of mind is unimpeded, it is called true (*chen*). Because it is something that is not established, it is said to be as it is (*ju*)." (7) It is the home consciousness (*chia shih*) and also the abode consciousness (*chai shih*) because this is where all false phenomena (*dharmas*) are based. (8) It is called the fundamental consciousness because it is the foundation of the false mind.[83]

From Hui-yüan's account of the seventh and eighth states of consciousness we can better understand the differences between his taxonomy and that of his predecessor, Fa-shang. The eight definitions for the *ādāna-vijñāna* and *ālaya-vijñāna*, respectively, indicate that the false belief in the ego and the *karma* that accrues resides in the *ādāna-vijñāna* but its foundation rests in the *ālaya-vijñāna*. The seventh consciousness encompasses a wide range of activities that are not explicated in Fa-shang's commentary on the *Daśabhūmika*, since Fa-shang had no mechanism of *manas* or *ādāna-vijñāna*. For Hui-yüan, the seventh consciousness, the *ādāna-vijñāna*, derives its basic form and content from the belief in an ego, and the eighth is a commingling of ethically pure and impure impulses and impressions, comprising the ontologically real and unreal, respectively:

Again, it is possible to say that there are nine [consciousnesses]. As the *Laṅkāvatāra-sūtra* states in the Sagāthakam section: "Eight or nine consciousnesses are like waves in the water." What is meant by this? False discrimination is twofold. (1) False and true discrimination that explain nine types [of consciousness]: in the false [discriminating consciousness] there are seven constituents, namely, the six functional consciousnesses (*pravṛtti-vijñāna*) and the false consciousness (*ādāna*); in the true [consciousness] there are two constituents, namely the *amala* and the *ālaya*. The principles were explained previously as combined into nine types. (2) False and true discrimination when separated from each other are of nine types, the true [consciousness] being designated as originally pure, the *amala-vijñāna*. When the true and false [consciousnesses] are combined, there are eight types.[84]

This essentially real nature of the *ālaya-vijñāna* is identified with the Tathāgatagarbha, the sagely wisdom, the supreme mind, the pure consciousness that is immaculate, the true essence, and the true reality of Suchness corresponding to the first six of the eight technical definitions of the *ālaya-vijñāna* and in consonance with Fa-shang's notion of Buddha Nature or Tathāgatagarbha and Paramārtha's notion of the ninth mode of consciousness, the *amala-vijñāna*.[85] The fourth of these definitions, that is, the pure and immaculate consciousness (*wu-kou*), is evidence suggesting that Paramārtha's *amala-vijñāna* influenced Hui-yüan's interpretation of Buddhist psychology but not in its attribution of this purity to the *ālaya*. In the last two of the eight technical definitions given in the *Ta-sheng i chang*, the text ascribes to the *ālaya-vijñāna* the evolution of false states of mental activity consonant with Fa-shang's characterization of the *ālaya-vijñāna* as well as with Paramārtha's system but adds on to the *ālaya-vijñāna* the pure dimension associated with Tathāgatagarbha.

Evidence that clearly illustrates the direct contribution Paramārtha made to Hui-yüan's philosophical development is seen in the description of the *ādāna-vijñāna*, a term not found in Fa-shang's extant work. Paramārtha uses this term throughout much of his corpus for the seventh level of ordinary, deluded conscious activity. The more usual terminology for this mental state or set of functions is *manas* or *kliṣṭa-manas*. Paramārtha focuses on the appropriating, narcissistic functioning and content of this set of operations, and as we shall see in the analysis of Paramārtha's thought, this notion is also fully incorporated into Hui-yüan's psychological model.[86]

The structure of consciousness in Hui-yüan's system, however, remains loyal to Fa-shang's ideological commitment to the true consciousness as the basis for phenomenal reality. Perceptual and ideational changes can only be brought about because of their reliance upon an absolutely real nature of mind that is identified with wisdom and truth: "The true mind changes into those false phenomena. Outside of the true there are no separate false conceptions. Consequently, the [*Hua-yen*] *sūtra*[87] states: 'All falsehood is only constructed by the One Mind, namely, constructs are only the One True Mind.'"[88]

Returning to the issue raised earlier, of a recognized need on the part of Hui-yüan to associate the *ālaya-vijñāna* with the Tathāgatagarbha, based primarily on Guṇabhadra's recensions of the *Laṅkāvatāra-sūtra* and the *Śrīmālādevī-sūtra*, we see the divergence of Hui-yüan's epistemological views from those of his Southern Ti-lun teacher. Why the conceptual changes in his psychological model? First of all, Fa-shang's system of mental operations represents an earlier Yogācāra tradition, preceding the complete translation into Chinese of many important treatises written by Vasubandhu and Asaṅga. The false consciousness or seventh level of mental functions that accumulates misconceptions is not examined in detail. The sixth state of ideation and the five functional consciousness or sensory faculties essentially represent the older Buddhist psychology of six levels of consciousness that predates Yogācāra. Superimposed upon seven deluded states is the religiously enlightened state of mind (*Tathāgatagarbha*) associated with the nature of reality as it is (Suchness). The evolution of the world ultimately is derived from a conscious source (*Tathāgatagarbha*), which itself is unconditioned and appears to be identified with the Buddha, and in a somewhat unclear fashion, with the Dharma Nature. Fa-shang's distinctive mark on southern Chinese Buddhism, presumably representative of early Southern Ti-lun Buddhism in general, is that the crowning consciousness possessed by all sentient beings is equated with the sublime reality of Suchness and its accompanying wisdom, the ground for all human experience. This consciousness, the Tathāgatagarbha, finally negates the defiled state of consciousness or *ālaya-vijñāna*.

Hui-yüan diverges from Fa-shang in splitting the *ālaya-vijñāna* into a bimodal set of operations, not unlike the bifurcation of the Tathāgatagarbha in the *Śrīmālādevī-sūtra* into an empty (*śūnya*) and not-empty (*aśūnya*) dimension.[89] It may have been the *Śrīmālādevī-sūtra* that, in fact, influenced Hui-yüan in developing his new analysis of the *ālaya*, since the *Śrīmālādevī* was one of his favorite texts and one on which he wrote a commentary, *Sheng-man ching i-chi*, although the portion of the commentary now extant does not mention either the *ālaya* or the Tathāgatagarbha. In the *Ta-sheng i chang* Hui-yüan does assert that within the true mind there is the eternally pure *amala-vijñāna* and the *ālaya-vijñāna*, which evolves into false states of conscious activity.[90] He cites liberally from Paramārtha's translation of the *Saṃgraha* whereas the *Ch'i-hsin lun i shu* never cites it. Like Fa-shang, he claims that all false concepts belong to an illusory world, the *ālaya-vijñāna* being the basis for the deluded world the mind creates. Unlike his predecessor, however, Hui-yüan had access to a richer set of resources, a more detailed phenomenological study of the appearance of sense data and the nature of an evaluative, judgmental ego, the *ādāna-vijñāna*, borrowed from Paramārtha's theories. However, the *ādāna-vijñāna* cannot store and retrieve past influential impulses or impressions.[91] Consequently, the accumulator or repository for these past habit impressions had to be located separately from the appropriating faculty of the ego. Fa-shang's model was found to be inadequate in this regard after Hui-yüan had access to the Yogācārin writings of Paramārtha.

One additional factor must be discussed with reference to Hui-yüan's divergence from Fa-shang's epistemology. Fa-shang committed himself to the position that reality itself must be the ground for mental operations if mind is to have any claim to access to true knowledge of the nature of things. He based this assertion on the premise that the support for human experience cannot be derived from what is void of any real content or ontological status. Hence, the *ālaya-vijñāna* is the mechanism for continual generation of ignorance while its ontological status can be nothing other than grounded in something factual and real, namely Suchness. Consequently, we can understand the statement made in Bodhiruci's translation of the *Laṅkāvatāra-sūtra*: "the Tathāgatagarbha does not reside in the *ālaya-vijñāna*" since the *ālaya-vijñāna* is devoid of any real existence. The *ālaya-vijñāna* only provisionally or temporarily exists as the source of epistemological error.

Hui-yüan vacillates in his enumeration of the modes of cognitive activity in a way that Fa-shang does not. In Fa-shang's system, there are only seven modes that initiate ignorance, all functioning epistemically but having no substantive self-existence. In numbering *all* modes of consciousness, including the ontologically real nature of our experiences as real and true, we then have an eighth mode of how things can be in the world, namely, as they are (Suchness), devoid of ego and false discriminations. Fa-shang in numbering his components of consciousness in this way is, I suspect, aiming for conceptual clarity. Seven modes represent a common structure for all ordinary human cognition;[92] but these are only temporary. The eighth mode represents the true structure inherent in all human cognition. I suggest that what Fa-shang had intended was to replace the term "Tathāgatagarbha" in the *Laṅkāvatāra-sūtra* with *tathatā* or Suchness. More precisely, he glossed the terms Tathāgatagarbha and Buddha Nature with Suchness to collapse the distinction between ontological and epistemological categories, a favorite technique in Yogācāra (and in some forms of Mādhyamika). The two sets of enumeration are presented in order to illustrate that the first seven modes are epistemically *distinct* from the eighth, although ontologically inseparable. Consequently, the *ālaya-vijñāna* must be distinct and separate from the Tathāgatagarbha in terms of its functions.

Hui-yüan, on the other hand, glosses Tathāgatagarbha with *ālaya-vijñāna*, a practice not found in Fa-shang but associated with *Śrīmālādevī-sūtra* exegesis.[93] Here is where we find Hui-yüan collapsing the distinction between the two terms, *ālaya-vijñāna* and Tathāgatagarbha, as an eighth mode. Yet, he often distinguishes a ninth mode as the *amala-vijñāna*, or what Paramārtha associated with *pariniṣpanna-svabhāva*. He would have then resorted to the same rationale in his enumeration of conscious processes used by Fa-shang, partly incorporating Paramārtha's philosophy of mind. It is his own innovation, however, to say that part of the functioning of the True Mind, understood as the *ālaya-vijñāna*, proclaimed in the *Ch'i hsin lun*, is to effect impure acts. The She-lun school did not accept this view, and the *Ch'i hsin lun* itself asserts that only good acts are brought about by the True Mind.[94] Unlike the She-lun system, which considered the *ālaya* a defiled faculty of the mind, Hui-yüan viewed the eighth conscious mode as both pure and impure. This is one of his most distinctive ideas, emphasized by his synthesis of the *ālaya-vijñāna* with the Tathāgatagarbha. T'an-yen, a teacher of She-lun philosophy, in accordance with that school of Yogācāra Buddhism, consistently maintained that the eighth consciousness was impure. Though the author of the *Ch'i hsin lun i-shu* shows his indebtedness to T'an-yen in citing the latter's work, on this issue he diverges from She-lun thought.[95]

The *Ta-sheng i chang* also adheres to the pure and impure dimensions of the *ālaya*. It is much more difficult to determine whether the mind of Suchness (*chen-ju shih*) or the eighth consciousness also effects impure acts in his *Ta-sheng i chang*, but that appears to be the implication since the *ālaya-vijñāna* and the Tathāgatagarbha are the same.

Although Hui-yüan diverges from Fa-shang as well as from Paramārtha by considering the *ālaya-vijñāna* bimodal, that is, a combination of true and false ideas corresponding to the essential and functional consciousness respectively, he also discusses an eight-consciousness theory of ordinary deluded states as headed by the *ālaya-vijñāna*. In other words, part of the eighth mode is false and consonant with Fa-shang's seventh mode and Paramārtha's eighth. When the real character of the *ālaya* is hidden, consciousness appears as false. Elsewhere, as we have seen in the *Ta-sheng ch'i hsin lun i-shu* and *Ta-sheng i chang*, a nine-consciousness system attributes the support of all phenomenal reality in its undeluded nature to Suchness, identifying this ninth level with the One Mind or the aspect of reality (*chen-ju hsiang*), and with the *amala-vijñāna* in the case of the *Ta-sheng i chang*. This level is beyond language and concepts. Functionally, the *ālaya-vijñāna*/Tathāgatagarbha is the level where language and concepts come into play.

In both Hui-yüan's and Fa-shang's structuring of conscious processes, the support for ordinary conscious activity that enables them to function is consciousness as it really is, identified with Suchness and Buddha Nature (Tathāgatagarbha). However, when Hui-yüan proposes a bimodal *ālaya-vijñāna* associated with the Tathāgatagarbha, he radically diverges from Fa-shang, who depicted the *ālaya* as totally deluded and separate from the Tathāgatagarbha. Fa-shang denied reality to the *ālaya* as anything but a provisional support for phenomena. Hui-yüan, on the other hand, synthesized the deluded *ālaya* with a pure consciousness grounding all other conscious acts, namely, the Tathāgatagarbha, which the Northern Ti-lun school of Bodhiruci and Fa-shang vehemently denied. It remains problematic why Hui-yüan synthesized the *ālaya-vijñāna* with the Tathāgatagarbha in even his earliest writings such as the *Shih-ti ching lun i-chi*. Neither Fa-shang nor Paramārtha would have agreed with such a position of associating Tathāgatagarbha with the foundation for delusion.

NORTHERN TI-LUN

Bodhiruci's lineage, the so-called Northern Ti-lun school transmitted through his chief disciple Tao-lung, is very difficult to reconstruct even tentatively because there is a paucity of documentation on the history of ideas characteristic of this branch of Ti-lun. It never gained the currency of its southern counterpart. But from other monks' writings referring to "Ti-lun masters" we can postulate some basic doctrinal points of Northern Ti-lun.

Chih-i (538-97), the great T'ien-t'ai master during Sui, characterizes what probably is Northern Ti-lun, or Ti-lun thought before the schism, in the *Miao-fa lien-hua ching hsüan-i*: "The Ti[-lun] followers explain the *ālaya* as the true, eternal, pure consciousness."[96] "The Ti[-lun] masters selected the eighth consciousness as the ultimate [reality] but the She-lun masters have refuted them, saying that it [*ālaya-vijñāna*] is the foundation for *saṃsāra*."[97] From these two very brief passages we can surmise that the *ālaya-vijñāna* as the eighth, pure consciousness signifying the absolute result of religious practice is not at all compatible with Fa-shang's position, since he regarded the *seventh* consciousness as the *ālaya-vijñāna*, the foundation for *saṃsāra* and, consequently, the source of delusion. Nor is this description given by Chih-i compatible with Paramārtha's position. Is Hui-yüan being used as a paradigm of Southern Ti-lun Buddhism even though it perhaps could be argued that he is more an idiosyncratic thinker than a representative example of Southern Ti-lun? Such a depiction of Ti-lun doctrine suggests Southern Ti-lun of Hui-yüan's system since Fa-shang maintained the *ālaya* was a seventh, not an eighth state, and was defiled. The notion of the *ālaya* as an eighth, pure state may have been a Southern Ti-lun tenet Fa-shang did not accept, or it may have been a Northern Ti-lun tenet. However, Paramārtha has been associated with doctrines that are attributed to Northern Ti-lun so that, by implication, since She-lun refuted "the Ti-lun" position, the Southern Ti-lun is indicated. Evidently, Hui-yüan's system is the form being described since Fa-shang's ideas would not correspond to this brief description.

Chi-tsang (549-623), the most renowned San-lun master during Sui, commented on Ti-lun and its disagreement with the She-lun school of Paramārtha in his commentarial study, *Chung-kuan lun shu*:

> Moreover, the old Ti-lun masters considered the seventh consciousness to be false and the eighth consciousness to be truly real whereas the She-lun masters considered the eighth consciousness to be false and the ninth to be truly real. In addition some others say that there is a twofold principle to the eighth consciousness, one is false [consciousness], the second is true [consciousness]. The meaning of the nature of enlightenment is the true; the retributive consciousness is the functioning [of consciousness] as false. The *Ch'i hsin lun* states: "The arising and ceasing plus the non-arising and non-ceasing are combined in the essence of the *ālaya*."[98] The *Laṅkāvatāra* [Bodhiruci's edition] has two passages: One asserts that the *ālaya-vijñāna* is the Tathāgatagarbha; the second that the Tathāgatagarbha is not the *ālaya-vijñāna*. The first part [of the passage] refutes the principles of the Ti-lun followers but does not refute other commentaries.[99]

According to the text, the "*old* Ti-lun masters" are given a position similar to Fa-shang's, if one construes the seventh false consciousness as the *ālaya*, and the eighth consciousness as the Tathāgatagarbha. This view would also be consonant with Bodhiruci and Northern Ti-lun who separated the *ālaya* from the Tathāgatagarbha. This is the view held by many Japanese Buddhologists who argue that the original form of Ti-lun was that advocated by Bodhiruci and that Southern Ti-lun (with the exception of Fa-shang in my opinion) deviated from these ideas. However, if one reads this text in another way, then Southern Ti-lun is the "old" school. Namely, if the seventh consciousness is not the *ālaya* but rather the eighth consciousness is the *ālaya*, then the ultimately real is the *ālaya-vijñāna* or Tathāgatagarbha, the identity maintained in Guṇabhadra's translation, presumably used as a scriptural source for Hui-yüan, who combined the two notions of *ālaya* and *Tathāgatagarbha*. The Southern Ti-lun upon which Hui-yüan added the notion of the *ādana* then can be viewed as a system that had eight consciousnesses, the eighth being the *ālaya-vijñāna/Tathāgatagarbha* as real. This use of

Guṇabhadra's translation on the part of Southern Ti-lun means that Fa-shang, for some unknown reason, deliberately chose Bodhiruci's translation over that of Guṇabhadra, the choice of his own master, Ratnamati. This remains problematic.

Northern Ti-lun may have deviated from the original doctrinal proclivities of the unified Ti-lun system by separating the *ālaya-vijñāna* from the Tathāgatagarbha as did Fa-shang. Another unidentified school is depicted as interpreting the *ālaya-vijñāna* as bimodal, an eighth consciousness partly real as the nature of liberation and partly unreal as the functioning of retributive consciousness. Citing the *Ch'i hsin lun*, Chi-tsang could be implying here the school of thought Hui-yüan proposed, as evidenced from the latter's commentary *Ta-sheng ch'i hsin lun i-shu* and also his *Ta-sheng i chang*. In citing the *Laṅkāvatāra-sūtra*, which makes the two assertions contradicting each other that the *ālaya* is and is not the Tathāgatagarbha, Fa-shang seems to be taking one side of the issue (*ālaya* is not the Tathāgatagarbha) based upon Bodhiruci's translation, and Hui-yüan seems to be taking the other side (*ālaya* is the Tathāgatagarbha), based upon Guṇabhadra. According to Chi-tsang, identification of the *ālaya* with the Tathāgatagarbha would be contrary to Ti-lun's doctrinal thesis, if one takes the referent for the seventh consciousness as the *ālaya* and the eighth as the Tathāgatagarbha and notes the last two lines in the passage quoted above from the *Laṅkāvatāra-sūtra*. Ti-lun in some of its early forms did not equate the two conscious faculties, and this thesis is the one upheld by Fa-shang. Since one branch of Ti-lun considered the *ālaya-vijñāna* a faculty of pure consciousness and Hui-yüan, in my opinion, may have attempted to synthesize Northern and Southern Ti-lun in his own interpretation of Buddhist psychology, perhaps Northern Ti-lun originally separated the two categories, *ālaya-vijñāna* and Tathāgatagarbha, and this provided the rationale for Hui-yüan later to analyze the *ālaya-vijñāna* as a pure consciousness that was the absolute result of religious practice. Southern Ti-lun, beginning with Hui-yüan, collapsed the two categories, claiming that the Tathāgatagarbha was *ālaya-vijñāna*.

The thought of Northern Ti-lun remains problematic because the referents for the seventh and eighth states of consciousness are unclear. It seems that Bodhiruci of Northern Ti-lun believed in only seven consciousnesses, the seventh being the *ālaya-vijñāna*, according to several Japanese Buddhologists such as Katsumata and Sakamoto.[100] Since Bodhiruci's translation of the *Laṅkāvatāra-sūtra* distinguishes between the *ālaya* and Tathāgatagarbha, the latter must be a type of eighth consciousness that is truly real. However, the most famous of early Southern Ti-lun proponents, Fa-shang, seems to be in wholehearted agreement with this. Northern Ti-lun has also been characterized as maintaining the *ālaya* as the phenomenal support of reality, implying that either this support is ultimately false or that it is true. In either case, there is a critical distinction between Fa-shang and Northern Ti-lun since the support of reality cannot be located in the *ālaya* for Fa-shang. It seems reasonable to hypothesize that Northern Ti-lun considered the *ālaya* a seventh consciousness that was false but nonetheless a support for phenomenal appearances. Southern Ti-lun diverged with regard to this notion of support. Fa-shang had two types of support for the world as we experience it. The ground for our ordinary world is a false system of support, being only the foundation for delusion (*ālaya-vijñāna*)—hence his retention of the Northern Ti-lun's numbering system of the seventh consciousness as the *ālaya* but with the denial of the *ālaya* as the support for all phenomena. The Tathāgatagarbha, then, is the ultimate support for all phenomena, the *ālaya* only temporarily supporting delusion. This results in the Buddha's wisdom (*jñāna*) being unconditioned (*asaṃskṛta*) for Fa-shang, whereas in the Northern Ti-lun, more consonant with Abhidharma, the *ālaya-vijñāna* and all knowledge (*jñāna*) are conditioned (*saṃskṛta*) and separate from the Tathāgatagarbha.

Northern Ti-lun considered the *ālaya* the support of phenomenal reality. Chan-jan says in his *Fa-hua hsüan-i shih ch'ien*: "The school [of Ti-lun] north of Hsiang-chou considered the *ālaya* as the support [of the phenomenal world]; the school [of Ti-lun] south of Hsiang-chou considered *tathatā* the support. Both sets of masters derived their theories from Vasubandhu, but their differences were like fire and water. In addition, the She-lun [school] also considers the *ālaya* in accordance with the Northern school."[101] In his *Fa-hua wen chu i*, Chan-jan describes the two forms of Ti-lun in the following manner: "The southern school considered Dharmatā as the producer of all phenomena. The northern school considered the *ālaya* as the producer of all phenomena."[102]

As we have seen from Fa-shang's fragments of writings, however, his views not only considered the Dharmatā as the ultimate and final support for all phenomena but also acknowledged the *ālaya* as the support for all *defiled* states. Chan-jan's commentaries do not seem to take this into account. But the opinions in Fa-shang's commentary contradict the characterization of Southern Ti-lun and, in fact, are compatible with the description given of Northern Ti-lun!

TI-LUN AND SHE-LUN BUDDHISM COMPARED

Hui-yüan was undoubtedly indebted to Paramārtha's philosophy of mind in developing his own interpretation of Yogācāra Buddhism in his later works. Before we turn to Paramārtha's epistemological model in the next chapters, a few comments on the relationship between Ti-lun and She-lun philosophical assumptions will enable us to place Paramārtha's ideas in the intellectual environs of his time. Chih-i makes the following analysis of the controversy between Ti-lun and She-lun Buddhist intellectuals in his *Mo-ho chih-kuan*:

> The [Southern] Ti[-lun] proponents say: "All understanding and delusion, the true and the false, are supported by the Dharma Nature. The Dharma Nature supports the true and false and the true and false are based upon the Dharma Nature." The She[-lun] proponents say: "The Dharma Nature does not become defiled by delusion or purified by the true. Therefore, the Dharma Nature is not the support. The support is the *ālaya*, the insubmersible ignorance that contains all the impressions [of past experience]."
>
> If one follows the Ti[-lun] masters, then mind constitutes all phenomena. If one follows the She[-lun] masters, then conditions (*yüan*) constitute all phenomena. [Chih-i's position:] These two sets of masters are selectively one-sided. With regard to the position that the Dharma Nature generates all phenomena, the Dharma Nature is neither mind nor conditions [since what generates mind and conditions must be separate from these two]. If it [the Dharma Nature] is not mind yet the mind generates all phenomena [according to Ti-lun's own premises], then since it is also not a condition, conditions should generate all phenomena [since by substituting the word "condition" for mind in the preceding clause, the same line of reasoning is valid]. How is it possible to say the Dharma Nature is the support for the true and the false?
>
> With regard to the position that the Dharma Nature is not the support but that the *ālaya* is the support: If the *ālaya* is a support apart from the Dharma Nature, then it [the *ālaya*] is unrelated to the Dharma Na-

ture. [But this is not true since every *dharma* is not separate from its *dharma* nature.] If the Dharma Nature is not separate from the *ālaya*, then the *ālaya* as a support is equal to the Dharma Nature as a support. How is it possible to say that only the *ālaya* is the support?[103]

Leaving aside Chih-i's criticism of both Ti-lun and She-lun philosophical problems, the Ti-lun here is in harmony with Fa-shang's schematization of conscious processes if Dharma Nature is used as an equivalent for the Tathāgatagarbha, supporting all experiences both deluded and enlightened, and the *ālaya* is taken to be false. It would be an oversimplification of Fa-shang's position, however, since the *ālaya* does provide the root cause for ignorance and is a type of temporary support for epistemological errors in an ever repetitive cycle. She-lun criticized the [Southern] Ti-lun position by making the counterclaim that the *ālaya* is indeed the insubmersible ground and contains all the past influences that trigger ignorant acts, and the Dharma Nature is not affected by ignorance. The *ālaya* is impure, whereas for Southern Ti-lun represented by Hui-yüan, it is both pure and impure. We shall see in analyzing Paramārtha's structures of consciousness that there is a support overriding that of the *ālaya-vijñāna*, namely Pure Consciousness or *amala-vijñāna*, which necessitates the cessation of the *ālaya* before functioning on its own. The She-lun school postulates a pure state, the *amala-vijñāna*, to counteract the impure *ālaya*. This is the most distinctive feature associated with this school's doctrines.

What is more significant in Chih-i's portrayal of the two schools of thought relates to the constituency of phenomenal reality. For Ti-lun—and we shall assume that he is referring to Southern Ti-lun—*mind* constitutes the nature of phenomena. It will subsequently be argued that for She-lun Buddhists, *conditioning* operations constitute the nature of phenomena. In other words, She-lun is not, strictly speaking, idealist in the same sense as Ti-lun or much of later Yogācāra, but is founded on a philosophical position that all things are conditioned reality and that the *ālaya-vijñāna* is simply one very important set of operations in that conditioning process (*paratantra-svabhāva*) and does not constitute the final reality (*parinișpanna-svabhāva*). In accordance with Mādhyamika, Paramārtha is asserting not the primacy of mind over matter but the primacy of conditioning principles governing both.

Southern Ti-lun and She-lun Buddhist scholarship shared an affinity in identifying the source of all reality and experience with the essentially good and real, although Fa-shang preferred to use the term Suchness for this support whereas Paramārtha usually used Pure Consciousness or *amala-vijñāna* together with the term Suchness for the ground of experience that can neither be defiled nor purified because it is always simply as it is, unoriginated and intrinsically pure. According to this position, the process of unfolding our manifold experiences results from the functioning of the world of mind and objects conditioning each other. Stated very simply, Ti-lun asserted that mind *is* the world we view as objects, whereas She-lun would assert that only mind, in analyzing its own conditioning process, can understand the nature of being both a conditioned object and a conditioned subject. According to Chan-jan, in his *Chih-kuan fu hsing ch'uan hung chüeh,* the sets of conditions in Paramārtha's system are partly described as follows:

Paramārtha says: "The *ādāna,* the seventh consciousness, is said to be the consciousness that grasps an ego. This is the nature of delusion whose essence is a conditioning cause. The *ālaya,* the eighth consciousness, is called the storehouse consciousness (*tsang-shih*), which can retain the impressions of knowledge (*chih*) so they are not lost. Its essence is insubmersible ignorance. The nature of ignorance is the adequate cause. The *amala,* the ninth consciousness, is Pure Consciousness, the perfect cause." The T'ang scholars do not permit this interpretation, asserting that the ninth consciousness is another name for the eighth. Consequently, the new translation of the *Mahāyāna-saṃgraha* does not preserve the ninth [consciousness]. In the Ti-lun texts there also is no mention of a ninth [consciousness], but only of an eighth, which is the perfect cause, the seventh being the adequate cause.[104]

The entire controversy of postulating a support for all experience and of enumerating sets of operations by which conscious acts were regulated was not simply scholastic fastidiousness on the part of Ti-lun and She-lun intellectuals nor a penchant for schematization and constructing taxonomies. At the time that we find Paramārtha's writings being disseminated rapidly during the Sui dynasty, the theory that mental acts created reality had become an engrossing existential question. Was there philosophical and psychological evidence to postulate that human nature was intrinsically good, so human beings could become socially cooperative and religiously fulfilled? Was this too optimistic a world view of either human potentiality or human action, given the surrounding circumstances of the day? For Buddhists like Hui-yüan and his teacher Fa-shang, the antisocial and unethical acts of human beings were essentially illusory and dependent upon the real and the good. To this extent, we may conclude that for Southern Ti-lun, evil was a judgmental error in evaluating the actual nature of human existence.

Paramārtha also belongs to this perspective of optimism in viewing human nature as do the Tathāgatagarbha followers in general. While eight out of nine cognitive modes he enumerates are caught within a closed system of reinforcing habits of misperception and misconceptualization, the ninth cognitive mode lies beyond all conceptual error and is the irreducible structure of the mind, the innate goodness that enables self-knowledge to occur. Unlike later Yogācārin philosophers such as Hsüan-tsang, K'uei-chi, and to a lesser extent Wŏnch'ŭk, Paramārtha did not deny to any sentient being this innately good capacity of the mind.

This notion of an innately or intrinsically pure mind had permeated all the various Mahāyāna Buddhist schools dealing with Bodhisattva practice and Buddha Nature. In the succeeding school of Hua-yen, Buddha Nature was to be structured and defined according to Paramārtha's phenomenological analysis of mind. Paramārtha's line of transmission via T'an-ch'ien and Hui-yüan was to be transformed by the time of Fa-tsang, the renowned Hua-yen master. Instead of an emphasis on a taxonomy of cognitive states, Hua-yen Buddhism would resort to an organic model. It would take us too far off the topic here to demonstrate the transformation of Paramārtha's schema into that of Fa-tsang. For our purposes, we shall in the the next two chapters examine Yogācāra's inquiry into the nature of language and concept formation, investigating the distinctive features of Paramārtha's thought according to his short treatise entitled *Chuan shih lun* (The Evolution of Consciousness).

III

Theory of Language in Yogācāra

THE MOST PROMINENT treatises of early Indian Yogācāra have been examined by scholars in the field, most notably the treatises *Mahāyāna-saṃgraha*, the *Triṃśikā*, and the *Viṃśatikā*.[1] Paramārtha in his translations of these works presents some of his own ideas on the relationship between language and perception and their concomitant effects on attitudes and actions. The Yogācārin theory of language plays a central role in the analysis of conscious processes and needs to be discussed before presenting the overlying phenomenological structure of mind in the short treatise, *Chuan shih lun* or "Evolution of Consciousness." Since Paramārtha does not sufficiently develop a theory of language in his CSL, I shall be using the *San wu-hsing lun* (SWHL) as my primary exegetical source for assessing Paramārtha's views on language, which are only briefly discussed in the CSL.

Many Buddhist works contain views about language and its influence on how we conceive ourselves and the world in which we live. Some of these texts have declared that if we could exchange the linguistic traps of our vulgar usage of language for a more strictly defined and exact language, we would be able to conceive ourselves and our world more accurately. The Abhidharmists, among the early Buddhist sects, are the clearest example of this view. They argue that language may express truth —may articulate reality—*if* we construct the language according to very strict definitions of terms.[2] Other Buddhist philosophers, most notably those of the two great Mahāyānist schools, Mādhyamika and Yogācāra, viewed language in a very different sort of way. For them, language distorts our self-conceptions and world views;[3] restructuring a language, no matter how precisely or strictly one defines the system's terms, can never eliminate the conceptual traps in which we are ensnared.

According to Mahāyāna Buddhism, one way out of misunderstanding the world is to explore the foundation of language and to realize that the linguistic structures in which our thoughts are embedded have no claim to expressing truth or articulating reality. Rather, language fulfills a useful social and communal function, enabling us to communicate with each other, to have interpersonal relations, and to promote mutual understanding in the societies we live in. Reality, however, must be experienced in a very personal and direct manner, and not through the medium of language. Mental discourse that is influenced by our language is not the personal, direct sort of knowledge the Mahāyānists advocate. A prelinguistic, self-conscious knowledge of reality is free of mental discourse that is based on ideas and formed through false discrimination. Such immediate knowledge enables us to view the world without the distorting medium of language.

Many theories of meaning and truth make implicit ontological claims, treating language as having a relationship with a purely objective world. In contrast, communication-oriented theories of language have often criticized these theories of meaning and truth for making unjustifiable ontological claims, for being unaware of the metaphysical presuppositions to which a given theory is committed,[4] and for neglecting to describe the structures of natural languages as modes of behavior for everyday practical communication. Moreover, such theories fail to analyze the intentions to communicate. According to communicational views of language, such as those advocated by many Mahāyāna Buddhists, any correspondence or relationship between language and objects is ultimately paradoxical and incoherent.

Yogācārin views on language focus on the communicative function of language, particularly the arbitrary nature of word formation, the intentional nature of reference of language, and the influence of language on our attitudes and behavior. Like all Mahāyāna Buddhists, Paramārtha was skeptical about the purported truth-expressing dimension of language and sharply criticized the realist's view of language for referring to objects in the empirical world; the Abhidharmists, for example, were subject to this attack.

The Yogācārin interpretation of language is given in two of Paramārtha's shorter translations, the *San wu-hsing lun* (SWHL)[5] and the *Chuan shih lun* (CSL).[6] The purported relationship between language and objects that forms part of the common sense notion of language and reference will be treated below in order to bring into sharper focus Yogācāra's main concern with the communication process of language.

The Relationship between Language and Truth

"NAME-GIVING"

At the outset of the SWHL, two questions are raised: Does labeling of things in the world provide a key to knowledge of the world? Do properties (*hsiang*), ascribed by language and imputed to particular things, yield accurate knowledge of objects in the world?

Paramārtha answers these two questions in the following manner. Labeling or "name-giving" is purely an arbitrary process. Practical knowledge, or knowledge for purposes of communication, is obtained through direct apprehension of properties and not through naming or mere labels: "The nature of discrimination refers to the self-nature of phenomena presented through language. . . . With reference to discrimination, it is called natureless (*niḥsvabhāva*) because its characteristics (*lakṣaṇa*) are without any nature. Why? Because the characteristics that appear [in the discrimination] do not really exist."[7]

Properties or characteristics are the means by which we perceive in similar ways through the agency of perceiving consciousnesses. The similarity of our perceptions forms the basis for mutual understanding and communication. The sense or meaning of a term exists only in a *psychological* manner and does not in itself constitute grounds for the existence of a referent. One cannot conclude that there is an external referent or object simply because there is a sense or meaning. Language can be intelligible, meaningful, and practical, without bringing truth-value into consideration.

According to Yogācāra, what enables us to communicate with

one another is the *functional* relationships between things, expressed as their properties or characteristics (*lakṣaṇa; hsiang*). Properties or aspects of phenomena refer to those characteristics of a particular thing in relation to that thing's dependency on or conditioning by another set of things. The properties of a thing are only dependent on others (*paratantra*) (*i-t'a-hsing*) for change: "The characteristics [or properties] are the varieties of phenomena, which are the basis for language."[8] The nature of dependence on others (*paratantra*) or on functionally related phenomena is equated with the apprehension of properties of things.[9] "Names" or "signs" are not necessarily related to elements of reality or "referents" but are arbitrary designations for their referents. Labeling is the process of designating some nonlinguistic reality, according to rules established by the users of a given language. Paramārtha comments on name-giving in the following manner in the SWHL: "Conventionally (*saṃketa*) means that names are established (*prajñapti*) by the contemporary fashion so that all of them are constructed by mutual consensus, in order to ensure a shared understanding."[10]

In Paramārtha's time there was a common-sense attitude, prevalent in Indian thought, that things had natural names through which knowledge was possible.[11] Yogācāra denied any but an arbitrary relationship between name and the nature of the referent and refuted notions of natural names attached to objects.[12] The name, often mistaken for the nature or properties of its referent, has no intrinsic structure to indicate the nature of a thing. The relationship between name and nature is one of reference. Senses or meanings[13] are assigned to referents because of a given functional relationship of properties and because of certain perceivable qualities, according to Yogācāra. Names do not exist in the same way that their referents do because names are arbitrarily assigned, whereas referents have functional relationships among themselves as well as with language users. Senses or meanings are the agreed-upon characterizations of these functional properties of the referents by the linguistic community.

THE "OBJECT INTENDED" OR REFERENT

Yogācāra presents the following thesis: Language is fundamentally intentional, that is, language is constructed by human minds for the purpose of expressing objects of consciousness and categorizing them, whether or not those objects actually exist. Referents, then, are objects of consciousness or "intended objects."

The Chinese term *i* is commonly used for the referred object, that to which a name is given. It denotes "intention," "meaning," or "principle"[14] and is a translation of the Sanskrit term *artha*, which may denote either sense or referent. *Artha* does not connote "name," and in many Indian theories of language name plays no necessary or essential part in conveying the sense of an expression. In both the SWHL and CSL the opponents' arguments, in the vast majority of instances, take the position that names convey the *artha* or sense *and* reference, thus conflating the two.[15] The word *artha*, for the opponent, illustrates the fusion between sense and reference; however, standard Yogācāra doctrine avoids committing this logical error.

In order to understand the Yogācāra line of reasoning in translating passages from the SWHL, it is essential to be able to indicate which one of the several meanings of *i* (or *artha*) is being expressed. The Chinese term *i* gives us an important key for interpreting some of the more turgid arguments since *i* always denotes an "intention" or "meaning" and never an object in the nonlinguistic world. To the degree that *i* may be a referent for a name, the implication is that such referents are intentional (that is, contingent upon the intentions of minds and dependent upon a language user), a point of some importance to Paramārtha and to Yogācāra in general.

Naming is a process involving the assignment of a name to a referent that is an intended object, an object of consciousness, rather than to a referent that is an external object. In order for mutual understanding and identification to succeed, it is necessary for the language users to agree on the intended object rather than on an external object:

Having attention (*manasikāra*) as the [immediate] cause (*samantara-pratyaya*?); and external sense data (*viṣaya*) [or matter] as the [secondary] condition (*ālambana-pratyaya*), consciousness (*vijñāna*) occurs. If one's attention, at first, desires to apprehend the two sense data of form ("color") (*rūpa*) and sound, then vision and hearing occur simultaneously and there will be two types of sense data [imputed onto an "external" object]. If one's attention is directed toward a certain locus, to see forms, hear sounds, and to smell odors, then these three [vision, hearing, and smell] occur simultaneously and there will be three types of sense data and so on; all the five [sense] consciousnesses may occur simultaneously or sequentially in a similar fashion.[16]

An example will help to clarify the Yogācāra position. In a given culture, certain sorts of spirits and demons are said to exist and communication about those spirits is possible. The consensus of the community to believe in these spirits facilitates meaningful discourse and predisposes them to have certain kinds of perceptions attributable to spirits and demons, even though spirits and demons do not exist in themselves.

The CSL argues that one does not need the notions of truth and objective reference for communication purposes. All one needs are intended objects and agreement about them for communication; consequently, there is no need to bring in the question of existence or nonexistence. In the following section we shall look at some of the key arguments used to refute the notion of the necessity of objective reference, replacing that notion with the intentionality of reference.

REFERENCE PRESUPPOSES INTENTIONALITY

In the Yogācāra system, the referent is presupposed to exist although it may or may not be an actual object: "If one explains discrimination per se, one means the mind and mental phenomena of the triple world. Its support and object then are not separate [from the discriminating mind] because the support [for discrimination] is the intended object that appears as if it were matter, and the object of discrimination is the name of that intended object that appears as if it were matter."[17] According to this account of intentionality as a *sine qua non* for communication and identification, the language process can be effectively described in terms of the acts of intending and of agreement among language users. The intended object is the assumed referent that is necessary and logically prior to the properties we perceive as being properties of the object and the basis for the sense. The act of intending objects in ways similar to other language users is due to the perceived properties of things that constitute the foundation for effective communication.

Yogācāra argues that the attribution of a name psychologically predisposes the name-giver to believe in an existing referent for that name. Naming, therefore, by its very nature of referring to something, assumes objects, that is, presupposes that there is an object corresponding to the name, an object of the referring process. This object of one's act of labeling is the "object intended" (or "intentional object").

In arguing that all objects are intentional and that names have only purported referents, Yogācāra posits that there is no objective relationship between language and objects. The existence of a name is often mistaken for the existence of a referent since a strain of realism pervades our ordinary language usage.

SENSE: UNDERSTANDING THE FUNCTIONAL ASPECTS OF THE INTENDED OBJECT

In the SWHL the psychological character of the sense is briefly discussed. Discrimination and apprehension of sensible forms in the world take place because the individual is attached to language, particularly naming, and because the mind's structure is predisposed to intend objects and to realism.[18] In other words, discrimination of and attachment to phenomena occur as a result of habitual and repeated language usage. Such discriminations are constitutive of the impressions ("seeds") fundamental to the structure of the mind (specifically, the *ālaya-vijñāna*). The uncritical attitude that prevails is such that names given to the objects we intend accurately describe the nature of the objects: "There is only the name that has no [relationship with the] object intended. Why? The world establishes names in the context of objects intended. The ordinary person is attached to the name and discriminates the nature of the object intended, saying the name is the same as the object intended. This is an incoherent way of thinking."[19]

To support the Yogācāra claim that names do not denote the world of objects but that the intentions of individual and collective language users are the foundation for objects and for mutual understanding and communication, Paramārtha presents three arguments, distinguishing between name and sense in order to refute his opponent. Arguing from logical priority, Paramārtha presents the first argument, paraphrased as follows:

(*a*) If, as the opponent claims, name and referent are necessarily related, cognition could not arise before naming. (*b*) If a name signifies the nature of an object intended, then one should not be able to understand the object intended without hearing the name. (*c*) Because one can understand the object intended without hearing the name, the name does not signify the nature of an object intended. (*d*) It is not the case that when one understands the object intended, one also should understand the name.[20]

The argument against the position that name and referent are necessarily related is found in Asaṅga's *Mahāyāna-saṃgraha*[21] and can be restated as follows: Names are arbitrarily assigned to objects by convention and have no basis either in the sense or in the properties of an object. The process of reference is therefore an arbitrary one, not one indicating a necessary relationship between name and referent. If there were a strictly necessary relationship between name and object, the name would be the *only* medium through which one could understand the nature of an object. If the name were the only medium through which one could understand the object, one would be unable to understand the object without hearing the name. Names, however, are assigned to objects arbitrarily and are not based upon either meaning or the properties of an object. Consequently, one can understand the object (either through its sense or through the properties upon which the sense is based) without knowing the name. Therefore, names do not signify the nature of an object and names are not the *only* medium through which one can understand an object. Yogācāra therefore recognizes an intermediary between name and object, namely, the properties of an object, forming the basis for sense and enabling one to apprehend the intended object.

The perceiver understands and apprehends the object intended without resorting to the name of the object. The necessary component for understanding and apprehending an object is the ability to perceive and to understand the functional aspects of the intentional object, what we may call the properties of a thing: how that thing is affected in the world and how it affects others.

Yogācāra has refuted the belief that if one does not know the name for an object, one cannot have full knowledge of the object. There is no concern with expressions of truth since one can account for ordinary language usage without discussing the existence or nonexistence of objects in the world but by discussing the arbitrariness of word formation and the intentional nature of sense and reference. When we attach meanings to names of objects, we arrive at functional, practical characteristics of objects, not the real properties of objects. These characteristics belong to intended objects rather than to existing ones and provide the basis for mutual understanding and knowledge of the world we experience as a community of language users.

Paramārtha's second argument, from spatiality, also implicitly delineates the tripartite structure of name, sense, and reference:

> (*a*) If, as the opponent claims, the name signifies the nature of the object intended, then if there is one thing with many names, there should be as many substances [having natures or essences] as there are names [since each name signifies the nature of an object intended for the opponent].[22] (*b*) If there are as many substances as there are names, then different phenomena could occupy one locus in space [since for every name there is a corresponding phenomenon, if there is a necessary relationship between names and their referents].[23]

The second argument can be expanded in the following way: The name, for the opponent, signifies the [complete] nature of an object, yet one object may have many names [and many senses]. The Yogācāra text counters that, if an object has only one nature [essence], then the name [and sense] does not signify the [complete] nature of an object since there are many names [and senses] but only one nature. Therefore, no single name can completely describe the nature of an object. If there are as many objects as there are names given to them, then each name should refer to a distinct object in one locus in space (and there would be many objects in one space) or each object would have to be in more than one locus to correspond to each name. But no object can occupy more than one locus in space at any one time and two objects cannot occupy the same space. We apply many names [in many languages] to refer to a particular individual that occupies only one space. While names are many, any given object has only one nature. Therefore, names are not in a one-to-one correspondence with the objects they denote, or with the natures of those objects (but are in a superficial relationship, *āgantuka*). Names are not distributed over space (and time) whereas objects are.

Paramārtha presents the Yogācāra argument that it is the *sense* of a name, not the name itself, that is based on the properties of the presentation of a commonly apprehended object. Objects to which many senses and names may refer have only one nature upon which the senses, not the names, are based. Names may be multiple, often implying more than one referent, but if the sense of two or more names is the same, the referent has to be the same. This is so because the sense is based upon the properties presented as characteristic of an intended object whereas names, being arbitrary, are not. An additional claim is made: names refer to objects according to the *intentions* of language users whereas senses are based upon the functional aspects of intended objects. It is because of the sense and reference that there is basis for mutual understanding and communication through language.

The third argument, from general names or homonyms, is similar in its line of reasoning:

(*a*) Since [general] names are indefinite [in terms of their reference], if the name signifies the nature of the object intended, the substance of the object intended would also be indefinite. (*b*) A name may refer to a variety of things besides the particular being denoted. (*c*) Therefore, according to the opponent, one could know the name but the object intended would be indefinite.[24]

The line of reasoning in this third argument takes into consideration the case of homonyms or homophones. A given homonym may suggest many referents to the listener besides the one the speaker wishes to denote. Since general names are distributed over many individuals, they have indefinite reference, that is, their reference is also distributed over many individuals. Therefore, singular reference, that is, definite reference, would be impossible since no general name or homonym, having only indefinite reference, could possibly denote a singular intended object or its particular nature. It is when the sense of a name is singular and definite that one is able to denote a particular object. General names do not signify the object intended since one homonym may refer to a variety of objects.[25]

Yogācāra makes the distinction between the class of names and that of their denoted objects. Name and reference do not belong to the same logical class since one is a linguistic entity while the other is not: ". . . name and the object intended are not necessarily related (*āgantuka*) ('adventitious to each other'). The reason for this is that the name is not necessarily related to the object intended and it is not of the same [logical] class as the object intended. The object intended, with regard to the name, also is not necessarily related and it is not of the same [logical] class as names."[26] The intermediary principle between the name and the intended object is the sense, which is neither a mental image (idea), that is, wholly subjective, nor the referent, which is objective. The sense is connected with our actual practice in the employment of language and is partly subjective and partly objective. In Yogācārin terms, the discrimination of various aspects (*hsiang*) of the thing in contrast to another, as a functional relationship between various phenomena and their relationship with the perceiver, is the criterion for constituting the sense or meaning of the intended object; this is an indirect, proximate knowledge of reality.

Yogācāra maintains that consciousness of the object intended is logically prior to perception of aspects or properties such as blue or yellow, "this" or "that." Perception, in turn, is logically prior to the attribution of a name. Stated otherwise, the implication is that attention to the referent precedes the sense of the referent, which in turn is logically prior to naming.

As you [the non-Buddhist] have said: "If the intended object really exists, one applies a name to reveal the intended object just as lamplight illuminates form." This does not hold. Why? Because first of all, one must have the object intended and afterward one establishes the name. When one does not have the object intended, one cannot establish the name. Even though one first perceives the object intended and later establishes a name, still one cannot completely ascertain the object intended through perception. Still less, how could one possibly ascertain the intended object from its name? The metaphor of the lamplight illuminating a thing is not analogous to the intended object. First of all, one can definitely ascertain a thing because of the lamplight. One does not first ascertain the thing and then afterward need the lamplight. . . . [Paramārtha's exegesis:] . . . The consciousness first has an object intended and then perceives blue or yellow, "this" or "not this." From these perceptions, one afterward establishes a name. If one can perceive and ascertain the object intended, then prior to perception consciousness should not have an object intended. Moreover, if there can be ascertainment of the intended object through names, when other people are not aware of the name, they should not understand the intended object without hearing the name. In the metaphor of a lamplight illuminating form, a given person should be able to reveal and ascertain the form because of the lamp, yet other people would not be able to see the form by this means. But this is meaningless [for the lamp *does* permit everyone to see the illuminated thing]. Therefore, it is definite that although a lamp can reveal form, this is not analogous to names' revealing intended objects.[27]

The analogy of the lamp for explaining naming is used by the opponent to try to support the notion that names complete one's knowledge of an object. The lamplight is compared to a name, having instrumental value in acquiring knowledge of an object.[28] Just as lamplight reveals colors and form, so does a name reveal an object. The opponent's analogy does not hold, as Paramārtha clearly demonstrates. It is not the name that completes one's knowledge of an object but rather the sense, at least for purposes of everyday communication. Paramārtha, in his exegesis, takes the position that since reference only occurs after perception has taken place, the analogy with the lamp does not hold: if one were to apply the lamp analogy to the relationship between perception and reference, it would mean that one sees the object [perception] before using the lamp [reference]. The relationship of perception to sense to reference is therefore subordinated to the act of intending—that is, first one directs one's attention toward and presupposes an object, then perceives the aspects of the object as in a functional relationship with other objects and with the speaker, which in turn provides the basis for the sense. From the sense, one then applies a name to the object, even though names for referents are assigned by convention.

From the above arguments we can understand that it is the epistemological structure of the mind, not the ontological structure of the world, that must be investigated in order to understand the foundation for the linguistic structures we use. In his interpretation of Yogācāra, Paramārtha then maps out the underlying structure for epistemological or "intentional" objects.

Paramārtha's Views on Yogācāra's Innate Structure of Mind

According to the SWHL, we habitually think in terms of our linguistic structure as if the phenomena we discriminate, by virtue of our linguistic categories, had natures intrinsically linked to the way we categorize them. We talk about the plurality of phenomena through our language systems as if phenomena were unchanging. Following Yogācāra's thesis that the discriminating consciousness requires both intentional objects and language in order to function, intentional objects become the content of a discriminating consciousness, and language is the tool by which we express the contents of our discriminations. Conversely, if there were no process of discrimination, there would be no language, no intentional objects, and no attachment to objects as subsistent entities.

Unlike certain contemporary philosophers of language who are concerned with meaning and sentence structure in order to understand public discourse, Yogācāra's ultimate aim in discussing linguistic structures is not to analyze the communication process per se. Although language does indeed serve a practical purpose in enabling us to engage in public discourse, language also affects our behavior and values in the world in which we are active. Our everyday discourse generates emotions and certain predispositions to act in various ways.[29] Because of the psychological relationship between words and our behavior and attitudes, the connotative qualities of language are often mistakenly assumed to be inherent in the object themselves. We become attached to certain things because they evoke pleasant feelings. The words themselves may often conjure up these feelings. Discrimination based upon the affective associations with and continual conditioning by certain types of words and their referents becomes habitual. We become conditioned to behave in set patterns because of the verbal stimuli we receive. Language patterns condition us to think in certain categories and to evaluate our environment according to the affective associations we attribute to certain words and concepts. These categories and feelings become an inflexible framework for producing predictable responses to similar verbal stimuli. In Yogācārin terminology, the individual becomes "attached" to persons and phenomena because of the "seeds" incurred from past actions (*karma*).[30]

Implicit in Yogācāra's epistemological theory is a course of action to eliminate the psychological bonds associated with elements in our language and to change our attitudes toward more ethical forms of social behavior. Here Paramārtha is concerned with presenting the philosophical and religious objectives implied in Yogācāra's analysis of language. His epistemological investigation does not focus on the description of language usage per se but on how all mental functions are affected in some way by language usage and by discrimination of intentional objects.

Yogācāra attempts to demonstrate that language sets up psychological barriers to understanding the world of intentional objects. It is the intentions of the language users, not the truth-expressing function of language, that makes communication an effective process. Therefore, in order to change certain modes of behavior, one must change one's way of intending objects, and in so doing also change one's way of communicating.

Since the intentionality of objects occurs prior to common agreement about them and prior to formulating their sense, the world of objects is inherently intentional, a dimension of the functioning process of mental states. An understanding of the relationship between objects intended and the subject who is intending them is a correct understanding of entities in the world as they really are. Ultimately, the knowledge that the two aspects of the world of entities, material and mental, are interdependent, contingent upon mental processes, is Paramārtha's interpretation of Yogācāra; other philosophers belonging to the Yogācāra tradition placed more ontological import on mental entities. The world we live in is not actually divided into two worlds—a world of appearance (senses) and a world of ideas (suprasensory)—but is a single unified structure.

On the ontological level, Paramārtha claims that the object intended has no ontological status independent of mental functions. He would not accept the view that names or their senses express truth. There is no notion of an ideal formal language or ideal science in Paramārtha's philosophical theories. Paramārtha believes that we use language in such a way that we presuppose the existence of actual objects as referents; he explains the Yogācāra Buddhist position that such ontological presuppositions are based upon the act of intending objects, not upon any notion of truth.

In accounting for the discrimination of intentional objects, Paramārtha presents the Yogācāra classification of factors contributing to the act of intending and its resulting discrimination into two types: (1) presupposing the existence of an object based upon nominal distinctions, that is, names we give to varieties of phenomena (*artha-nāmābhiniveśa-kalpa*); and (2) contrasting intended objects based upon perceptual distinctions (*svabhāva* and *viśeṣa-vikalpa*).[31] The first group, in Paramārtha's treatise SWHL, focuses on how the mind functions as the underlying structure that supports discrimination and daily linguistic discourse. Yogācāra Buddhism is, by implication, criticizing language theorists who assert that our (natural) language can provide an adequate account of reality, because these theorists have not satisfactorily investigated whether or not there is a prelinguistic foundation for name-using other than the means by which we perceive a referent, the aspects or properties of a thing. Notions of plurality of phenomena are paradoxical and incoherent when expressed through language.

Paramārtha presents five kinds of distinction with regard to the act of intending, based upon nominal distinctions.[32] This subgroup includes communication with others by explaining through names, labeling one's discriminations and becoming attached to those discriminations as criteria for making further discriminations, and defining and categorizing things based upon past linguistic information concerning classes and characteristics of objects. This subgroup is an expansion of the first item in the second subgroup listed below, namely, the discrimination of self-existent entities (*svabhāva*).

The second subgroup, contrasting intended objects, is based upon perceptual distinctions. This subgroup includes discrimination of self-existent entities that are based upon an assumed relationship between name and object; grasping the differences between sense data in any single intended object; perceiving an intended object and communicating its name to others; perceiving an intended object but being unable to communicate the object to others, as in the case of animals; discriminating based upon the emotive effects of past actions; and discriminating through name-giving or through observation without name-giving.[33] This subgroup of distinctions based upon contrasts between intended objects describes the act of discriminating both in terms of immediate, direct perception and in terms of habitual conditioning resulting from past psychological experiences in an individual's life. An interesting implication, which cannot be dealt with here, is that emotive influences from past experiences can distort or decidedly alter acts of perception.

Acts of intending are the ground for discriminating objects as unchanging and substantially real. Yogācāra contends that if we understand the conscious processes constituting intentional acts, we will be able to change the attitudes that we have developed owing to our unreflective dependency upon language and conceptualization.[34] In order to understand these conscious processes that constitute intentional acts, we must investigate the two structures involved in acts of intending, those based upon nominal distinctions and those based upon making perceptual distinctions between objects that are functionally related to each other.

Nominal distinctions intrinsic to language are the more indirect means by which discriminations arise. At this level, the influence of language on our view of the world is a misleading one to the extent that we are not conscious of the degree or range of this influence. We suppose that there is a more or less persistent entity corresponding to the referent to which we assign names and that the attributes assigned to a referent accurately denote the changing properties of that referent.

Discrimination by grasping one of the many clusters [of sense data] (*piṇḍa-graha-vikalpa*) [as one entity] refers to attachment to an ego (*ātma*), to sentient beings (*sattva*), to life (*jīva*), and to one who has sensations (*jantu*) relating to the aggregate (*skandha*) of form (*rūpa*). All names are conventionally established (*saṃketopasaṃhita*). Grasping this cluster, discrimination occurs. Moreover, among the many clusters of phenomena, grasping a given cluster [as one entity] is reason for saying: "this is a house," "an army," "a cart," "a garment," "food," "drink," etc. Such names are all conventionally established. Grasping these, discrimination occurs. This is called discrimination by grasping one of many clusters [of sense data as one entity]. These [correlative] pairs signify internal and external discrimination; the former is attachment to personhood, the second is attachment to phenomena.[35]

We are naïve in not realizing that if our linguistic structure did not involve a subject-predicate grammatical form, we would not have the tendency to construct a metaphysics that reflected our grammar. Paramārtha makes this claim but in a less direct and explicit manner in his exegesis; Hsüan-tsang's recension, HYSCL, does not have the following commentary:

Take the case of a person who does not yet have the intended object but previously has had the name "form." He has heard the following explanation of the characteristics (*hsiang*) of form: "It has a shape that is resistant. It can be sustained and it can be destroyed."—Something with such characteristics is called "form." This person afterward sees the appearances of the various types of "form" as substance. According to what he has heard in the past, he recognizes it as "form." That is to say, one can discriminate the substantive nature of "form" based upon names. . . .[36] Take the case of a person who already knows the name and the intended object and afterward discriminates again with regard to what he had previously known as the name and the intended object: namely, this is the substance of form and this is the name "form."[37]

In Mahāyāna Buddhist terms, the linguistic structure of all natural languages involves us in a metaphysics that posits persons and phenomena as substantial entities because we express ourselves and our world in terms of subjects and objects persisting through time. If we reflect upon the structure of consciousness, we can become aware of the capacity of consciousness to intend objects over and against subjects. These acts of intending are influenced by the nominal distinctions we construct. We can in that way understand how language reinforces a dualistic view of the world, a world of subjects as contrasted to objects.

Since the structure of consciousness, in its everyday involvement with its world, is fundamentally intentional, nonexistent entities can be objects, that is, intended objects. If we have preconceived notions of persons and phenomena as having unchanging essences, we impute these essences to the objects we intend. The door to subjective idealism is consequently opened, because we then believe that objects intended are integral parts and processes of consciousness, formulated by nominal distinctions and by perceptual distinctions. Yogācāra wants to make the further claim, in attacking the empiricist position, that the structures of consciousness already give us the means whereby we intend objects—namely, through our capacity to make nominal distinctions and perceptual distinctions.

Perceptual distinctions are more primitive and basic to the act of intending than are nominal distinctions to the degree that perceptual distinctions are based upon contrasts the senses make and are logically prior to linguistic, that is, nominal, distinctions. Naming is arbitrary and not based upon perceptual distinctions ascribed to the referent. Even perceptual distinctions are inherent in the structure of consciousness and do not really constitute the essences or real natures of objects.

Therefore, every act of intending is conditioned by acts of consciousness that are language-dependent or perception-dependent. One intends objects of the world according to prescribed mental structures. In its perceptual structure, consciousness intends an object by means of its capacity to contrast one object over and against another. The perceiving consciousness discriminates properties attributed to an object, based upon the sense data of the object it intends, and contrasts that object as external to the contents of consciousness. These aspects or features of the intended and perceived object appear to the intending consciousness by virtue of consciousness' direct attention or apprehension of an object as existing. The awareness or recognition of the primacy of the intending role of consciousness is not acknowledged at the primitive level of immediate sense perception. Consciousness as an agent that contrasts has a dialectical relationship with the objective content of its contrasts. There is as yet no acknowledgment of the nature of consciousness as intending objects and formulating categories through which the world is perceived.

Acts of consciousness that are language-dependent provide a possible means for understanding certain structures of the mind. In contrast to the more primitive and basic level of immediate sense perception, at the level of communication one can more readily become aware of the role of the mind as the producer of linguistic objects based upon the language-formulating structure. At this level one can recognize and acknowledge that it is the language user who sets up categories for objects intended. Upon reflection and self-consciousness, investigation of these linguistic categories affords us the opportunity to understand the world of objects as basically intentional, as presupposed to exist in certain categorical schema patterned after the way our language is structured.

A study of language is significant for Paramārtha and for all Yogācāra Buddhists because, by means of a philosophical investigation of language, one can be led to an investigation of the mental capacity for constructing not only linguistic entities but also ontological ones. It is by means of an initial critical reflection on language that Paramārtha anticipates leading the reader to understanding the contrasting, discriminating nature of consciousness and its unifying, intentional structure of consciousness, which underlie both nominal distinctions and perceptual distinctions of our world of objects:

Thus, "from one to another [form], evolving from each other" means that consecutive moments [in the evolution of the discriminating consciousness] are not the same. Therefore, one says "through mutual interaction." All the various constructs are [evolved from] consciousness without an objective world. "Into varieties of discriminations" means that in each single [act of] consciousness there is both a discriminator and a discriminated object. The discriminator is identical to consciousness and the discriminated object is identical to the sense object. . . . Therefore, one says "into varieties of discriminations and discriminated objects." For this reason, outside of consciousness, there are no other sense objects.[38]

Yogācāra's Contributions to the Philosophy of Language

Paramārtha, in the CSL and SWHL, defines language as having both a private and a public dimension. The private dimension of language involves the intentionality of reference; the public dimension involves mutually agreed upon intentional objects of practical communication and mutual identification. It is Paramārtha's analysis and comments on Yogācāra's theory of language that make his philosophical theses innovative and worthy of study. For him, steeped in the Yogācārin tradition, the limits of language are *not* the limits of our world. However, a close study of our language dependency does shed light on the important question of how we think in preconceived ways about our world. These a priori forms of knowledge establish the basis for understanding the structures of the mind, devoid of empiricist biases.

Paramārtha views the matter not as a question of an *interface* between mind and object but as a unified foundation, namely, the act of intending, which is the basis for his psychological theories. Though much of Western philosophy has been mainly concerned with truth and the laws of truth or science, Buddhist philosophy has on the whole been concerned with intentions and the psychological predispositions that influence our attitudes and behavior. Whereas truth is public and readily comprehensible to those who know the laws of logic, intentions are personal, yet shared through daily communication. Sense impressions, feelings, and attitudes are not the concern of logic.

Yogācāra epistemology negates the dualistic structures of inner (subjective) versus outer (objective) worlds. The act of intending is construed as a unifying structure, underlying the subject who intends and the object that is intended.[39] According to Paramārtha's presentation of Yogācāra, the world of intending is only conceptualized as inner and outer spheres when, according to Paramārtha's presentation, the structure of the mind as language-dependent and perception-dependent discriminates in dualistic patterns formed by habitual conditioning and reinforced by daily communication. Instead of analyzing acts of intending as entities or static forms, Paramārtha interprets the unfolding of the world of language as a dynamic process in which subject and object are moments of a process dominated by linguistic structures of mind. Paramārtha's interpretation of Yogācāra presents the unfolding of perceptual properties functionally related to objects, moments of a process dominated by perceptual structures of the mind in which sense data are contrasted to one another. Acts of intending, therefore, cannot be bifurcated into inner and outer worlds but are processes in continual momentum. They do not constitute an interface or tertiary type of entity, an entity that is neither wholly subjective nor wholly objective, nor do they bridge two logically and ontologically different classes.

Paramārtha replaces a common Western tripartite model, in which an intermediary agent such as sense interacts between the world of minds and the world of objects, with a "systems-oriented" model.[40] This new model, characteristic of Yogācāra's philosophical position, is a system in which various components as variables perform specified functions according to the structures of the system. The system is one of "intending," of directing attention toward the components comprising the system itself. Language and perception perform specified functions of communication and categorization according to the discriminative structures of the system and conceal reality. Consequently, both language and perception are viewed as vital mechanisms through which the system maintains its operations.

Concluding Remarks

In Paramārtha's analysis, the prelinguistic self-conscious structures of the mind are viewed as fundamentally intentional, influenced by language and by perception in practical discourse. In order to understand the underlying mental structures upon which language and perception are based and to investigate the way we use language in communicating with one another, Paramārtha commented on, as well as translated, Yogācāra treatises. The focal points of his linguistic analysis are the notion of intentionality and the paradoxical nature of language. The primary condition involved in all labeling, categorizing, and ascribing of properties to things is mutual agreement about perceived properties in objects assumed to exist. What we find in Yogācāra arguments against opponents who claim that language provides an essential key to the nature of things, is a rudimentary distinction between sense and reference.[41]

In this early Yogācāra Buddhism, sense and reference are distinguished in order to demonstrate that a referent is presupposed to exist but that sense can be established without raising the question of existence and nonexistence. Truth-expressing aspects of language were believed to be unnecessary for the achievement of communication. Our understanding of objects is influenced by personal, psychological factors, and they must be altered if our behavior is to be altered. Consequently, behavioral and attitudinal changes were the goal of understanding the intentional nature of language and perception. Intentional and psychological variables involved in practical communication were viewed by Paramārtha as relevant not only to an analysis of meaning but, more importantly, to an understanding of the psychophysical nature of human beings.

IV
Philosophy of Mind

FROM EARLIEST times, spiritual liberation in Buddhism has been defined in terms of three requirements: discipline (*śīla*), meditation (*samādhi*), and wisdom (*prajñā*).[1] The objective of this threefold process of liberation is the elimination of all anxieties, compulsions, and attachments, since they are the source of suffering. Positively stated, the spiritual path culminates in an insight (*prajñā*) into reality as it is (*tathatā*) and a direct awareness of one's true self (*anātman*).[2] Liberation is the realization of the true nature of self free from attachment and delusion. This knowledge is attained by analyzing the process of consciousness that brings about attachment. To understand the process is to be free from it. The basic problem in all Buddhist systems is to understand the conditions of ignorance and delusion in order to develop the capacity for the perception of reality as it is.

Though all Buddhist schools acknowledge that the problem of ignorance and attachment must be dealt with in terms of the tripartite path to spiritual freedom, theories do not agree on how consciousness is influenced by ignorance[3] nor on how to identify the structures of consciousness and how to refine the powers of the mind.[4] This chapter will discuss the relationship between spiritual liberation and the structures of consciousness, as seen in some significant early Yogācārin texts translated by the sixth-century philosopher Paramārtha.[5]

Textual Materials

Although Paramārtha's largest and most complete works were his translations of the *Mahāyāna-saṃgraha* and the *Abhidharma-kośa-bhāṣya,* there is a very close relationship between the *Mahāyāna-saṃgraha* and the anthology attributed to him, consisting of the *San wu-hsing lun, Chuan shih lun,* and *Hsien shih lun,* which were collectively called the *Wu-hsiang lun.*[6] These three texts are not specifically dated in any of the catalogues of Chinese Buddhist scriptures, but Paramārtha seems to have written them during the period between his translating the *Saṃgraha* and the *Koṣa,* that is, between 563 and 567. These texts can therefore be taken as representative of Paramārtha's most highly developed and significant philosophical views. Moreover, the trilogy shares the most distinctive feature of Paramārtha's thought, namely, the identification of a transcendent, pure consciousness called the *amala-vijñāna.*[7]

CHUAN SHIH LUN

The *Chuan shih lun* (CSL) is an adaptation from the *Triṃśikā* by Vasubandhu. Although some specialists have regarded the CSL as a translation of the *Triṃśikā,* it is more accurately described as a prose paraphrase of the thirty Sanskrit verses collectively entitled the *Triṃśikā,* together with liberal exegetical comments not found in the Sanskrit original.[8]

The CSL defines eight evolutionary modes of conscious activity in connection with a glossary of terminology for various good, bad, and neutral mental states.[9] Discrimination, that is, mental construction through conceptualization of phenomena, is explained in terms of the Yogācārin framework of Consciousness-Only. Functional dependency between perceiver and perceived object is also discussed. A description of reality that is devoid of mental construction is equated with a transcendent, pure state of consciousness. This text appears to be a self-contained and coherent outline of Paramārtha's interpretation of Yogācārin philosophy, and it is especially significant to Buddhologists because we also have Hsüan-tsang's translation, the Sanskrit verses with Sthiramati's commentary, and Paramārtha's own exegesis to work with.

SAN WU-HSING LUN

The *San wu-hsing lun* (SWHL) is the most difficult text in the *Wu-hsiang lun* as well as the most detailed tract on early Yogācārin thought.[10] Unlike the CSL, it does not seem to constitute a self-contained discussion of Yogācāra's general schema of consciousness but is, rather, only a portion of a larger work that Hsüan-tsang, in his translation, entitles the *Hsien-yang sheng chiao lun*.[11] As the title *San wu-hsing lun* (The Three Naturelessnesses) suggests, this treatise is primarily concerned with the nonsubstantial nature of reality.[12] It discusses, in considerably more detail than the CSL, the nature of mental construction or discrimination and expands the discussion by arguing that discriminative acts are language-dependent. Language use, as we have seen in chapter 3, is established by distinguishing functional relationships between perceiver and perceived. This network of operations yields a closed system until one breaks the cycle of repeated patterns of discrimination conditioned by habitual ignorance and attachment. The way to gain release from this cycle constitutes the spiritual path of the Bodhisattva.

HSIEN SHIH LUN

The latter half of the SWHL and the entire text of the *Hsien shih lun* (HSL)[13] define the variety of the seeds of experience (*bīja*), which are the stimuli for conditioned habits of discrimination, yielding recurrent responses of ignorance and attachment but also capable of yielding wisdom. It is not clear what text the HSL is based upon, although Ui compares portions of it with the *Mahāyāna-saṃgraha*.[14] The same system of seeds can yield two different sorts of response. The relation between this closed system of cyclical ignorance and the release from it turns on the understanding of the system itself. The operations programmed by certain structures of consciousness can be terminated by those same structures through the practice of meditation.[15]

The Structures of Consciousness

The Mahāyāna Buddhist consensus with regard to the phenomenal world is that everything can be understood by thoroughly investigating the way the system of consciousness works. To control and finally eliminate certain states of consciousness or certain activities of consciousness, one must become aware of the process of their emergence and formulation. The mode of operation that determines behavior and perception is termed "conditioning" (*pratītya-samutpāda*).[16] This "conditioning" is an ongoing process of change in a world viewed as impermanent and not self-existent. To understand the system of consciousness therefore requires analyzing the process of conditioning that determines how various structures of consciousness function. Once the system is understood, one is able to change habitual behavioral and perceptual patterns by locating the causes for them. Although the religious goal of Yogācāra, in general, is to perceive reality through meditation and discipline, Yogācāra also devotes much attention to the processes of consciousness that are compulsive acts of ignorance and attachment.

In accordance with the Buddhist project of investigating the conditioning factors of a given system in order to understand the operation of that system, the CSL defines consciousness in terms of the variety of processes that emerge as perception and behavior. The text describes an eightfold process of consciousness, with three levels or structures that are categorized according to the conditions necessary for each level or structure to operate.[17]

The CSL begins with the statement: "Consciousness evolves (*pravartate*) in two ways: (1) it evolves into selves (*ātman*); (2) it evolves into things (*dharma*). Everything perceived [or cognized] is included in these two objects [of cognition]. These two really do not exist, but consciousness evolves into these two [false] representations."[18] In this opening statement the world of beings and things is defined as mentally constructed: the activity of consciousness evolves (*vijñāna-pariṇāma*) into mistaken apprehensions (*upacāra*) of personhood (*ātma*) and into a world of phenomena (*dharma*). Everything is construed either as a self or as a substantial object, and both are objects of consciousness. The relationship between consciousness and the world is fundamentally constructed by consciousness. This mental activity or evolution of consciousness "conditions" perception and behavior. For Vasubandhu, in the *Triṃśikā*, the relationship between sentient beings and their world is continually undergoing a series of changes in a mentally constructed system (*vijñāna-pariṇāmo 'yam vikalpo*) and is nonexistent outside that system (*tena tan nāsti tenedam sarvaṃ vijñapti-mātrakam*). This is what is meant by the statement that sentient beings and phenomena "are really nonexistent." Everything is therefore a by-product or an evolved product of an activity of consciousness.

The function of consciousness is to condition, that is, to be a conditioner or conditioning power, to be affecting or constructing things. The text goes on to state: "Next, we shall explain the three kinds of perceiver [or cognizer; also termed *vijñāna-pariṇāma*]: (1) the retributive (*vipāka*) consciousness, namely, the *ālaya-vijñāna*; (2) the appropriating consciousness, namely, the *ādāna-vijñāna*; (3) the consciousnesses of sense data, namely the six [sense] consciousnesses (*vijñaptir viṣayasya*)."[19] According to this classification, the structures of consciousness operate on three levels. From the religious perspective of Yogācāra in general, the retributive structure of consciousness is primarily an ethical domain and is regarded as the basic or fundamental function of all conscious activity. This underlying structure is to be investigated until a cessation of its activity occurs in the highest forms of meditation, according to Paramārtha in his CSL, or a transformation (*āśraya-parāvṛtti*) in the case of Hsüan-tsang. We shall return to the shift from the function of consciousness that constitutes ignorance to the function that is pure wisdom.[20]

Technically known as the *ālaya-vijñāna*, this underlying structure in the evolution or developing process of consciousness (*vijñāna-pariṇāma*) represents the capacity of consciousness to construct future acts on the basis of past habits and behavior. The *ālaya-vijñāna* is defined functionally as the activity of consciousness that maintains certain modes of behavior and perception and certain ideologies or conceptions. In Buddhist terminology, the *ālaya-vijñāna* is metaphorically called the receptacle for *karma* because it is the result (*vipāka*) of past *karma* in the form of "impressions" (*vāsanā*) or habits, which condition future *karma* as "seeds" (*bīja*) or stimuli.[21]

Paramārtha states that we can know only indirectly of the existence of this structure through its effects on an individual's behavior.[22] From a deluded act or thought we infer a preparatory stage in which a latent habit-impression in the "clearinghouse" of the *ālaya-vijñāna* influences one to behave in a deluded or ineffectual manner. An example may be helpful. Take the behavior of a liar who habitually distorts the facts of a given incident. In order for the act of lying to have taken place, there must have been a stage in which a dormant habit-impression, from a past act of lying, influenced the person to behave in a similar manner, thus acting as the "seed" for the new lie. This seed's potency or energy in turn becomes a habit-impression when the new act of lying takes place, and so the cycle continues until it is broken.

The second level or structure in the evolution of consciousness, namely, the *ādāna-vijñāna*,[23] is likewise defined in terms of its function, which is "to appropriate" or "to acquire." This level is based upon the *ālaya-vijñāna* and is the activity of egotism or of appropriating for "me." Through the *ādāna* all conceptualizations are intertwined with a false self-identity, and one's existence is then seen in terms of what one acquires or appropriates, whether it be material possessions, other persons, or ideas and values. In the case of our habitual liar, he lies because of his past propensity to lie but also because he believes he will thereby gain something of value, perhaps status or material benefit. His repeated lying is influenced by a self-image dependent on status and wealth.

The third level or structure in the evolution of consciousness, namely the six *vijñānas*, functions in both sensory and ideational processes, since sensation and ideation involve the same mechanism. All sense data are, in this analysis, basically mental. Sensation or ideation takes place when three elements of the process interact: a sense faculty (*indriya*), sense data (*viṣaya*), and a consciousness (*vijñāna*).[24] This threefold process of interacting elements is the evolution of consciousness that appears to be an objectified world of objects and persons. How we perceive and construct our world is influenced by associations from past experiences and by the linguistic terms we use to categorize the world we live in. For example, a child's fear of the dark may be due to perceiving monsters lurking in his room at night. These "monsters" may in turn have been shaped by a previous experience in which the child's parents said a monster would spank the child if he or she misbehaved. Every time the child misbehaves, there is the recurrent fear of the dark associated with fear of punishment. This fear affects the child's perception, that is, monsters in the room; the word "dark" can evoke all of these feelings, perceptions, and ideas in the child.

Sensory and ideational processes are also related to other cognitive states: attention (*manasikāra*), sensation (*vedanā*), volition (*cetanā*), and conceptualization (*saṃjñā*).[25] The underlying structure for these activities of consciousness is the *ālaya-vijñāna*, which is the "current," while the five cognitive states are the "waves,"[26] disruptive and delusory. Intellect or *mano-vijñāna* is always active except in certain states of meditation, sleep, and unconsciousness.[27]

Consciousness-Only

The *amala-vijñāna*, literally "Pure Consciousness," is equivalent to Consciousness-Only. That is, "Consciousness-Only" is defined negatively as the elimination of all anxieties, compulsions, and attachments by means of the elimination of both the sense object and the sensing, functioning consciousness. The positive definition is the wisdom of things as they are, the activity of consciousness no longer controlled by ignorance. The CSL states: "The meaning [of Consciousness-Only], fundamentally, is to dispense with sense objects and to dispense with the mind." The text continues: "For this reason, outside of consciousness, there are no other sense objects. . . . one dispenses with sense objects in order to empty the mind. . . . [When] both the sense object and consciousness are dissolved, this [state of affairs] is identical to the true nature [*tattva* or *tathatā*]. The true nature is identical to Pure Consciousness (*amala-vijñāna*)."[28]

Paramārtha's description of "emptying" consciousness of subject-object concepts is similar to Nāgārjuna's description of the term "Emptiness."[29] "Consciousness-Only" is used to denote the understanding of both the arising and cessation of ignorance as an activity of consciousness. The meditative state of mind operates in the same system as the ignorant state. Nāgārjuna's negative dialectic is a device to dispel the misconception that phenomenal and mental entities are self-existent things unaffected by one another. Paramārtha also uses a negative dialectic to correct these same habitual misconceptions but reformulates the dialectical method in terms of the activities of consciousness that evolve into simulating persons and things as self-existent entities.[30] Additionally, there is a critical distinction between the two uses of the negative dialectic: Paramārtha has a distinctively religious intention in affirming a "Pure Consciousness," and this spiritual affirmation supplements Nāgārjuna's view of Emptiness.

Mental Construction and False Discrimination

The goal of Yogācāra practice is to weaken and finally to eliminate the usual patterns of experiencing the world filtered through the five senses and the idea-creating intellect. These patterns are the grossest forms of ignorance and unethical behavior and, therefore, the easiest to eliminate. The religious intention behind analyzing this activity of consciousness is to determine the retributive impact of actions that either increase or release from suffering.[31] By no means do all activities of consciousness have retributive value. For example, the activity of a Bodhisattva is no longer shaped by past experiences. Freed from past actions and their effects, the Bodhisattva experiences the liberating effect of understanding reality without conscious effort.[32] However, the ordinary consciousness at this level is a structure involving retribution for every psychological event.

All perceptions and ideations have certain accompanying mental states that contain some conceptual (*saṃjñā*) and some affective (*vedanā*) components. In other words, all sensations and ideas entail mental constructions and depend upon or are conditioned by emotions or feelings. Yogācāra analyzes the relationship between mental construction (*vikalpa, parikalpita*) and the overall system of mental states. All sensations and perceptions are considered indirect, since they are constructed by categorization; the external object is only inferred. The only mental processes without construction occur in meditation, even in the early stages, but conceptualization (*samjñā*) and feelings (*vedanā*) are totally eradicated only in the last stage of meditation (*nirodhasamāpatti*).[33]

Let us begin with the relationship between the conditioning subject that senses and perceives and the conditioned object that is sensed and perceived. That is, we shall look at the func-

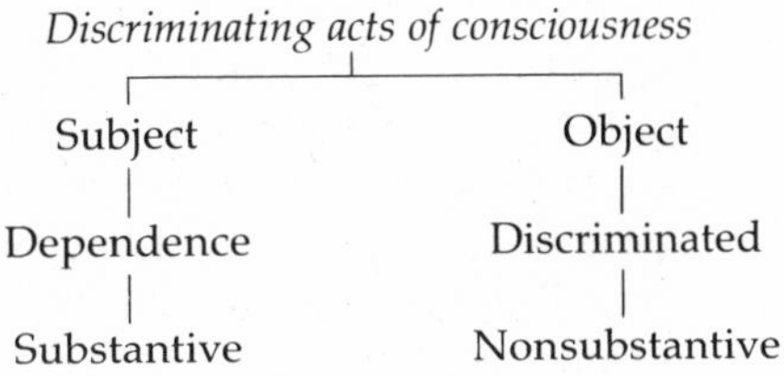

FIGURE 1

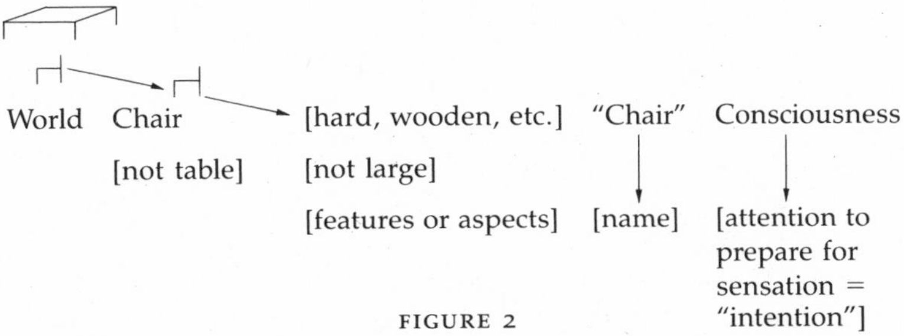

FIGURE 2

tions of consciousness engaged in the perception of an object.[34] The relationship of perceiver or subject (consciousness) to the perceived or object (sense field)[35] is described by Paramārtha in terms of the correlates "nature of dependence" (*paratantra*) and "discriminated nature" (*parikalpita*), respectively. This is the standard Yogācāra formula for dualistic constructs. Paramārtha also adds a new set of correlative terms, "substantive" and "nonsubstantive," for the same process of being conscious of an object (fig. 1).

To discuss the conditioning process between subject and object, one must understand what is meant by "discriminated nature."[36] Discriminating an object is conditioned by the features or aspects that distinguish and contrast it from other objects. That is, one makes distinctions about an object such as a chair on the basis of contrasts with other things (cabinet, table, etc.). The contrasting process of apprehending features or aspects of one object in relation to those of another is called the "discriminated nature" and is the basis for constructing names and referring to objects.

Figures 1 and 2 illustrate the dynamics of the relationship between the sensing, concept-forming, language-using consciousness and the object or content of consciousness. At this level the conscious agent does not realize that to be conscious is to be conscious of something that has already been constructed and categorized by the inner dynamics of the system itself. To be able to apprehend a sense field and then later infer a sense object requires a previous stage of being attentive to an object, of directing or "intending" an object as external to the conscious subject.

"Intention" or the mental preparation preceding sensation and ideation is not yet understood at this level. The individual is not aware of the fact that objects (of consciousness) are of a discriminated nature. Knowledge of consciousness' imputation of properties or aspects onto objects is lacking or deficient. At first, the discriminated or contrasting nature of objects is assumed to be radically different in nature from the subjective consciousness; the subjective consciousness is posited as other than its object, that objects are self-existent outside the mind yet knowable. Consciousness is dependent upon this "other" or object and is consequently called "dependent in nature,"[37] from the perspective of making still another contrast or discrimination. That is, just as the mind can contrast between tables and chairs, the mind can also make contrasts between itself as a subject and itself as an object. It is of paramount importance to analyze the system of evolving things and persons rather than to attempt to analyze the evolved products or objects in themselves, since they cannot be known apart from mental construction.

Interdependency and Self-Consciousness

Knowing the power of consciousness to evolve a manifold of objects results in objects being subjective or mental in content. When consciousness reflects upon itself as an object, that is, becomes "self-conscious," all objects also can be reduced to objects of consciousness. A world outside of consciousness can only be hypothesized.[38] Stated otherwise, everything knowable is knowable because it evolves from or is constructed by an activity of consciousness. To understand that the world of one's experience is mentally constructed and knowable only because of the discriminating and constructing nature of consciousness is to be no longer attached to a world of objects as having self-existing powers over one's life.[39] Because of past experiences, one misconstrues a world of objects by assuming that they are totally external to mental construction. Yet at the same time these objects are viewed as necessary for one's personal identity. The nature of one's true self as a self-conscious being is the only appropriate content of knowledge and is the religious goal of Yogācāra Buddhism.

Eliminating the assumption that an object is a self-existent entity and the assumption that consciousness can know self-existent objects without any mental construction is the spiritual liberation of "Consciousness-Only." When the CSL states that "The meaning [of Consciousness-Only], fundamentally, is to dispense with sense objects and to dispense with the mind,"[40] this is what is meant. If objects and consciousness were radically different from each other and only contrastive in nature (*parikalpita-svabhāva*), not dependent on each other (*paratantra-svabhāva*), one could not have any type of knowledge whatever, either of objects or of conscious processes (*self-knowledge*). For Paramārtha, one could not have consciousness itself as an object: that is, self-knowledge or self-consciousness[41] would be impossible to attain. The functions of consciousness would be unknowable, relegating an individual forever to a realm of ignorance of the true nature of self and of existence. In brief, the Yogācāra Buddhist wants to conclude that objects and consciousness cannot be so different from each other if any sort of knowledge is attainable.

The self-awareness of the relationship between subjective and objective world is a pivotal stage in Yogācāra Buddhism because the religious character of consciousness comes to the forefront of the argument. The critical distinction between consciousness and its contrastive objects is that consciousness can take itself as an object—that is, it can become self-conscious. In Yogācāra, the more refined and advanced forms of this self-investigation take place in meditation. Consciousness and self-consciousness enter a different relationship with each other than do consciousness and its objective world. Consciousness and self-consciousness cannot differ from each other in the same way as objects differ from each other. Consciousness can be contrasted to objects; nonetheless, it is also dependent on objects as much as objects are dependent upon consciousness in order to be known.[42] The relationship is mutual; in Yogācārin terminology, this relationship is "dependent in nature" (*paratantra-svabhāva*). Nāgārjuna's notion of mutual dependence between subject and object, both having no self-existence, is similar.

The Absolute and Consciousness-Only

Understanding the process of becoming self-consciousness is approached in several ways by Paramārtha. The first argument in the CSL concerns the contingency between subject and object, based upon the functions of contrasting and discriminating sense data. The most critical arguments to support the Yogācārin position of Consciousness-Only, however, center on the self-generating operations of consciousness.

The self-generating process of consciousness is a closed system of operations, metaphorically represented by "seeds" or impressions that constitute the conscious energy[43] from which all sensation, perception, and feelings emerge. All phenomena—persons and things—derive from the same source, namely, from the seeds of the fundamental conscious structure. When consciousness recognizes itself as a "seed-consciousness,"[44] that is, becomes conscious of the true nature of self, then the spiritual journey to transforming this seed-consciousness to a pure, "seedless," structure is well under way. This stage (*yoniśomanaskāra*) must be realized before enlightenment and is acquired in all the stages of the path of insight (*darśana-mārga*) known as the stages of effort (*prayoga-mārga*). Phenomena can be retained in their true nature inasmuch as conditioning by seeds has been understood, and therefore may be controlled. The assumption is that the seeds no longer give rise to ignorance when this self-consciousness is fully attained. We shall turn to this presently, but first we need to explain the complex structure of the seeds as a metaphor of Consciousness-Only.

The multiplicity of phenomenal experiences was described above as ordinarily conditioned by ignorance (or "seeds" of ignorance) in such a way that compulsive tendencies, dogmatic ideological positions,[45] and unethical behavior were the consequences. Owing to the backlog of these latent habit-impressions and their imminent effects, this entire system of thought and action is repeated endlessly. The latent aspects of these habit-impressions are "appropriated" by the second structure of conscious activity, the *ādāna*. "Seeds" have the energy to be activated in two simultaneous counterparts: the appropriating sub-

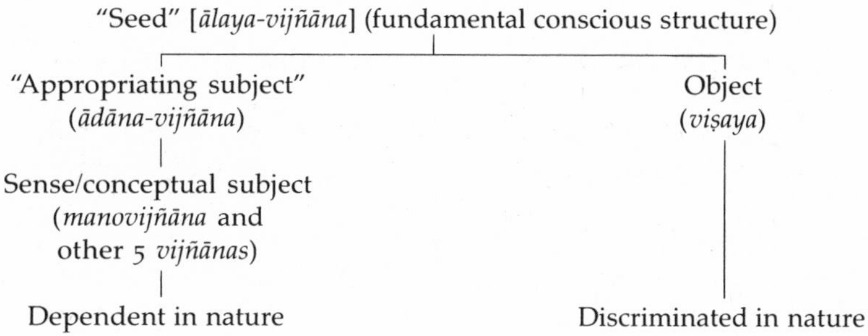

FIGURE 3

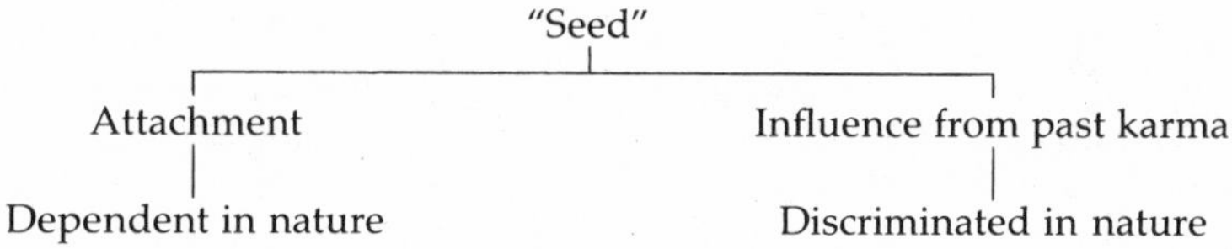

FIGURE 4

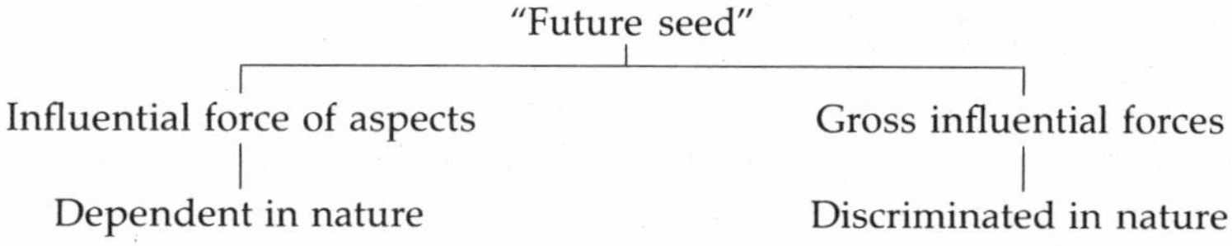

FIGURE 5

ject or *ādāna* and its objects filtered through the six sensory and conceptual consciousnesses (*pravṛtti-vijñāna*). The "seed" or energy of consciousness responsible for subject-object relationships thus has a definite twofold structure (fig. 3).

Figures 4 and 5 show the behavioral effects of a seed. In its dormant stage (fig. 4), the conditioning process from the accumulation of past *karma* reflects the dual structure of the seed as revealed in its perceptual effects. And in its active stage (fig. 5), the conditioning process creates future *karma* (*kleśa*) also in a dual mode of operation, with "influential forces of aspects" balancing "gross influential forces."[46]

The significance of this simultaneity of counterparts in the seed structure is threefold:

1. Figure 3 illustrates the overall structure of the three cycles

or structures of conscious activity. The fundamental structure can only be *inferred* as the underlying, unifying one based upon its dualistic effects.

2. Figure 4 illustrates a subset of the effects of figure 3 with reference to past *karma*. This represents the conditioning process of how an individual's responses are affected by the past. Past appropriation or attachment by the ego yields future responses of a similar nature.[47]

3. Figure 5 also illustrates a subset of the effects of figure 3 but with reference to future *karma* or *kleśa*. Although past *karma* may have been extinguished, there is still future retribution from past *karma* illustrated in figure 4. In other words, this level (fig. 5) is the more readily controlled one. In the second level (fig. 4), the Arhat has not thoroughly controlled or eliminated the seeds, since subtle influences from past experience still affect perception, ideas, and feelings.[48]

A thorough understanding of Consciousness-Only synonymous with spiritual freedom entails eliminating subject-object constructs that affect our lives. In other words, one must get to the source of the conditioning process that yields attachment to things and to self by eliminating the "seeds" that underlie the dynamics of the system. We infer that these seeds exist because the operations of subject-object interactions are not possible without the ability to contrast a discriminating subject over and against its object. The ability to understand mental constructions of this kind can only reside in a structure that can take itself for an object of investigation. What is ultimately and finally knowable, therefore, is of the very nature of "seeds," namely, the *ālaya-vijñāna*, which simultaneously produces the subject, discriminating consciousness, and its objective world. In other words, understanding the nature of the "seeds" is the teaching of Consciousness-Only.

The Emptiness of the Ālaya-Vijñāna

Since a fixed entity of selfhood is denied by Paramārtha, as it is by almost all Buddhist schools, the task set before him is to give a sufficient account of the notion of self or personhood as a series of effective and morally accountable activities without a permanent substrate. The question is therefore concerned with the plurality of psychological and physical events within a single, continually changing organism, held together by a name and by an economy of mental procedures. It is the series (*saṃtāna*) itself, a sum total of conscious events and evolving processes of conscious activity, that is designated as a "person" or "self."

Notions of "self" or "person" have only nominal existence (*prajñapti-sat*). The evolving processes of sensation and ideation (*pravṛtti-vijñāna*) are communicable through language. The subconscious processes of the *ālaya-vijñāna* that shape sensations and conceptualizations together with the sensory and ideational activities of the operating cognitive faculties (*pravṛtti-vijñāna*) constitute the sum total of the stream (*saṃtāna*) of consciousness, erroneously construed as a permanent self or ego. In other words, the *ālaya-vijñāna* and its analysis are an expansion of the earlier Mādhyamikan doctrine of Emptiness.[49]

Each act or event leaves a mental impression (*vāsanā*) which in turn discharges its energy or "seed" (*bīja*) as a future evolution (*pariṇāma*) in the consciousness-series. *Pariṇāma* refers to the transformations or changes in the consciousness-series (*saṃtāna*) that manifest themselves as things or selves because of the powers of the *ālaya-vijñāna*, *ādāna* (or *manas*), and *pravṛtti-vijñāna* in the subjective side of conscious processes.[50] In the context of morally qualified acts, the seed of any given act remains dormant in the subconscious clearinghouse (*ālaya-vijñāna*) after the act has been committed. Later, the seed will mature as compensation or retribution (*vipāka*) derived from the previous act which left a residual impression (*vāsanā*). In light of the accepted tradition throughout the history of Buddhism that trance-induced states (as well as the unconscious states of dreamless sleep and comas) suspend all normal functions of consciousness, Buddhist philosophers had to account for the retention of retributive seeds, memory, and past habits until consciousness was resumed. The replenishment of "seeds" occurs on a momentary basis even though normal conscious states have been temporarily suspended during meditation. Seeds of influential events from past experiences also are replenished, to be later retrieved in the case of memory or habitual responses, when conditions associated with the past event are met.

Early Yogācāra accounted for the continuity of the "seeds" of retribution, memory, and so on after normal functioning of consciousness had temporarily ceased, by resorting to the notion of the *ālaya-vijñāna*, metaphorically, the uninterrupted series of latent "seeds" that influence behavior and perception. This series of subconscious moments continues to function in a momentary but steady stream throughout states of unconsciousness. Hence, the "seeds" of past experiences continue to replace themselves without interruption during meditation, dreamless sleep, and so on.

Paramārtha's innovation, namely, the ninth consciousness, which is transcendent and pure (*amala-vijñāna*), eventually terminates the functions of the seed-system of the *ālaya-vijñāna*, replacing it with the absolute nature of reality, the *amala-vijñāna*.[51] This new structure of consciousness, also called "Consciousness-Only," is what remains when the seeds of defilement are no longer produced. The *ālaya-vijñāna* is the subconscious receptacle for karmic seeds stored for subsequent release, but the continuum of this karmic cycle and of rebirth ceases when the functioning of the *ālaya-vijñāna* ceases. What remains is the absolutely real, the *amala-vijñāna*, the "seedless" state of consciousness: "If an objective world does not exist, what produces any effects? For example, seeds can produce a sprout. If the seed does not exist, how can a sprout emerge? Therefore, there is no production [of effects]. The nature of the absolute (*parinișpanna-svabhāva*) is called 'the state devoid of any substantial nature' with respect to the nature [imputed on to a thing] because it neither exists nor does not exist [as some sort of substantial entity]."[52]

The *ālaya-vijñāna* and its processes of producing "sprouts"[53] of attachment and delusion no longer function when the wisdom of the *amala-vijñāna* has been attained, according to Paramārtha's interpretation of the *Triṃśikā*. The nature of the *amala-vijñāna* is different from the nature of the *ālaya-vijñāna*. One set of activities of consciousness does not simply transform its content from misconceived notions to knowledge of reality; rather, the entire mechanism that the *ālaya-vijñāna* represents no longer functions. Pure consciousness is identified with reality (*parinișpanna*) or Suchness in Paramārtha's exegesis. To know the structures of consciousness as inherently "pure" is to understand that the nature of reality is ultimately knowable and is an expression of mind, separate from the defilement in the *ālaya-vijñāna*, according to Paramārtha.

The Bodhisattva path consists in the process of understanding the relationship between mind and its world, eliminating false views and attachments. A detailed account of the elimination of the obstacles of defilement and of knowledge is described in the *San wu-hsing lun*.[54] This process of obstacle-elimination culminates in the nondiscriminative wisdom (*nirvikalpa-jñāna*)[55] of the advanced stages of Bodhisattvahood and finally of Buddhahood. Such wisdom, said to require a revolution or transformation (*āśraya-parāvṛtti*) of the basic structure of consciousness, is identical to the shift from an *ālaya-vijñāna* mechanism to that of the *amala-vijñāna* for Paramārtha. The karmic cycle ends when the system of discrimination has ended. Stated in another way, the *amala-vijñāna* is the mode of operation for one who has the wisdom of the source of ignorance and attachment: the system of seeds in the *ālaya-vijñāna*. This type of wisdom is realized only in meditation. All other activities of consciousness admit some degree of mental construction.

Since the doctrine of action, or *karma*, was the foundation for the ultimate explanation of ordinary mental states, when the *ālaya-vijñāna* as the karmic receptacle ceased, the introduction of another, non-karmic consciousness was felt to be needed by Paramārtha. This diverges from the standard forms of Yogācāra that changed or transformed the *ālaya* itself. Action or *karma* had always been essentially construed as thought or volition, able to be qualified morally.[56] Each completed action or thought was necessarily related to some sort of retribution. The notion of the *ālaya-vijñāna* explained the continuity of the retributive mechanism without positing a permanent substrate. For the Mādhyamika, actions were never completed—hence no retribution nor a receiver of retribution. For Yogācārins like Paramārtha, the overt action influences the *ālaya-vijñāna* through a habitual impression (*vāsanā*) of a seed (*bīja*) in the evolution of the ongoing stream of consciousness (*saṃtāna-pariṇāma*).

Paramārtha sees the *amala-vijñāna* as the true nature of self devoid of all misconceptions and defilements. It is the religious state of mind cultivated in meditational insight through the Bodhisattva path and culminating in Buddhahood. *Amala-vijñāna* is the wisdom of the Buddha, reminiscent of the earlier

Mahāyānist doctrine of Tathāgatagarbha[57] and of the Sautrāntika prototype found in the *Abhidharma-kośa,* that the good or pure seeds (*kuśala-bīja*) persist throughout the series of consciousness.[58] Liberation, being inherent in the structure of the mind, becomes accessible to all.

The incorruptible nature of the good seed or intrinsically pure nature of mind has a long history in Buddhist thought, most notably in Mahāsāṃghika (*prabhāsvaram cittam*),[59] Sautrāntika (*kuśala-bīja*), and Tathāgatagarbha thought. Paramārtha's philosophical and religious purpose for establishing the notion of *amala-vijñāna* appears to have been twofold: (1) to account for the possibility of good habits being produced after bad habits have been formed; (2) to account for actions without karmic residue, *nirvāṇa* without remainder. The *ālaya-vijñāna,* as a structure of consciousness entailing the propensities for habitual ignorance, could not, in Paramārtha's opinion, account for the mental states devoid of karmic retribution since by definition the *ālaya-vijñāna* represented that system of retribution. Though other Mahāyāna Buddhists preceding Paramārtha, most notably but not exclusively Tathāgatagarbha proponents, certainly had postulated an underlying, fundamentally spiritual character to the mind, none of the earlier theories had developed a systematic, phenomenological analysis of mind as intrinsically capable of salvation by its very nature. It was only with the brilliant compositions of Vasubandhu and his transmitters such as Paramārtha that a new philosophy of mind developed.

The *amala-vijñāna,* the fundamentally good structure of mind no longer chained to a cycle of retribution, was the expression Paramārtha created to embody that most cherished of Chinese Buddhist beliefs, the belief in universal enlightenment or self-cultivation as the natural capacity of the mind to know its own true nature. The notion that mind is capable of knowing its own processes as the natural evolution of mind toward its own self-discovery has been a dominant feature of much of Classical Chinese thought, particularly in the analysis of *hsing* or the true nature of things.

In summary, the structures of consciousness were the paramount object of study for the early Yogācārin philosophers in general since the natural evolution of the mind was to gravitate toward knowledge of itself. For the Chinese Buddhist intellectual, this strain of thought became increasingly provocative and challenging. Mind capable of knowing its own processes, of understanding the nature of mental constructions through the language developed in a given culture and through the interdependency between mind and its objects became the subject of vigorous study and controversy. The only subject matter that is knowable, in the final analysis put forth by Yogācāra, is mind, since only a world of mind-created symbols is ours to know. For Paramārtha and Yogācāra Buddhism, this world is opened up to us through philosophical investigation and through meditation. Both types of inquiry aim at the understanding that to be spiritually free is to develop the ability to ascertain the true nature of mind—the true nature of self—free from the conscious processes that constitute attachment and delusion, binding the individual to a never ending cycle of existence filled with ignorant and unethical habits of behavior.

V

The *Chuan shih lun*: An Analysis

OF ALL THE oldest catalogues of Buddhist literature and the biographies of prominent monks, only the *Ta-chou lu* (TCL),[1] compiled in 695, and the *K'ai-yüan lu*,[2] compiled in 730, list Paramārtha's *Chuan shih lun* as an entry. No biography in the *Hsü kao seng chuan* refers to the text. According to the KYL, this text was published originally as part of the *Hsien shih lun* (HSL) (A Treatise on Consciousness as Perception), the words "translated by Paramārtha" (*chen-ti i*) having been added to both texts at the time of the composition of the KYL in 730. Neither the dates of translation nor the places of translation are given for either text. The HSL, in turn, is described as itself an extract from a larger text titled *Wu-hsiang lun* (WHL) (A Treatise on the Unreality of [Phenomenal] Characteristics), with the subtitle *Hsien shih p'in* (*p'in* indicating that the HSL was originally only a section or part of that larger work). The *San wu-hsing lun* (SWHL) is also considered an extract from the WHL, and the place of translation is given in KYL as the Chih-chih temple in Kuangchou. We may assume that the other two texts, CSL and HSL, were composed at the same place as the SWHL, since all three texts were originally published together under a single title. The translation date could not be earlier than 562, when Paramārtha, under the sponsorship of Ouyang Wei, settled at the Chih-chih temple to begin his translation of the *Mahāyāna-saṃgraha* three months after arriving in Kuangchou. Since the *Saṃgraha* was completed in the seventh month of the fifth year, T'ien-chia, 564, the CSL, HSL, and SWHL must have been translated after that.[3] During this period, Paramārtha's most famous and most complex translations, the *Mahāyāna-saṃgraha* and the *Abhidharma-kośa*, were completed. Therefore, these concise treatises, comprising at one time the WHL, reflect Paramārtha's most mature philosophical views, set down in the last six years of his life, after he had completed his translations of the two great Buddhist compendia.

Scholars in the field of Buddhist studies now generally agree that the CSL was part of the lost treatise *Wu-hsiang lun*.[4] The subtitle in the Kao-li manuscript of the CSL adds the words "extracted from the *Wu-hsiang lun*." The three manuscripts from Sung, Yüan, and Ming as well as the Old Sung manuscript and Tempyō manuscript from Chion-in omit these words.[5]

In addition to the evidence given in the TCL and KYL and in the Kao-li manuscript, a very close association of this trilogy (CSL, HSL, and SWHL) with the WHL is confirmed by authors of other primary source materials. We shall limit ourselves to the sources that give citations attributed to the WHL and also corresponding to the extant CSL. The earliest of these sources is Fa-tsang's *Ta-sheng ch'i hsin lun i-chi*: "As the *Wu-hsiang lun* states: 'What kind of aspects (*ākāra*) and objects (*ālambana*) does this consciousness [*ālaya-vijñāna*] have?' Its aspects and objects cannot be [clearly] discriminated because they are identical and not different [from the *ālaya*]."[6] This passage is found in the CSL as part of a description of the *ālaya-vijñāna*,[7] asserting that one cannot know of the existence of the *ālaya* except by inference from its effects. Similarly, Fa-tsang uses this quotation as a gloss for the first of three aspects of the unenlightened mind delineated in the *Ta-sheng ch'i hsin lun*, namely, the constant movement of the unenlightened mind engaged in conceptualization (*nien*) and therefore inextricably related to suffering.[8] Using the CSL statement of the identity between the *ālaya* and its aspects and sense objects, Fa-tsang maintains that conceptualization in an unenlightened mind is identical to suffering, just as the *ālaya* and its resulting objects are indistinguishable. The implication is that we know of the subtle movements of the mind (*ālaya*) from its effects as suffering.

Hui-chao (650-714), in *Ch'eng wei-shih lun liao-i teng*, cites the following: "The third, the 'abode' [consciousness] is also [discussed] in the *Wu-hsiang lun*, which says: . . . 'because it is the residence for all impressions.'"[9] This is a very close paraphrasing of the CSL passage that reads: "It is also called the 'abode' consciousness because it is the place where all seeds rest."[10]

Another excerpt from the WHL citing the *Chuan-shih p'in* is quoted by Shingō (934-1004) in the *Yuishikigi-shiki*:

The *Wu-hsiang lun, Chuan-shih p'in,* says: "There are three kinds of perceiver: (1) the retributive consciousness, namely, the *ālaya-vijñāna;* (2) the appropriating consciousness, namely, the *manas;* (3) the sense consciousnesses, namely, the six consciousnesses or *viṣayasya vijñaptiḥ*. When both the object and consciousness are dissolved, this is the nature of Emptiness. This nature of Emptiness is the *amala-vijñāna*. . . . Only the *amala-vijñāna* is Suchness.[11]

The *Chuan shih p'in* must refer to the extant CSL since this citation corresponds to the CSL text,[12] with the notable difference that the CSL refers to the appropriating consciousness as the *ādāna-vijñāna,* rather than as the *manas*, the more usual technical term. This choice of terminology may have been an idiosyncracy of Paramārtha's, although a few other texts also refer to the appropriating consciousness or *ādāna-vijñāna*.[13]

None of the biographies of monks collated in the HKSC lists the CSL, HSL, and SWHL as part of their scriptural studies. The WHL is mentioned, however, in the biography of Ching-sung (537-614) among the forty texts he studied during the Ch'en dynasty under the tutelage of Fa-t'ai (d. 601), one of the most influential direct disciples of Paramārtha.[14] From this information, we may speculate that the division of the WHL into a number of separate texts could have taken place after the era of Ching-sung and Fa-t'ai, no earlier than the very end of the sixth century and before 695, when the TCL was compiled. Since sources composed toward the end of the seventh century during the T'ang dynasty still cited the WHL, the WHL must have continued to be circulated even after the separate sections were released. No catalogues after the LTSPC list the WHL. Since the KYL[15] asserts that the CSL and HSL were published as separate texts during the Ch'en (that is, before 589 when the Ch'en dynasty came to an end), Ching-sung may have been one of the last monks to study the WHL before it began to be circulated in separate segments. Moreover, it appears that the CSL was formerly part of the HSL and later extracted. In other words, the WHL was divided into an unknown number of separate texts before 589, one of which was the HSL, which was then further broken up into what is now called the HSL and the CSL, some time before 695 when the TCL lists these separately. Paramārtha must originally have intended to study the contents of the CSL, HSL, and SWHL in an integrated context under the collective title *Wu-hsiang lun*. Since the preserved edition of the CSL cites the SWHL, the CSL must have been transcribed after the SWHL, or else the quote from the SWHL was a recent addition to the text.

In addition to the established relationship between the purported trilogy of CSL, HSL, and SWHL, other texts are associated with the lost WHL as part of the original work, but on the basis of very limited evidence. For example, the WSL, which may be the extant *Ta-sheng wei-shih lun*,[16] has been considered by Ui to be incorrectly identified with the extant latter work.[17] Ui argues that the subject matter in the two texts must have been different because quotes attributed to the WHL cited in other sources are not found in the extant text entitled *Ta-sheng wei-shih lun*. These quotes, according to Ui, appear to be similar, from a philosophical point of view, to the CSL and HSL. But Ui does not mention the possibility that the *Ta-sheng wei-shih lun* in its present form may be an abbreviated text or that the lost WHL may have been similar in philosophical content to the CSL and HSL yet was not necessarily part of the WHL.

From the passages quoted above and from others attributed to the WHL corresponding to material found in the HSL and SWHL, we can definitely conclude that the CSL, HSL, and SWHL were once part of the WHL. But because many other passages cited as belonging to the WHL do not correspond to any of the three texts (CSL, HSL, and SWHL), we can conclude that either there were other extracts now lost that were part of the original or else that when sections of the WHL were published separately, some textual materials belonging to the WHL were omitted. Ui suggests that perhaps Paramārtha never completed the entire WHL, but Ui's arguments are not compelling.[18]

The T'ang dynasty Korean scholar Wŏnch'ŭk, one of Hsüan-tsang's most important students, identified the SWHL as another translation of a core text corresponding to the *Hsien-yang sheng chiao-lun: [ch'eng] wu-tzu-hsing p'in* (HYSCL), a work translated by Hsüan-tsang in 645.[19] Wŏnch'ŭk and others considered this text to be a composition of Asañga's, although Wŏnch'ŭk identifies both the SWHL and the *Triṃśikā* as compositions by Vasubandhu.[20] Furthermore, Wŏnch'ŭk goes on to say, because Vasubandhu based his views of insubstantiality (*wu-hsing; asvabhāva*) on his brother Asaṅga's and Maitreya's systems of thought, the discrepancies on the nature of existence and nonexistence reflect Paramārtha's misinterpretations and are not the errors of the great masters. But then Wŏnch'ŭk says that Paramārtha's SWHL is from a text other than Hsüan-tsang's HYSCL. This raises the question of what Wŏnch'ŭk meant by identifying Paramārtha's translation with Asaṅga's HYSCL yet at the same time claiming that the SWHL was a work of Vasubandhu's. If we look closely at the HYSCL we see that Paramārtha has clearly omitted what corresponds to the verses in Hsüan-tsang's recension.[21] But though the exegesis in Paramārtha's version seems to account for these omissions, it is puzzling in that it could belong both to Paramārtha (when it diverges from Hsüan-tsang's understanding of Yogācāra) and, as Wŏnch'ŭk also implies, to Vasubandhu, even though Hsüan-tsang's edition does not have parallel commentary.

Since Wŏnch'ŭk claims that Paramārtha's SWHL is derived from a different core text, could the SWHL be based more closely on Vasubandhu's interpretation of his brother Asaṅga's work, whereas Hsüan-tsang focused exclusively on Asaṅga's views? Many Buddhist thinkers published commentarial material separately, and that may account for Hsüan-tsang's producing two redactions of the HYSCL, one including a commentary plus the verses and the other consisting of only the verses. Ui hypothesizes that the exegesis is derived from notes students recorded of Paramārtha's own views.[22] Yūki criticizes both Fukaura and Ui for their unquestioning acceptance of portions of the WHL as simply a derivation from sections of the HYSCL.[23] Yūki theorizes that Paramārtha may have intended the SWHL to be Vasubandhu's views on Asaṅga's verses in HYSCL, which would explain what Wŏnch'ŭk meant in referring to the SWHL as part of Vasubandhu's commentarial remarks on his brother's verses; in other words, in saying that the SWHL is and is not the same text as the HYSCL, Wŏnch'ŭk was implying that the SWHL is Vasubandhu's interpretation of the HYSCL.[24] But Yūki's argument seems to overlook the fact that certain comments in the SWHL, especially those referring to the *amala-vijñāna*, do not express beliefs held either by Vasubandhu or by Asaṅga but are, at least according to tradition, beliefs ascribed to Paramārtha. A closer analysis of Hsüan-tsang's and Paramārtha's redactions along with the *Yogācārabhūmi* is essential for determining where there are additions to Asaṅga's views and whether these additions belong to Vasubandhu or to Paramārtha.

Tun-lun's compendium on Yogācāra, *Yü-chia lun chi*, compiled during the T'ang, gives the following information: "The master [Wen-] Pei also says: 'In the past tradition, the *amala-vijñāna* in the *Wu-hsiang lun* was given as evidence of nine consciousnesses. That *Wu-hsiang lun* is identical to the *Hsien-yang lun:* [*ch'eng*] *wu-hsing p'in* yet in that section (*p'in*) there is no term *amala*.'"[25] Again, the passages that relate to an *amala-vijñāna* most probably belong to Paramārtha's interpolations since there is no basis whatever for claiming that Vasubandhu ever held such a belief or ever used the term. Both Wŏnch'ŭk and Tun-lun's works confirm the close association between the SWHL and the HYSCL, on the one hand, and the WHL and the HYSCL on the other. Although these T'ang works were contemporaneous, one cites the later separate publication SWHL while the other refers to the earlier WHL. Clearly, the WHL—that is, the portion separately titled SWHL—had a close connection with Asaṅga's HYSCL and with his *Yogācārabhūmi*, while the position of Vasubandhu's purported exegesis remains problematic.

To compound the difficulties of placing the three texts within a larger whole, we find that the following, much longer passage, from the CSL, is very similar to a Tunhuang manuscript discussed below:

If the nature of discrimination is posited as identical to the nature of dependence, then the nature of discrimination would never exist nor could it include the five sets [of phenomena]. The nature of dependence could never exist either. If this were the case, then there could be no life or death, liberation, good or evil, morality or discipline. This cannot be. Therefore, since this is not the case, the nature of discrimination and the nature of dependence are not to be posited as identical.

If one maintains that they are different, then given the nature of discrimination, one could not dispense with the nature of dependence. This follows because, if we view the nature of discrimination as devoid of existence, then and only then will we see that the nature of dependence is also devoid of existence. Therefore, we are not to posit that they are different.[26]

A passage from the SWHL corresponds almost exactly to the same Tunhuang manuscript although the latter work does not indicate an ellipsis of material found in the SWHL. The entire passage reads as follows:

Because the nature of discrimination is always nonexistent, the nature of dependence is also not existent. These two are both nonexistent. This is identical to the *amala-vijñāna*. Only this consciousness belongs to the unchanging and is thus called Suchness. This previously mentioned Suchness dispenses with the twelve entries (*āyatana*) [in the sensory realm]. What the Hīnayāna discusses as the entire range of phenomena are only the twelve entries. These are not incoherent views. Now the principle of Mahāyāna refutes these entries, asserting that all are nonexistent because they are only constructs of a confused consciousness. If these twelve entries were incoherent, then there would be only the one confused consciousness. Since they are not incoherent, they are called Suchness. The essence of this consciousness still is changing. Then, by the natures of discrimination and dependence one can dispense with this confused consciousness. Only the *amala-vijñāna* is not incoherent and is unchanging. This is the true Suchness. Within the previously mentioned principle of Consciousness-Only, one should be able to understand this consciousness. First, by using only the confused consciousness, one dispenses with the external object. Next, the *amala-vijñāna* dispenses with the confused consciousness. Finally, there is only the pure consciousness.[27]

A Tunhuang manuscript, simply titled *She ta-sheng lun chang*,[28] quotes a *Wu-hsiang p'in* as part of the WHL, similar to the immediately preceding two passages: "The nature of discrimination is always nonexistent and the nature of dependence also does not exist. This is identical to the *amala-vijñāna*. . . . Therefore, in the final analysis, there is only the one pure consciousness."[29] This passage is found in the SWHL, thus identifying that text with a chapter or section once entitled *Wu-hsiang p'in* of the original WHL.[30] Just as the CSL and HSL were parts of the larger work WHL bearing the subtitle *p'in* (later changed to *lun*), the extant version of the SWHL originally was subtitled *Wu-hsiang p'in*. Perhaps this title was used to indicate that the most salient teachings in the original WHL were those in the section bearing the subtitle *wu-hsiang p'in*, or SWHL. Now, in addition to Tun-lun's associating the WHL with a section titled [*cheng*] *wu*-[*tzu*-] *hsing p'in* from the HYSCL and Wŏnch'ŭk's also associating the SWHL with the latter text, we see a curious alternation between *wu*-

hsiang and *wu-hsing* in both sets of documents. The extant version of the HYSCL has no section titled *wu-hsiang* but only *ch'eng wu-hsing p'in*. In conclusion, the SWHL was originally the *Wu-hsiang p'in*, the HSL was the *Hsien-shih p'in*, and the CSL was the *Chuan-shih p'in* of the larger corpus titled WHL. The first of the three (SWHL), identified with material in the HYSCL, was composed at least in part by Asaṅga, and it is very close in content to *chüan* 73 and 74 of the *Yogācārabhūmi*. No parallel portions of the HYSCL occur in the documents for the HSL and CSL.

Other passages attributed to the WHL but not located in the CSL, HSL, and SWHL must have been part of the original treatise, perhaps including the *Wei-shih lun* material that Ui speculates was once part of the WHL. The SWHL alludes to other sections or *p'in*: *Li k'ung p'in* (Establishing Emptiness), *Fa wu-tzu-hsing p'in* (The Insubstantiality of Phenomena), and a *Wu-hsing p'in* (Insubstantiality). The HYSCL has a section called *Ch'eng k'ung p'in* (The Attainment of Emptiness), but there is no way of determining whether that section or the other *p'in* mentioned above in the SWHL would also have corresponded to extant sections in the HYSCL or would have referred to other texts. In addition, the CSL cites the SWHL on one occasion, although this could have been either a later addition to the text or a separate subtitle associated with the *Wu-hsiang p'in*. The *Shih-pa k'ung lun*, part of the *Madhyānta-vibhāga*, also mentions the SWHL by title so that it is not clear whether Paramārtha himself actually used the title WHL but referred instead to the separate sections by their own title headings. According to Katsumata, one of Paramārtha's disciples may have applied the title WHL to this group of short treatises.[31]

What can be tentatively reconstructed from the fragmented sections formerly constituting the WHL is that there were several sections, one corresponding to the *ch'eng wu-hsing p'in* of the HYSCL by Asaṅga, namely the SWHL, with commentary perhaps by Vasubandhu and notes on the *amala-vijñāna*. This segment is a portion of the *Yogācārabhūmi*. Another section, *ch'uan-shih p'in*, corresponded to Vasubandhu's *Triṃśikā*, namely the CSL, with unidentified passages of commentary perhaps by Paramārtha. That section known as CSL may have been published separately but also embedded within the HSL, as the TCL and KYL indicate. Portions of the HSL define various functions of the *ālaya-vijñāna* resulting in nine types of imputations or *vijñapti*, bearing a striking resemblance to the eleven *vijñapti* described in the *Saṃgraha*.[32] Then, at still a later stage, the CSL was published independently of the HSL.

It is difficult to establish the nature of the relationship between the HSL and the CSL, the former probably closely aligned with Asaṅga's *Mahāyāna-saṃgraha* and the latter a redaction of Vasubandhu's *Triṃśikā*. What would have been the reason for joining portions of the *Yogācārabhūmi*, *Mahāyāna-saṃgraha*, and *Triṃśikā* into one corpus? Just what kind of text can be imagined that would have included these and other texts as subsections? Why produce the HSL after completing the entire *Saṃgraha*? We are left with the impression that the lost treatise WHL was a curious type of anthology, including the *Triṃśikā* by Vasubandhu and the HYSCL and HSL by Asaṅga with commentary by Vasubandhu. Perhaps Paramārtha's constant traveling from place to place resulted in his assembling texts in this rather hodgepodge way. It is also possible that, as Paramārtha was at least sixty-four years old at that time and despondent over failing in his efforts to return to India, he pieced together several unfinished projects into one ill-matched whole.

Outline of the Text

For all its curious history as at one time part of the *Hsien shih lun* which in turn was a chapter in the lost *Wu-hsiang lun*, the *Chuan shih lun* can be still read as a self-contained and coherent treatise on the basic tenets of Yogācāra. In nearly every respect, except for being written in prose rather than in verse, it follows the *Triṃśikā-kārikās*, which serves as its model and source of inspiration. But though it paraphrases Vasubandhu's text and follows the same order of subject matter, it is perhaps better to consider it an exegetical and interpretative work rather than a literal translation. Yūki, for example, makes the point that since Paramārtha in all his other translations preserved the corresponding literary form, he was not in this instance simply changing the form from verse to prose. Other Buddhologists, including Fukaura[33] and Ui, maintain that the CSL is not just a translation of a line-by-line commentary on the *Triṃśikā* but Paramārtha's own exegesis.

The use of prose rather than the verse style of Vasubandhu is, indeed, the striking feature of the CSL. In a sense, the prose style itself makes Paramārtha's version a type of interpretation. The exegetical comments in the CSL of course present a problem of authorship. Chinese Buddhist historians have traditionally ascribed these and other exegetical interpolations to Paramārtha, and modern scholarship in the field has on the whole not departed from this traditional assessment. However, an alternative view of the comments found in the CSL and not located in the *Triṃśikā* may also be given some credence. As will be indicated in the notes to my translation of the CSL, the text contains some ideas found in other Sanskrit literature of the Yogācāra tradition. These include the idea of a so-called ninth consciousness called the *amala-vijñāna*; though this idea is not explicitly indicated in Sanskrit sources, the notion of nine consciousnesses as well as of a pure consciousness is occasionally represented. Also, we should consider the equation of the *amala-vijñāna* with Suchness (*tathatā*) and the absolute nature (*pariniṣpanna*). These topics will be discussed after we look at the form and the fundamental philosophical themes of the treatise.

The text opens with a striking statement, found in verse I of the *Triṃśikā*, paraphrased as follows: "Consciousness evolves in two ways: (1) it evolves into selves (*ātman*); (2) it evolves into things (*dharma*)" [34] Mind fabricates or constructs both animate and inanimate objects, which are only representations of its own creation. Everything is mentally conditioned, the exegesis adds, and not truly existent independent of consciousness and its own fabrications.[35] This is a description of the objective content of cognitive acts.

Verse II of the Sanskrit is a description of three kinds of evolution of consciousness (*vijñāna-pariṇāma*) as a generating faculty creating moral retribution, "appropriating" or possessing [what ultimately is fictitious], and perceiving and conceptualizing a world of sense objects.[36] These three mental activities correspond to the *ālaya-vijñāna* (*-vipāka*), *manana* (*-manas* or *ādāna*), and *vijñaptir viṣayasya* (*pravṛtti-vijñāna*). The CSL's exegesis expands upon the descriptions: the retributive function of mind originates in defilement and *karma*; it is the most fundamental of all functions, because it is a repository for all hidden or latent impressions (*bīja* or "seeds") bearing moral valuation.[37] In sum, verse II with its commentary discusses the subjective side of mental acts.

The next line, corresponding to verse III, defines the nature of the "retributive consciousness"[38] as the place for the seeds. The question of how the aspects (*ākāra*) and objects (*ālambana*) of this consciousness become knowable is raised in the exegesis in the CSL (and in Sthiramati's commentary). The exegesis in the CSL argues that by inference from its observable effects we know of its existence. One cannot directly apprehend the images and objects of this retributive faculty,[39] but its effects such as ignorance are knowable. The exegesis in the CSL mentions that there are eight names for this state of consciousness or *ālaya-vijñāna*, citing the *Chiu shih p'in* (Chapter on the Meaning of the Nine Consciousnesses), but only one of the eight names is listed. In the second line of verse III, the processes of sensory contact, attention, sensation, volition, and conceptualization are associated with the *ālaya*. The CSL, in the exegesis to verse IV, metaphorically compares attention (*manaskāra*) and volition (*cetanā*) to a galloping horse: "Attention is like a galloping horse and volition is like the rider. A horse only gallops straight ahead but cannot avoid a wrong place or head toward the right place. Because of the rider, a horse can avoid the wrong and head toward the right place. Volition [like a rider] thus can enable one's attention to avoid reckless actions."[40] The citation of the *Chiu shih p'in*, a work believed to be not a translation but an original tract composed by Paramārtha, is evidence that this exegesis may be Paramārtha's and not some other commentator's. Verse IV asserts that these mental states associated with the indeterminate (*anivṛtāvyākṛtam*) moral quality of *ālaya-vijñāna* are constant and ever moving, momentary, like the current in a river.[41] Verse V asserts that the continuity of the *ālaya* ceases at the stage of Arhatship, and Sthiramati's commentary is in agreement. Verses I and II and their interpretation encompass a brief treatment of the first of the three evolutionary cycles of consciousness, namely, the *ālaya-vijñāna*.

In verse V, the second of the three evolutionary cycles of consciousness, the *ādāna-vijñāna* (called *manas* in the *Triṃśikā*),[42] is based upon the *ālaya*. The CSL in the exegesis asserts that "appropriating" (*ādāna*) is its essence.[43] Verse VI presents the four types of delusion—ignorance (*ātma-moha*), views of self or ego (*ātma-dṛṣṭi*), conceit or self-pride (*ātma-māna*), and self-love (*ātma-sneha*)—these being the accompanying states associated with the *manas*, described as indeterminate, as was the *ālaya*, but hidden (*nivṛta*) (because of defilement), unlike the *ālaya* (which is *anivṛta*).[44] Verse VII acknowledges that the Arhat eliminates these four defiled states[45] as well as those entering "cessation-meditation," *nirodha-samāpatti*. The exegesis adds: "When the path of insight (*darśana-mārga*) destroys the defiled consciousness and its mental states and when there is the attainment of the transcendent path (*lokottara-mārga*) of the sixteen practices [of meditation on the Four Noble Truths] then it [the defiled consciousness] is ultimately eliminated."[46] Verses V, VI, and VII with commentary end the description of the *manas* or *ādāna-vijñāna*, the second of the three evolutions of subjectivity posited in verse II.

The first two words in verse VIII refer back to the second evolution (*dvitiyaḥ pariṇāmo'yam*) and then the verse presents the last of the three dimensions of subjectivity or evolutions stemming from consciousness (*vijñāna-pariṇāma*). Six kinds of sensory consciousnesses (that is, the five sense consciousnesses and ideation as a sixth "sense") appear as sense data (or matter, *viṣaya*). The exegesis relates these sense objects to the three natures (*trisvabhāva*). Ten kinds of good and bad actions together with major and minor forms of defilement are associated with this sensory-ideational complex in verse IX.[47] Verses IX through XIV list good and bad actions and the major and minor forms of defilement (*kléśa* and *upakléśa*). The exegesis comments on the ten good actions together: "These ten pervade the mind of the triple world [of desire, matter, and spirit] and the mind [in the realm] without outflows [from defilement, namely *anāsrava-dhātu*] and are classified as the great mental elements. Their nature is intrinsically good."[48]

As Sthiramati's commentary notes, Verse XV is substantially different from the translation given in the CSL. The Sanskrit reads: "There is the arising of the five [consciousnesses] in the fundamental consciousness (*mūla-vijñāne*) according to conditions, either simultaneous or not, like waves in the water."[49] Paramārtha's translation of verse XV reads as follows: "The five [sense] consciousnesses [subsumed] in the sixth consciousness—the intellect (*manovijñāna*), the fundamental consciousness, and the appropriating consciousness—these three [groups of] faculties ensue from causes and conditions. They occur either simultaneously or sequentially." The exegesis elaborates on the conditioning process for sensation, taking attention as the (immediate) cause and the external sense data as the (secondary) condition for consciousness to occur. In the exegesis on this verse given in the CSL, the interior process of creating a sense datum and projecting it as an external object is described for the five sense consciousnesses, which may occur sequentially or simultaneously. Each sense consciousness has a corresponding sense datum (vision to form, hearing to sound, and so on). Multiple sense consciousnesses must occur simultaneously with multiple sense data in order to register as a single, coherent image. All seven consciousnesses (in these subjective-objective dynamics of consciousness/sense data series) interact with each other in the *ālaya-vijñāna*,[50] and are "reflected together as in a mirror."

In verse XVI, conditions or situations are given for when the faculty of the intellect (*mano-vijñāna*) no longer occurs: the two kinds of highest meditation (*samāpatti*), sloth or extreme lethargy (*acittikaṃ middhaṃ*), and states of unconsciousness (*acittikā mūrchā*).[51] The CSL adds to this list a sixth state, "dreamless sleep." All thought processes associated with the intellect (such as language, symbol making, integrating sense data, and concept formation) cease in these five or six situations.[52] Verses VIII through XVI complete the description of the third cycle of mental development or evolution in which the sensory and ideational functions of consciousness are in operation.

Verse XVII, beginning a discussion of the dual aspect of discrimination, which is synonymous with *vijñāna-pariṇāma*, says that the evolution of consciousness is twofold: (1) the discriminator and (2) the discriminated object.[53] This repeats the model found in verse I of the *Triṃśikā*; that is, consciousness splits itself into two, imputing an actor or self creating the content of its own world as imputed objects. This twofold dynamic is critical to Paramārtha's entire interpretation of Yogācāra or Consciousness-Only. The exegesis adds: ". . . the discriminator also does not exist. Without a sense object to be grasped, consciousness cannot occur." Then the CSL cites the last part of the verse: "Therefore, the principle of Consciousness-Only can be upheld."[54] This passage, as I shall explain later on, may be an indication that Paramārtha is here developing a new idea that departs from the tenets of Sthiramati's and Vasubandhu's school of thought. The CSL elaborates: "What does it mean to establish the principle of Consciousness-Only? The meaning, fundamentally, is to dispense with sense objects and to dispense with the mind."[55] This passage, frequently cited in the literature, is evidence that this was a significant redefinition of *vijñaptimātratā* not common to other Buddhist treatises and perhaps unique to Paramārtha's own thought. It is a much more radical statement than either verse XVII or Sthiramati's exegesis.

Paraphrasing verse XVIII,[56] the CSL states: "As for the consciousness containing the seeds of all phenomena [namely, the *ālaya-vijñāna*], it creates and evolves from one to another [form], evolving from each other onward and onward into varieties of discriminations and discriminated objects through mutual interaction [of the *ālaya* with the other states of consciousness]."[57] In verse XVIII, for the first time in the CSL, "the commentary states" (*shih yüeh*) is used to comment on each separate line. Following this, original ideas on the *amala-vijñāna* and the *trisvabhāva* (*niḥsvabhāva*) theory are presented in detail. (These innovations are not found in Sthiramati's commentary on the relationship between *paratantra* and *parikalpita*.) The subject matter in the last twelve verses serves as allusions to support the CSL's position on the *trisvabhāva* theory, and indeed beginning at this point the commentary in the text contains more substantive additions than the verses themselves. From this point on, beginning with the textual passages that parallel verse XIX, Paramārtha begins to quote his own works and translations, the SWHL and *Chiu shih i p'in*, in support of the ideas expressed, using *shih yüeh*. Some of these portions of the text marked off by *shih yüeh* must signal either a lost Indian tradition not compatible with Sthiramati's commentary or a highly original creation by Paramārtha.

Acquiring wisdom begins with the knowledge that there are no objects independent of mind. A rhetorical question is then raised in the CSL: "If one dispenses with sense objects but retains consciousness, then one can say that there is a principle of Consciousness-Only. But if both the sense object and consciousness are to be dispensed with, how can consciousness [of any kind] be maintained?" The response: "One establishes that

Consciousness-Only temporarily dispenses with the sense object but retains the [existence of] mind. In the final analysis, however, one dispenses with sense objects in order to empty the mind." The issue of dispensing with the subjective component of consciousness is explained: "[When] both the sense object and consciousness are dissolved, this [state] is identical to the true nature (*tattva* or *tathatā*). The true nature is identical to Pure Consciousness (*amala-vijñāna*)."[58] Here is the identity between the *amala-vijñāna* (Pure Consciousness) and reality or Suchness that is the core of Paramārtha's thought and the foundation for the She-lun school of Chinese Buddhism.

The CSL's prose translation of verse XIX begins with the nature of the influences from past *karma* and with the twofold influences of perception (*grāha-dvaya-vāsanā*), metaphorically called "seeds" residing in the *ālaya-vijñāna*.[59] These impressions produce both our interior world and our so-called "exterior world."

There are two kinds of influences (*hsün-hsi*) from past *karma* and two kinds of influential forces (*hsi-ch'i*). The text makes the distinction between twofold latent influences from past acts of a moral nature and latent energy (*vāsanā*) that produces a dualistic apprehension of the world and attachment to that world. Verse XIX, however, discusses only the twofold *vāsanā*[60] of perception (*grāha*) and does not consider the *vāsanā* produced from *karma* as twofold. The CSL interprets *hsün-hsi* as *vāsanā* of *karma* and *hsi-ch'i* as defilement. These are then considered synonyms for the seeds (*bīja*) of *karma*.[61] The CSL comments that the *vāsanā* of attachment from past *karma* is the discriminator, the *vāsanā* from past *karma* being the discriminated object. (The *vāsanā* of *karma* is not construed as twofold in either Sthiramati's commentary or Vasubandhu's verse. Sthiramati's gloss on the varieties of *vāsanā* describes the twofold *vāsanā* of perception[62] as perceiver and perceived; the *vāsanā* of *karma* propels an individual into another rebirth.) The CSL, in contrast to Sthiramati, implies that the *vāsanā* of *karma* is twofold: attachment to past *karma*, which is identical to the discriminating subject, and the *vāsanā* of *karma* itself, which is its object. This is a very unusual divergence from the Sanskrit. Moreover, the CSL elaborates on influential forces of habit (*hsi-ch'i*) that have a defiled character, a notion that has no analogue in the *Triṃśikā* or its commentary. These influential forces (*hsi-ch'i*) are of two kinds: the influential habits of imputing features or characteristics on things, and primitive (or gross), latent defilements. The former is the subjective side of consciousness, dependent in nature; the latter is the objectified side of consciousness, the discriminated nature.[63] By eliminating both types of influences and their defilement, one arrives at the absolutely real nature.

Each seed or impression (*bīja*), according to this exegesis, has a twofold dimension corresponding to the *vāsanā* of *karma* and *vāsanā* of perception.[64] This means that the CSL construes each seed as dual (*dvaya-vāsanayā*), including the *vāsanā* of *karma* and not only what strictly corresponds to *grāhavāsanā* or the *vāsanā* of dualistic perception as Sthiramati and Vasubandhu construe the twofold nature of this latter category of *vāsanā*. The CSL mentions that the SWHL gives different names to the influential forces of habit (*hsi-ch'i*) and reverses their ascription to the *parikalpita* and *paratantra-svabhāva*.[65]

The CSL paraphrases verses XX through XXI on the three natures theory. The nature of discrimination is essentially nonexistent, and the nature of dependence is defined as being dependent upon others. The CSL's translation of verse XX reads: "Whatever is discrimination: if one discriminates this or that kind of thing, these kind of things are called the nature of discrimination. These only have names, but the essence [of a thing] that the name indicates does not really exist."[66] The CSL's translation of verse XXI: "The essence [of a thing] that is indicated [by a name] does not really exist; this discrimination is generated contingent upon others. Therefore it is called the nature of dependence. Both natures are inseparable; this is identical to the nature of the absolute (*pariniṣpanna-svabhāva*)." Verses XXI and XXII of the *Triṃśikā* on the relationship between *paratantra-svabhāva* and *pariniṣpanna* and Sthiramati's commentary on these verses contend that *paratantra* can be separated from *parikalpita*, resulting in *pariniṣpanna*.[67] The Sanskrit asserts that there is a separation between *paratantra* and *parikalpita* and an inseparability between *paratantra* and *pariniṣpanna*. The Chinese text states emphatically that no such separation between *parikalpita* and *paratantra* is possible. This is a peculiarity of the CSL that the exegesis defends at some length. When one realizes that these two reciprocally condition each other, the absolute reality (*pariniṣ-*

panna) is apprehended: "If one does not view the nature of discrimination, then one does not view the nature of dependence." Sthiramati gives *paratantra* and *pariniṣpanna* as the referents for the latter part of verse XXII, which simply reads: "When one is not seen, the other is not seen." In Sthiramati's commentary, the pivotal role of apprehending the absolutely real by extricating it from the mental fabrications of *parikalpita-svabhāva* belongs to *paratantra*.

Arguing against the separability of these two natures, *parikalpita* and *paratantra*, the CSL opposes what constitutes the position of Sthiramati: "If they were separable from each other, then the principle of Consciousness-Only would not be upheld, because sense objects would be different from consciousness. Because they are inseparable, there is Consciousness-Only without an objective world. Because there is no objective world, consciousness also does not exist. Because the sense object does not exist and neither does consciousness, the principle of Consciousness-Only is established."[68] The CSL does not affirm the existence of either a mental or a material world, both being contingent upon each other, suggesting a strong Mādhyamikan line of reasoning. This interdependency is termed absolute reality, Pure Consciousness (*amala-vijñāna*), or Consciousness-Only, all of which have positive connotations that Prāsaṅgikan Mādhyamika would not accept. The form of Yogācāra that the CSL represents also does not grant independent existence to consciousness since such an independence cannot be supported by experience or philosophical scrutiny.[69]

A digression from verses XXI and XXII follows, similar to the examples in Sthiramati's commentary on verse XXII comparing the identity and difference between impermanence (*anityatā*) and the composite elements of existence (*saṃskāras*) to that between *parikalpita* and *paratantra*, in the CSL, and *paratantra* and *pariniṣpanna*, in Sthiramati.[70] The first two natures are conventional truth, and only *pariniṣpanna* is absolute truth according to the CSL, whereas Sthiramati maintains that both *paratantra* and *pariniṣpanna* are absolute truths when *paratantra* is no longer involved with *parikalpita*.

Verse XXIII presents the relationship between the three natures (*trisvabhāva*) and the three "naturelessnesses" (*triniḥsvabhāva*). Verse XXIV lists two of the three "natureless" states—

states devoid of substantiality—(*lakṣaṇena niḥsvabhāva* and *svayaṃbhāva niḥsvabhāvatā*)—and verse XXV lists the third (*paramārtha-niḥsvabhāvatā*).[71] The CSL expands at some length on each of these three naturelessnesses: "The essence [of an object in consciousness] appears as the aspect of matter. Matter is the nature of discrimination. Since discrimination does not exist, the essence [of an object] does not exist. Since the causes do not exist either, the sense object, being derived from the nature of discrimination, can bring about effects on consciousness."[72] The CSL explains in paraphrasing verse XXV that the nature of the absolutely real in all phenomena is equivalent to these three states that do not have substantiality.[73] The CSL comments on this verse by saying: "In order to indicate these three states devoid of substantial natures, we explain the principle of Consciousness-Only."[74] The important difference between the Sanskrit and the Chinese is that the CSL substitutes the term "three states devoid of substantial nature" for only the third of the three states, *pariniṣpanna-svabhāva*. All three states are Suchness for Paramārtha whereas only the third is for Vasubandhu and Sthiramati. According to the CSL, the absolutely real nature or Consciousness-Only is synonymous with Suchness, manifested in all three states of nonsubstantiality.[75]

The propensities (*anuśaya*) to attachment to subject and object must be completely eliminated if one is to be firmly grounded in Consciousness-Only, according to verse XXVI paraphrased in the CSL.[76] The exegesis adds: "One establishes the One Vehicle in which all are able to learn the Bodhisattva path." Verse XXVII warns against asserting "this is Consciousness-Only" from conceited views and from insufficient understanding, for discriminative acts will continue to occur. The CSL paraphrases verse XXVII in the following manner: "If one says 'there is only the existence of consciousness' based upon attachment to what is presented before him [as an object], then since he has not yet eliminated this attachment [to dualistic perceptions], he does not enter Consciousness-Only."[77] Verses XXVIII and XXIX translated in the CSL define knowledge of Consciousness-Only as devoid of the perception of sense objects and the absence of dualism. Commenting on this knowledge, verse XXIX describes this wisdom as transcendent (*jñānaṃ lokottaram*): the state of mind is entirely transformed (*āśraya-parāvṛtti*), devoid of obstacles to enlightenment. Verse XXX, the *Triṃśikā-kārikās*, adds additional descriptions to this wisdom: it ascribes to this state of mind the qualities of goodness, permanence (*dhruva*), the body of liberation (*vimukti-kāya*), the element devoid of defilement (*anāsrava-dhātu*).[78] The concluding exegesis discusses the nature of the obstacle to enlightenment located in the *ālaya-vijñāna*, citing the *Śrīmālādevī-siṃhanāda-sūtra* as an authority on the foundation of ignorance and its cessation. The CSL ends with some of its most frequently quoted lines, on how both the sense object and consciousness do not exist;[79] and this is the definition of both Consciousness-Only and the *amala-vijñāna*.

The Major Differences between the CSL and Hsüan-tsang's CWSL

Although there are many contrasts between Paramārtha and Hsüan-tsang when we look at each philosopher's corpus of writings, we shall investigate here only three major points of difference between the CSL and the *Ch'eng wei-shih lun* (CWSL), the work translated by Hsüan-tsang in 659.[80] These three important differences have to do with the notions of *āśraya-parāvṛtti*, *tri-svabhāva*, and *vijñāna-pariṇāma*.

ĀŚRAYA-PARĀVṚTTI

The compound *āśraya-parāvṛtti* means "change (or transformation) of the basis," that is, of the basic consciousness or *ālaya-vijñāna*.[81] Sthiramati glosses the word *parāvṛtti* as the cessation of the twofold *vāsanā* of evil retribution (*dauṣṭhulya-vipāka*) and the transformation of the *ālaya* by the nondualistic knowledge of the *Dharma-kāya*, the activity of truth.[82] In Chinese, Paramārtha renders it *chuan-i*, "the evolving basis" or "evolved basis," using the same character *chuan* to translate *pariṇāma* or "evolution" and *pravartate*, "to function" or "to occur." The term *chuan-i* appears only once in the CSL (63c5), just as *āśraya-parāvṛtti* occurs only once in the *Triṃśikā* (verse XXIX). In both the *Triṃśikā* and the CSL this psychological change in the *ālaya-vijñāna* entails cessation of all obstructions caused by the seeds of ignorance and defilement. Sthiramati's commentary is in agreement. This change culminates in identity with the Buddha's pure knowledge, or nondiscriminative wisdom, equivalent to reality or Suchness itself.

Hsüan-tsang acknowledges this theory but adheres to or emphasizes another interpretation:

The "basis" (*āśraya*) (*i*) means that upon which something is based, or *paratantra* [-*svabhāva*], because it is that upon which pure and impure phenomena are based. The impure refers to the false or *parikalpita* [-*svabhāva*] and the pure refers to the absolutely real or *parinispanna* [-*svabhāva*]. "Transformation" (*parāvṛtti; chuan*) means that the two [*svabhāva*] are transformed by elimination [of the falsehood of *parikalpita*] and by attainment [of truth or *pariniṣpanna*]. Because of repeated cultivation of nondiscriminative wisdom, the two obstacles [the obstacle of defilement and the obstacle to knowledge] in the fundamental consciousness are cut off. Therefore, one can evolve [the character of the fundamental consciousness] by eliminating the discriminated nature (*parikalpita-svabhāva*) superimposed upon the dependent nature (*paratantra-svabhāva*) and can evolve [the character of the fundamental consciousness] by attaining the absolute nature (*pariniṣpanna-svabhāva*) within the dependent nature. . . . Some say that the basis is Suchness, [found] in Consciousness-Only, because this is the basis for both *saṃsāra* and *nirvāṇa*. The foolish, with incoherent views, are deluded with regard to Suchness, having endured suffering in *saṃsāra* from beginningless time whereas the sage has separated from incoherent views and is awakened to Suchness, attaining Nirvāṇa, the ultimate bliss. . . . Therefore, one can evolve [the basis of consciousness] by destroying the basis as *saṃsāra* and can evolve [the basis of consciousness] by experiencing the basis as *Nirvāṇa*. This is Suchness, separate from the defiled. Although it is naturally pure, it is characterized by defilement. Therefore, when it [the basis of consciousness] is separated from defilement, we conventionally explain that it is recently purified and this recent purification is explained as *āśraya-parāvṛtti*.[83]

Hsüan-tsang advocates the first interpretation of *āsraya-parāvṛtti* and Paramārtha, the second. Sthiramati in his commentary on verses XXI and XXII also eliminates *parikalpita* or discriminative ways of thinking in order to view the conditioned world of phenomena (*paratantra*) as real (*pariniṣpanna*), but he does not apply the term *āśraya-parāvṛtti* to this process of change. The CWSL interprets *āśraya-parāvṛtti* in conjunction with a twofold *paratantra*, but the Sanskrit original was less systematic in its presentation. The term as used in verse XXX has no relationship at all with *parikalpita* since it is identified with the *Dharma-kāya*. For the CSL, the absolute reality cannot be defiled in any way whatever, but the *Triṃśikā* commentary by Sthiramati begs the question in verses XXI, XXII, and XXIX. Hsüan-tsang gives *paratantra* an impure and pure dimension, placing emphasis on verses XXI and XXII in agreement with Sthiramati; Paramārtha's text, as noted in the above summary of the CSL, diverges significantly from both thinkers. Paramārtha does not recognize a pure aspect to *paratantra* or to the *ālaya* but only to *parinişpanna*. *Āśraya-parāvṛtti* is associated with Pure Consciousness or *amala-vijñāna*. Paramārtha does acknowledge the twofold *paratantra* in his *Saṃgraha*.[84] For Hsüan-tsang, the *ālaya* is both *paratantra* and *parikalpita*. As *āśraya-parāvṛtti* it counteracts the defiled aspect of itself.

Sthiramati does not explicitly identify *paratantra* with a dimension of the *ālaya* (nor *parinişpanna* with the *ālaya*), but he does equate *āśraya* with the *ālaya*.[85] By inference, the *ālaya* in this mode, since it contains all the dualistic seeds of false perceptions, is both *parikalpita* and *paratantra*. In sharp contrast to both Hsüan-tsang and Sthiramati, Paramārtha asserts that the *ālaya* is only defiled, as *paratantra*, and therefore cannot have absolute reality.[86]

All three philosophers agree on the absolutely pure nature of *āśraya-parāvṛtti*, but they disagree on the mental faculty that is the locus for this enlightened state. Hsüan-tsang associates the theory of the three natures with his interpretation of *āśraya-parāvṛtti* and labels the pivotal transition of *paratantra* from *parikalpita* to *paratantra* by the term *āśraya-parāvṛtti*. Paramārtha remains close to the verse itself and to Sthiramati in identifying *āśraya-parāvṛtti* with the *Dharma-kāya*. He also agrees with Sthiramati in not identifying *āśraya-parāvṛtti* with the *ālaya*, but rather with its transformation into something else. The term *parāvṛtti* has different connotations in the two forms of Yogācāra. In Paramārtha's interpretation, the conditioned *ālaya-vijñāna* and its *āsrava-bīja* are replaced by the unconditioned *anāsrava-bīja* in the *amala-vijñāna*. According to Hsüan-tsang, the conditioned seeds are terminated because of the power of the unconditioned *anāsrava-bīja* by slowly acquiring the great mirror-wisdom, *ādarśana-jñāna*, that transforms the *ālaya*. Yogācāra in general is of course concerned with the *ālaya*, its transformation being the ultimately real or Suchness and *Dharma-kāya*, but Paramārtha's interpretation calls for identifying Suchness in sentient beings with the *amala-vijñāna*, similar to the *Mahāyāna-sūtrālaṃkāra*'s identification of Suchness with the Tathagatagarbha and Vasubandhu's *Mahāyāna-saṃgraha-bhāṣya*, which identifies the purity of *pariniṣpanna-svabhāva* with Tathāgatagarbha. Neither Paramārtha nor Sthiramati associates the *paratantra-svabhāva* with *āśraya-parāvṛtti*.

VIJÑĀNA-PARIṆĀMA

One of Vasubandhu's most notable innovations was his theory of *vijñāna-pariṇāma*, first mentioned in the *Triṃśikā* (verse I). This theory is not found in the *Madhyānta-vibhāga*, *Mahāyāna-saṃgraha*, or *Sūtrālaṃkāra*, but it is found in the *Kośa* and the *Viṃśatikā*.[87] *Pariṇāma* means "change" or "transformation,"[88] but in the sense of developmental change rather than extraordinary, radical change, going against one's nature, as in *parāvṛtti*. *Pariṇāma* is translated by Paramārtha as *neng yüan*, the conditioning subjective side of consciousness that is threefold. The three types of subjectivity (*neng yüan*) occur simultaneously with their projected, objectified world (*so-yüan*), which also stems from consciousness. They evolve together (*pravartate*; *chuan*) in three ways as the *ālaya-vijñāna*, *ādāna-vijñāna*, and *pravṛtti-vijñāna*. The objectified world projected by these three evolutionary movements functions together with their subjective correlatives in the appearance of animate and inanimate things.[89] The simultaneous evolution of a subject with its object is *vijñāna-pariṇāma*, but false discrimination (*vikalpa*) assumes that the subject is different from the object. According to the CSL, when *pariṇāma* no longer takes place, that is, when the change in mental character (*āśraya-parāvṛtti*) is completed, one has understood the absolute, and the *ālaya* ceases. *Āśraya-parāvṛtti*, in the CSL, becomes synonymous with the cessation of the *ālaya-vijñāna*.

Hsüan-tsang translates the threefold changes of subjectivity as *neng-pien*, which is similar in connotation to Paramārtha's *neng yüan*. But where Hsüan-tsang translates the corresponding objective side (animate and inanimate objects) as *shih so pien*,[90] "changes based upon consciousness," Paramārtha's translation, *shih chuan*, suggests the functional development of conscious states into the appearances of things, the contents of consciousness being only momentary images or symbols. Paramārtha's term *chuan* here for the Sanskrit *pravartate* may be intentional, to bring the meaning closer to *pariṇāma*.

In sharp contrast to the CSL, the *Ch'eng wei-shih lun* accords to consciousness a substantial existence as the ground for all phenomena; the simultaneous relationship of subject and object is not recognized by Hsüan-tsang since the object is based upon consciousness, its ontologically prior cause and foundation. Only the discriminated object lacks absolute existence whereas consciousness does exist absolutely for Hsüan-tsang, in both its dependent and absolute natures.[91]

Interestingly, Paramārtha's three-natures theory seems to correspond to a heterodox view, described in K'uei-chi's *Ch'eng wei-shih lun shu-chi*: "Thus, we refute the two heterodoxical positions of affirming and negating: . . . We refute the affirming position that objects independent of mind truly exist and the negating destructive position of emptiness that posits mind as also nonexistent because its view of emptiness is heterodoxical and misconstrued."[92]

It seems that, on the one hand, *pariṇāma* involves a dualism in all three cycles (*ālaya*, *ādāna* or *manas*, and *pravṛtti-vijñāna*) except when the *āśraya-parāvṛtti* occurs. The subject or *ālaya* is taken as an object by the *ādāna* or *manas*; sense data (or seeds) created from the *ālaya* are taken as objects by the *pravṛtti-vijñāna*. *Vijñāna-pariṇāma* is simply the activity of consciousness, the contrasting of subject versus object which the Chinese translations by Paramārtha and Hsüan-tsang have rendered as *neng* and *so* correlatives (the Sanskrit equivalents are *vikalpa* and *yad vikalpyate*, as well as *grāhaka* and *grāhya*, in verses XVII, XVIII, XX, XXVI, and XXVII). Unfortunately, from the very beginning of Chinese Yogācāra, the term *pariṇāma* was translated with primary emphasis on the subjective or *neng* component that was correlated with the objective or *so* component. As a result, the stress on *neng yüan* or *neng pien* would lead to the danger of positing *pariṇāma* as a substantial entity, rather than as activity. This style of translating into Chinese by using *neng/so* pairs may have been devised to aid the reader who was being exposed to this philosophical system for the first time, though the Sanskrit does make allowances for justifying this translation style.[93]

Sthiramati in his exegesis on verse I asserts that *pariṇāma* is *pratītya-samutpanna*, but there is actually an ambiguity in the Sanskrit: the term *vijñānasya* may modify *pariṇāma*, or it may modify *pratītya-samutpanna*. If it modifies *pariṇāma*, which the compound from the verse, *vijñāna-pariṇāma*, certainly suggests, then conditioned co-arising is being equated with *vijñāna-pariṇāma* or evolutions of consciousness. If *vijñānasya* modifies *pratītya-samutpanna,* then conditioned co-arising *of conscious states* is evolutionary (*pariṇāma*) and momentary.[94]

If the first interpretation of verse I is accepted, then the identity between *vijñāna-pariṇāma* and *pratītya-samutpāda* (or *pratītya-samutpanna*) would be a redefinition of the Mādhyamikan stance on Emptiness (*śūnyatā*) or *pratītya-samutpāda* as the analysis of conscious states only. This would be an idealist's position and would be giving absolute existence or *svabhāva* to consciousness itself. *Vijñāna* is truly existent (*dravyato*) for Sthiramati also. If, however, we are simply discussing the conditioning process of consciousness as *pariṇāma,* then this does not necessarily accord to consciousness some kind of substantial existence. This view would be more compatible with Mādhyamika, and it is the position of Paramārtha that I shall argue below in light of the *trisvabhāva* theory.

TRISVABHĀVA

The three-natures or *trisvabhāva* theory is the theme most central to Yogācāra thought. This theory defines three ways that an entity or phenomenon can exist for consciousness and also three ways of looking at the world, progressing from delusion to enlightenment. Since the only reality recognized in Yogācāra is the reality of cognitive activity or thought, the three natures are aspects of reality that consciousness believes to be true at various stages of learning. This *trisvabhāva* theory is not presented consistently, however, from one text to the next. The first of these three natures is the discriminated nature that is totally false; the object is purely imagined (*parikalpita-svabhāva*) as existing outside consciousness. This would be the naïve realist's view that is the most common way of looking at the world. The second way an entity can be apprehended by consciousness is as dependent upon conditions (*paratantra-svabhāva*). This nature of a thing is partly real, insofar as it recognizes that things have no self-existence; but at the same time, this view is only a half-truth because it still depends on appearances that are falsely constructed. The ultimate reality behind all false appearances is the absolute nature (or *pariniṣpanna-svabhāva*) that is known only when all dualistic conventions of perception and thought cease.

The first occurrence of the *trisvabhāva* theory is probably that found in the *Saṃdhinirmocana*, but the exact meaning of each of the three natures is not explained. *Parikalpita* is naming things in terms of their essence, functions, and other characteristics. *Paratantra* is dependent upon origination, defined as the twelve *āyatanas*, and *pariniṣpanna* is the world of Suchness.[95]

In its presentation of the *trisvabhāva* theory, Paramārtha's CSL differs strikingly not only from the *Triṃśikā* and CWSL but also from Paramārtha's other translations, especially on the concept of *paratantra*. Verse XX is the first verse to use the term *parikalpita*: "Whatever thing (*vastu*) that is erroneously conceived (*vikalpyate*) by various discriminations (*vikalpena*), that nature is only imaginatively constructed (*parikalpita*) and does not exist."[96] Verse XXI introduces *paratantra-svabhāva*: "The nature of being dependent on another is discrimination (*vikalpaḥ*) that arises from conditions."[97] In the CSL Paramārtha states in his gloss on verse XVIII: "The discriminator (*neng fen-pieh*) is identical to consciousness and the discriminated (*so fen-pieh*) is identical to the sense object. The discriminator is the nature of dependence and the discriminated is the nature of being discriminated." Thus, the dualistic aspects of perception corresponding to *nimitta* and *darśana-bhāga* in Hsüan-tsang and *grāhya* and *grāhaka* in Sthiramati's commentary on the *Triṃśikā* become *so fen-pieh* and *neng fen-pieh* in the CSL. The former is *parikalpita-svabhāva* and its latter correlative is *paratantra-svabhāva*.

Both these natures make a distinction between the object seen and the self that perceives and introduce the delusion of perceiver and perceived. Dharmapāla and Hsüan-tsang attribute this delusion to the nature of dependence; Sthiramati's own position is not clear, although he implies that delusion is relegated solely to the falsely imagined nature.[98] Paramārtha views both natures as equally responsible for delusion, they being the components contingent upon each other for false discrimination (*vikalpa*) to occur. One nature (*parikalpita-svabhāva*) is the thing discriminated as external to consciousness; the second nature (*paratantra-svabhāva*) in a reciprocal relationship with the former is the discriminating subject. One is contingent upon the other, and in themselves they do not exist outside this relationship. Together they make up our empirical world, the level of conventional truth. However, the object as external to consciousness is illusory even in our experience because it is a judgment that goes beyond the information provided by the senses. The discriminating subject, though equally unreal outside the discriminating process, does appear as relatively real because moments of consciousness are causally efficient—that is, unlike *parikalpita-svabhāva*, one moment of conscious activity conditions the next (*pratītyasamutpāda*). This level of knowing the world is the basis for the falsely imagined and is also itself based upon another level of knowledge, that of the absolute or *pariniṣpanna*. For the CSL, this level of truth is no longer related to the distinction between subject and object; in other words, false discrimination has ceased.

Sthiramati's position on the nature of *paratantra-svabhāva* is that this level of truth and reality is pivotal to the whole system of Consciousness-Only. *Paratantra-svabhāva*, the development or evolution of consciousness from one moment to the succeeding moment, produces both *parikalpita-svabhāva* or falsely imagined objects and *pariniṣpanna-svabhāva* or the absolute. In the evolution of consciousness in which the subject grasping the object and the object grasped are produced from a latent potency (*vāsanā*) in the storehouse consciousness, this is the imaginatively constructed level of reality: "In false discrimination (*vikalpe*) the perceiver and the perceived (*grāhya-grāhaka-bhāvaḥ*) are imaginatively constructed (*parikalpitaḥ*). Thus, in false discrimination, one imaginatively constructs nonexistent perceivers and things perceived. This is called 'imaginative construction.'"[99]

If we compare Sthiramati's representation of *parikalpita-svabhāva* here with that in Paramārtha's CSL, we see that Paramārtha's interpretation of the dualism generated from perception is not only *parikalpita* but also *paratantra*. To be dependent in nature seems to imply not only successive moments of activity in conscious processes but also the contingent relationship between the subjective and objective sides of cognition:

> The essence [of a thing] that is indicated [by a name] does not really exist; this discrimination is generated contingent upon others. Therefore it is called the nature of dependence. Both natures [the imaginatively constructed and the dependent] are inseparable; this is identical to the nature of the absolute. If they were separable from each other, then the principle of Consciousness-Only would not be upheld, because sense objects would be different from consciousness. Because

they are inseparable, there is Consciousness-Only without an objective world. Because there is no objective world, consciousness also does not exist. Because the sense object does not exist, and neither does consciousness, the principle of Consciousness-Only is established.[100]

We see here that Paramārtha differs from Sthiramati on the interpretation of the *trisvabhāva*, although in at least one other work Sthiramati considers the twofold perceiver and perceived within the dependent nature.[101] For the CSL, *paratantra-svabhāva* and *parikalpita-svabhāva* are inextricably related, just as the dualism found in perception depends upon a perceiver and an object perceived. The interpretation of *trisvabhāva* put forth by Sthiramati in his commentary on the *Triṃśikā* requires that the level of knowing the world designated by the term *paratantra-svabhāva* can become the absolute level of truth (*pariniṣpanna*) by separation from this dualistic process: "Because always and in all times when there is a state of complete separation from the perceiver and the perceived by the dependent nature, that is the absolute nature."[102] Grammatically, this phrase in Sthiramati's *bhāṣya* could be translated in the following manner, making the interpretation closer to Sthiramati's views in his *Madhyānta-vibhāga-ṭīkā* and also more compatible with the CSL, although from the context of the *bhāṣya* this reading is unlikely: "Because always and in all times what is separate from the dependent nature through the agency of the perceiver and the perceived is called the absolute nature." This reading would support, in part, Paramārtha's interpretation, namely, that *paratantra-svabhāva* is part of the dualism between subject and object and *pariniṣpanna-svabhāva* is the complete separation from that dualism. Hence, *pariniṣpanna* is separate from *paratantra-svabhāva*. Ueda misconstrues the Sanskrit to make it conform to Paramārtha's interpretation, stating that by maintaining an inseparable relationship between *parikalpita-svabhāva* and *paratantra svabhāva* Paramārtha means to say that consciousness and its object simultaneously do not exist. This is a correct rendering of the CSL, but it does not translate the words of Sthiramati precisely.[103]

Sthiramati and Paramārtha seem to be in agreement over the simultaneous nature of subject and object in dualistic acts of perception rather than giving logical priority to the perceiver over the perceived, as Hsüan-tsang does. Nonetheless, this simultaneous generation of perceiver and perceived is to be found in the *parikalpita-svabhāva*, at least in Sthiramati's *bhāṣya*, whereas in the CSL schema each counterpart corresponds to either the *parikalpita-svabhāva* or the *paratantra-svabhāva*. Both are eliminated when one views the world in its absolute reality (*pariniṣpanna*), and this is the transformation, or more precisely, the cessation of the *ālaya-vijñāna* (*āśraya-parāvṛtti*) in the CSL. It is difficult to judge whether Sthiramati, in his *bhāṣya*, would have associated *pariniṣpanna-svabhāva* with the *āśraya-parāvṛtti*, but he does link the latter term with Suchness. Paramārtha identifies *pariniṣpanna-svabhāva* with Suchness, *āśraya-parāvṛtti*, and, most to the point, the *amala-vijñāna* or Pure Consciousness.

An Unresolved Question

Of all of the doctrinal differences between Paramārtha and other prominent Yogācārin thinkers in China, particularly Hsüan-tsang and his followers, the innovation attributed to Paramārtha that stands out most prominently is the positing of a ninth consciousness, superimposed on the more common eight-consciousness theory, constituting the force countervailing the defiled eight forms of mental acts. This so-called ninth consciousness was termed the *amala-vijñāna* or Pure Consciousness. Several texts from Paramārtha's corpus, now extant, do in fact mention the *amala-vijñāna*, but this consciousness is never enumerated specifically as a ninth consciousness, though this is the implication from the assertion that the *amala-vijñāna* is separate from all defilement and emerges only after the cessation of the *ālaya*. Paramārtha considers the *ālaya* to be defiled and to be eventually eliminated; in Hsüan-tsang's view, the *ālaya-vijñāna* is never abandoned.[104]

One text, now lost, entitled the *Chiu shih i p'in* (Chapter on the Meaning of Nine Consciousnesses) and attributed to Paramārtha, explicitly uses the number nine in the title. Scholars have usually taken this to be a reference to the *amala*. One Japanese scholar, Yūki Reimon, contends that if such a work actually did exist—and there is some question about this—the number nine does not necessarily refer to the *amala*, but rather may be a reference to the ninefold descriptions of the *ālaya-vijñāna* or "perceiving consciousness" (*khyāti-vijñāna*) given in Paramārtha's HSL.[105] The term may also have been an alternative to *viśuddha-jñāna*, found in the *Triṃśikā*, since the translation into Chinese would be pure consciousness or "pure knowledge," virtually indistinguishable to the Chinese reader. Still, Yūki is but one dissenting voice, opposing a tradition descending from the T'ang that associates Paramārtha with this creative novelty of a ninth consciousness. Other texts besides the *Laṅkāvatāra-sūtra*, previously mentioned, also allude to the theory of nine consciousnesses. Both Chinese recensions of the *Ghana-vyūha-sūtra*, for example, clearly state that there are nine states of cognition.[106]

The term *amala-vijñāna* does appear in the commentarial passages in the CSL glossing verse XVIII (though not anywhere else in the *Triṃśikā* or in Sthiramati's commentary): "[When] both the sense object and consciousness are dissolved, this is identical to the true nature. The true nature is identical to the *amala-vijñāna*."[107] In addition, since the elimination of both sense object and consciousness is equated with Consciousness-Only, it follows that *amala-vijñāna* is also synonymous with Consciousness-Only. Furthermore, the three states devoid of any substantial nature are explained as Consciousness-Only,[108] for which we may substitute *amala-vijñāna*. Attainment of Consciousness-Only is called *āśraya-parāvṛtti* (*chuan-i*) and wisdom of Suchness. Since Consciousness-Only is identical to Suchness according to verse XXIV of the *Triṃśikā*, we may postulate an identity between Suchness and *amala-vijñāna*, a position that the tradition does attribute to Paramārtha although the CSL makes no explicit identity between the two. The "true nature" is almost certainly an equivalent of *tattva* or *tathatā*, that is, Suchness or reality itself.

Paramārtha's alleged work, *Chiu shih i p'in* (or *Chiu shih i chi*), may have mentioned the term *amala-vijñāna*, but this is mere conjecture.[109] T'an-ch'ien and Ching-sung apparently wrote commentaries on nine consciousnesses but they are now lost.[110] A catalogue entry for *Chiu shih i chi* in two *chüan* is found in the LTSPC, dated as third year T'ai-ching (549) in Hsin-wu, Mei-yeh temple.[111] The same title and information are given in the NTL,[112] but no entry occurs in other catalogues, including the KYL, so it appears that some time between 664, when the NTL was compiled, and 730, when the KYL was completed, the text, if it ever existed, was lost. The omission of the text in catalogues contemporaneous with the NTL such as Ching-mai's KC and in catalogues even predating the NTL such as the Fa-ching catalogue is something of a mystery.

Wŏnch'ŭk, in his commentary *Chieh shen-mi ching shu*, cites both a *Chiu shih p'in* and a *Chiu shih chang*, which may have been attributed to Paramārtha:

> Paramārtha, based upon the *Chüeh ting tsang lun*, established a theory of nine consciousnesses. As the *chiu shih p'in* says: "As for the nine consciousnesses, those of vision through the sixth consciousness are generally the same as in other treatises on consciousness. The seventh, *ādāna-vijñāna*, is called 'appropriating' since it appropriates the eighth [consciousness] as 'I' and 'mine.' It is only an obstacle of defilement and not attachment to phenomena [as real things]. This definitely is not accomplishing Buddhahood. The eighth, *ālaya-vijñāna*, has three subunits: (1) the enlightened nature (*chieh hsing*) of the *ālaya*, which has the principle that can accomplish Buddhahood; (2) the retributive *ālaya*, which apprehends the objects in the eighteen spheres [of a sensory and mental world] . . . (3) the impure *ālaya*, which apprehends Suchness." From the four kinds of wrong views there is attachment to phenomena but not to selfhood. This is according to Sthiramati's school. The ninth consciousness is the *amala-vijñāna*. This is called the immaculate consciousness (*wu-kou*); Suchness is its essence. In this one Suchness there are two principles: (1) the perceived object, namely Suchness as the limit of reality; (2) the perceiver, namely, the immaculate consciousness, which is also called the fundamental consciousness. All this is cited in the *Chiu shih chang*, *Chüeh ting tsang lun*, and *Chiu shih p'in*.[113]

Wŏnch'ŭk gives the ninefold model found in the CSL and attributes it to the *Chiu shih p'in*. There is no discrepancy between his presentation and that of Paramārtha's until he describes the three types of *ālaya-vijñāna* not found in the CSL. He claims this characterization of the *ālaya* is attributed to Sthiramati, thus linking Paramārtha with Sthiramati's school, but the information he gives to show at what point Sthiramati's ideas are to be distinguished from Paramārtha's is hardly sufficient. Sthiramati certainly had no notion of *amala-vijñāna*, and on this issue, at least, we can make a doctrinal distinction between Sthiramati and Paramārtha. The definition that Wŏnch'ŭk gives of the *amala-vijñāna* is of particular interest here. Suchness is defined as twofold: its perceived object (*so yüan ching*) is the limit or parameter of reality, the appearances of objects to the enlightened mind. The perceiver is the *amala-vijñāna*, the one cognitive agent looking at itself as its own reality. This would appear, at a glance, to bear some similarity to Sthiramati's description of nondiscriminative wisdom: "Of course there is the transcendent knowledge devoid of false discrimination, having neither the object nor that which supports the object [namely consciousness]. There is only mind (*cittam eva*) abiding in the Dharma-Nature of itself, and the subtle propensities (*anuśaya*) of attachment to something perceived and to the perceiver are eliminated."[114]

Besides the CSL, some of Paramārtha's other translations mention an *amala-vijñāna*: the SWHL, *Chüeh ting tsang lun* (CTTL), and *Shih pa k'ung lun* (SPKL). A ninth consciousness is also mentioned in other works besides Paramārtha's translations, in the *Laṅkāvatāra-sūtra*[115] (although not identified as *amala-vijñāna*), in Prabhākāramitra's *Ta-sheng chuang-yen ching lun* (*Mahāyāna-sūtrālaṃkāra*), where the term *amala-vijñāna* is used, and in the *Ratnagotra-vibhāga*, which cites *amala-vijñāna* in verse XXVI.[116]

Let us take a look at the SWHL first, since it was at one time part of the WHL, and preceded the CSL in composition. The SWHL states, in describing the fifth characteristic of existence, namely *parinispanna*, the only ultimately real denotation for the truth: "The fifth characteristic is also included in the absolute nature (*parinispanna*). This does not grasp on to the two characteristics of name and intended object and therefore is identical to the nondifferentiation between cognizer and object, the *amala-vijñāna*."[117] This is the only instance of *amala-vijñāna* in the SWHL. In Hsüan-tsang's HYSCL, *ch'eng wu-hsing p'in* refers only to *parinispanna*.[118] This definition of *amala-vijñāna* as a characterization of the absolute corresponds to the CSL's definition of nondiscriminative wisdom: "This wisdom is called 'the transcendent wisdom devoid of false discrimination,' which means there is no differentiating between cognizer and sense objects. It is called the 'wisdom of Suchness' and also the transformation of the basis [of consciousness]."[119]

The CTTL mentions the term *amala-vijñāna* and is the same text as Hsüan-tsang's *Yü chia shih ti lun: She chüeh tse fen*,[120] that is, "The section on determining [the truth]" from the *Yogācāra-bhūmi*, *chüan* 51 through 54. In Paramārtha's translation, the term *amala-vijñāna* is discussed in six different passages, beginning with the following: "Eliminating the *ālaya-vijñāna* is changing (*chuan*) one's ordinary nature, abandoning ordinary things; the *ālaya-vijñāna* is terminated. Because this consciousness is terminated, all defilements are terminated. Because the *ālaya-vijñāna* is contravened, there is the attainment of the *amala-vijñāna*."[121] Where Paramārtha uses the term *amala-vijñāna*, Hsüan-tsang uses *chuan-i*, or *āśraya-parāvṛtti*. For Paramārtha, elimination of the *ālaya-vijñāna* and its defilements is the transformation of the basis of consciousness, evolving into the *amala-vijñāna*. For Hsüan-tsang, the movement of the dependent aspect of reality to the absolute reality of the Buddha is the transformation of the basis of consciousness. The *ālaya* has not been terminated.

The second discussion of *amala-vijñāna* in the CTTL is much longer:

> The *ālaya-vijñāna* is impermanent and has outflows [from defilement] (*āsrava*). The *amala-vijñāna* is permanent and has no outflows (*anāsrava*). Consequently, realizing the path in which the object is Suchness (*tathatā-viṣaya mārgaḥ*) is the attainment of the *amala-vijñāna*. The *ālaya-vijñāna* is the consequent of subtle evil. The *amala-vijñāna* is followed by subtle evil. The *ālaya-vijñāna* is the foundation for all defilement and is not the religious path or its foundation. The *amala-vijñāna* is not the foundation for defilement but is only the religious path. It is the attainment of the path and becomes its foundation. The *amala-vijñāna* constitutes the basic cause (*i-yin*) for the religious path but does not constitute the generative cause (*sheng-yin*). . . . when one abandons even retribution from subtle evil, one attains the necessary conditions (*yin-yúan*) for the *amala-vijñāna*.[122]

Hsüan-tsang does not use corresponding terms for *āsrava* and *anāsrava*, but grasping and nongrasping (*you ch'ü-shou*, and *wu ch'ü-shou*) and in his system, *anāsrava-bīja*, are located in the *ālaya-vijñāna*. Even more significant is the fact that he again uses *chuan-i* every time Paramārtha uses *amala-vijñāna*. The psychological transformation, for Hsüan-tsang, conditions (*yüan*) the path of Suchness, but no such conditioning is mentioned in the CTTL. This notion of the *amala-vijñāna* as the *anāsrava-bīja* may have been influenced by Tathāgatagarbha thought, which at times totally separates defilement from the true nature of mind. Although the term Tathāgatagarbha never occurs in the CSL, HSL, or SWHL, Paramārtha's influence from Tathāgatagarbha literature is clearly indicated in his translation of Vasubandhu's *Mahāyāna-saṃgraha-bhāṣya*, as is well recognized by Japanese Buddhologists.[123] This may in part explain why the CSL does not adhere to a twofold *paratantra-svabhāva* that is a mixture of purity and impurity, and consequently denies a "mixed" *ālaya-vijñāna*.

The third passage in the CTTL describes the simultaneous cessation of defilement and the *ālaya-vijñāna*: "Therefore, cultivate good thoughts, for this is proof of the *amala-vijñāna*. Know that the *ālaya-vijñāna* together with its defilement is terminated."[124] In Hsüan-tsang's translation there cannot be the co-termination of both the *ālaya-vijñāna* and its defilements but rather, only of the impure part of the *ālaya*, the pure part being *āśraya-parāvṛtti*. Paramārtha's translation evokes the analogous assertion in Tathāgatagarbha literature that the Tathāgatagarbha is unaffected by defilement and forever separated from it.

The fourth time the *amala-vijñāna* is mentioned in the CTTL, a contrast is made between the *ālaya-vijñāna* and the *amala-vijñāna*: "When one says there is a locus (*ch'u*) (*sthāna*?) this refers to all worldly things having the *ālaya-vijñāna* for their foundation. All things that are other-worldly, not eliminating the [religious] path, have the *amala-vijñāna* for their foundation."[125] Hsüan-tsang's work is quite different, referring to the seeds that must be eliminated, not to the termination of the *ālaya-vijñāna*.

A fifth passage from the CTTL indicates once again that Paramārtha has no place in his interpretation of Yogācāra thought for the continuation of the *ālaya* in an undefiled state: "When one says that other-worldly things arise in succession to each other on the basis of the *amala-vijñāna*, this can be maintained. Because of this succession [of the *amala*], there is the counteracting of the *ālaya*. This is nonabiding and it is the world devoid of fluctuations [in defilement], devoid of evil and constituting a definite separation from defilement."[126] Hsüan-tsang asserts that it is owing to the power of *āśraya-parāvṛtti* that religious acts arise. The *āśraya-parāvṛtti* overcomes the *ālaya* and its defiled seeds and is therefore *anāsrava* and separated from speculative reasoning (*prapañca*).

The sixth and final passage on the *amala-vijñāna* is an equation between *amala-vijñāna* and *viśuddha-vijñāna*: "The *amala-vijñāna* that counteracts the worldly consciousness is extremely and profoundly pure and said to be nonabiding."[127] Hsüan-tsang refers to the *viśuddha-vijñāna* as the state when the conditions or subtle propensities (*anuśaya*) have been discontinued, no longer producing form, sensation, and so on, contravening ordinary states of consciousness for an eternally pure one. The CTTL uses the term *amala-vijñāna* a total of nineteen times in six passages, making this text the most important available source on the *amala-vijñāna* theory.

Tsoṅ-kha-pa (1357-1419) in his writings mentions a nine-consciousness theory, which he refutes in favor of the more conventional eight-consciousness theory. The Buddhist who must have introduced this theory to Tibet was the Korean monk Wŏnch'ŭk through his commentary on the *Saṃdhinirmocana*, which Chos-grub translated from Chinese into Tibetan during the T'ang dynasty.[128] Tsoṅ-kha-pa also refers to Bodhiruci and to Paramārtha's translation, *Chüeh ting tsang lun* (*Rnam-par ṅes-pa's mdzod*) and to Hsüan-tsang's *Ch'eng wei-shih lun* (*Rnam-par-rig-pa tsam-du grub-pa*). In his discussion of Paramārtha's views on the *amala-vijñāna*, Tsoṅ-kha-pa does not quote from Wŏnch'ŭk's refutation of this concept but offers his own criticism—that if there were a ninth consciousness separate from the other eight, it would be a permanent entity (*nitya-bhāva*).[129] Since Paramārtha came from India, Tsoṅ-kha-pa thought that the theory of nine consciousnesses also originated in India and that both Indian and Chinese Buddhists believed in this theory. Except for tracts in logic, much of Yogācāra literature was never transmitted from India to Tibet, and so it is rather ironic that Paramārtha's idiosyncratic ideas were brought to Tibet via China and were still discussed as commonly held theories of Indian provenance almost nine hundred years after Paramārtha's death.

The final work of Paramārtha's to mention the term *amala-vijñāna* is the *Shih pa k'ung lun* (Treatise on the Eighteen Emptinesses), either an alternative translation or perhaps an exegesis of the *Madhyānta-vibhāga*, although it is difficult to ascertain why Paramārtha would have made two translations of the *Madhyānta-vibhāga*.[130] The term *amala-vijñāna* occurs twice: "Q: If its intrinsic nature is neither pure nor impure, why not say that the Dharmadhātu is neither pure nor impure? A: The *amala-vijñāna* is the intrinsically pure mind. Because it is defiled by extraneous defilement, it is called impure. Because extraneous defilement is exhausted, it is called pure."[131] The Sanskrit verses corresponding to this passage use the term *prabhāsvaratvāc cittasya*, "because of the intrinsically pure nature of mind," omitting any reference to *amala-vijñāna*.[132] The second occurrence in the *Shih pa k'ung lun* is as follows: "The second [meaning of Consciousness-Only] is the correct insight into Consciousness-Only. Dispensing with the false mind of *saṃsāra* and its world, all is entirely pure. Only this is the intrinsically pure mind, the *amala-vijñāna*."[133]

The term *amala-vijñāna* is so closely tied to Paramārtha and his transmission of Yogācāra that a great number of monks during the T'ang claimed that the theory originated with him. Modern Japanese Buddhologists tend to agree with the Sui and T'ang tradition with only an infrequent disclaimer.[134] Some of the great Sui and T'ang scholar-monks discussed the notion of the *amala-vijñāna* in their own writings. Perhaps the first such documents with a known author are those of Hui-yüan discussed earlier. His *Ta-sheng i chang* has a wealth of material that may be used to trace the development of the theory of *amala-vijñāna* during the sixth century. Some of his earlier works such as his *Shih-ti ching lun i-chi* adhere to an earlier model of seven states of consciousness borrowed from his teacher Fa-shang, with an additional eighth state that he calls both the *ālaya-vijñāna* and the *Tathāgatagarbha*. In Hui-yüan's *Ta-sheng i chang* there are also eight states of consciousness, the eighth state being denoted not only as the *ālaya-vijñāna* or *Tathāgatagarbha* but also as the supreme mind (*paramārtha-citta*) and the immaculate consciousness (*wu-kou*), used synonymously for the *amala-vijñāna* in Wŏnch'ŭk's work. Hui-yüan's two scriptural references supporting his interpretation are the *Laṅkāvatāra-sūtra* and the *Śrīmālādevī-sūtra*.[135] In discussing them, he elaborates on what is meant by the immaculate state of consciousness:

> The *amala-vijñāna* is said to be immaculate; also, it is explained as originally pure. . . . The true essence is externally pure and, therefore, is called "immaculate." . . . In the *Laṅkāvatāra-sūtra*, section on the verses, it says: "The eight or nine consciousnesses are like waves in water." . . . What is meant by nine consciousnesses is that there are seven false ones, namely, the six operative consciousnesses (*shih shih pien*) and the false consciousness [*manas* or *ādāna*]. There are two subdivisions of true [consciousness], namely, *amala-vijñāna* and *ālaya-vijñāna*, as explained before. Because of this previous interpretation, in total there are nine. The true and false can be separated or combined. When we say there are nine kinds [of consciousness], the true [state] is one, namely, *amala-vijñāna*. When the true and false are combined, there are eight kinds, as explained before.[136]

While in Hui-yüan's earlier works Fa-shang's influence is considerable, in his later work such as the *Ta-sheng i chang* we see a bimodal set of operations associated either exclusively with the *ālaya-vijñāna* or with the *ālaya* and *amala-vijñāna*. Notable in his discussion, however, is the reliance upon the *Laṅkāvatāra-sūtra* and the *Śrīmālādevī-sūtra* as the textual bases for the theories of nine consciousnesses and pure consciousness, respectively, rather than upon Paramārtha. Just as Suchness has two aspects, one pure and one impure, in both Tathāgatagarbha literature and in Paramārtha's texts, here the true consciousness also is twofold in nature.

The Tunhuang manuscript on the *Saṃgraha*, simply titled *She ta-sheng lun*, contains references to both the *Wu-hsiang lun* and the *Shih-ch'i ti-lun*, both of which consider the theory of nine consciousnesses a "foreign tradition." [137] But though the *Shih-ch'i ti-lun* is part of the *Bodhisattvabhūmi*, neither the extant Chinese nor the Sanskrit recension mentions the term. This text was allegedly Paramārtha's first translation effort, and his lost redaction may have been the reference for the Tunhuang manuscript. As I have already indicated, Wŏnch'ŭk closely associated the theory of nine consciousnesses with both Sthiramati and Paramārtha's *Chüeh ting tsang lun* and *Chiu shih chang*, that is, with an Indian transmission, but nothing in Sthiramati's extant works can be taken as evidence to support the notion that Sthiramati ever postulated such a theory.[138]

Chih-i, in his commentary on the *Suvarṇa-prabhāsottama-sūtra*, entitled *Chin kuang-ming ching hsüan-i*, states: "The term *amala-vijñāna* is the ninth consciousness, which is inactive (*pu-tung*) (*acala*?). If it discriminates, it is identical to the Buddha's consciousness. The *ālaya-vijñāna* is the eighth consciousness, which is subconscious ('insubmersible') (*wu-mo*), and has a combination of latent forms of defilement (*anuśaya*) and ignorance, being the Bodhisattva's consciousness." [139] The *amala-vijñāna* is interpreted in Ting-pin's *Ssu-fen-lu shu shih-tsung i-chi* as consisting of two parts, a conditioned object that is coextensive with Suchness and a conditioning subject that is coextensive with knowledge of Suchness.[140] This agrees with Wŏnch'ŭk's description cited previously. The implication is that the Buddha has a discriminating consciousness without defiling elements, in concurrence with Chih-i's interpretation of *amala-vijñāna*. The CSL would seem to attribute to Suchness that is coincidental with delusion (*samala-tathatā*) the two natures of *parikalpita* and *paratantra*. When all object-subject dichotomies are dissolved, this would be the Dharmadhātu as pure Suchness (*nirmala-tathatā*) that is unconditioned (*asaṃskṛta*). For thinkers such as Paramārtha it does not seem to have been a problem that the Buddha's knowledge (*samyak-jñāna*) is unconditioned (*asaṃskṛta*) and is at the same time *amala-vijñāna*, although from the point of view of Abhidharma, *jñāna* is always conditioned and *vijñāna* always takes an object. In the system represented by the CSL, the *amala* is itself unconditioned, but all conditioned things are based upon it.

According to K'uei-chi, in his *Ch'eng wei-shih lun shu-chi*, "the perfect mirror wisdom" or *ādarśana-jñāna* denoted by Hsüan-tsang is what "former masters" erroneously called the ninth consciousness. One of these masters may be a referent for Paramārtha. Though K'uei-chi considers this a false teaching, he nonetheless recognized the fact that the *Laṅkāvatāra-sūtra* had proposed a theory of nine consciousnesses. He renders the ninth as designating the mirror wisdom or transformed eighth consciousness. Tun-lun, in the *Yü-chia lun chi*, also claims that the *amala* is simply another name for the eighth consciousness after Buddhahood has been achieved.[141]

From the above sources, one can outline a genre of literature within Yogācāra postulating the existence of *amala-vijñāna*. The term is associated with qualities of the *Tathāgatagarbha* as a dimension of the *ālaya-vijñāna*; this association between the two latter terms is found in the *Laṅkāvatāra-sūtra*. The enumeration of nine consciousnesses is also supported by the *Laṅkāvatāra-sūtra*, as both Hui-yüan and K'uei-chi recognized. The *Śrīmālādevī-sūtra* (ŚDS) and the commentary *Ratnagotra-vibhāga*, both extremely important scriptural sources for Tathāgatagarbha thought, are also given as textual evidence for advocating an immaculate state of consciousness. The former is cited by Hui-yüan as a gloss on the immaculately pure mind, but it is also cited in the CSL. The Tunhuang manuscript, *She ta-sheng lun*, refers to both the *Shih-ch'i ti-lun*, purportedly a translation of part of the *Yogācārabhūmi*, and the *Wu-hsiang lun* as foundations for the theory of nine consciousnesses, which is said to be a theory that began as a foreign import, presumably from India. Wŏnch'ŭk implies that there was some doctrinal relationship between Paramārtha and Sthiramati, but he does not specify the exact affinity.

The *Yogācārabhūmi*, in Paramārtha's interpretation of portions of it entitled CTTL, is taken to be one of the primary sources for the notion of an affinity between his thought and Sthiramati's. Prabhākaramitra's translation of the *Mahāyāna-sūtralaṃkāra* mentions the term *amala-vijñāna*, but this translation is not cited as a scriptural source by the T'ang scholars we have discussed. But even though the extant recensions of the *Yogācārabhūmi* do not indicate a theory of nine consciousnesses, does this exclude the possibility that a tradition may have once existed that commented upon Asaṅga's (or Maitreya's) work, fusing ideas from *sūtras* such as the ŚDS and the *Laṅkāvatāra* with Yogācāra ideas presented by Asaṅga (or Maitreya)? The literary evidence suggests, at the very least, that Paramārtha, in his later works, was concerned with commenting upon Vasubandhu and Asaṅga's writings by blending the Tathāgatagarbha ideas found in *sūtra* literature such as the ŚDS and *Laṅkāvatāra* with Yogācāra treatises. Just as the *Ratnagotra-vibhāga* and Prabhākaramitra's translation of the *Mahāyāna-sūtrālaṃkāra* indicate a Tathāgatagarbha-oriented form of Yogācāra, works such as Paramārtha's WHL, CTTL, and SPKL indicate that a tradition may have once existed that glossed Yogācārin vocabulary with philosophical and religious terms denoting an omniscient state of mind or *amala-vijñāna*. The CSL is an example of that type of exegetical literature. Its originality may not consist in Paramārtha's inventing the notion of nine consciousnesses or of *amala-vijñāna*. Rather, it thoroughly maintains this lost tradition's fusion of two sets of theoretical views on the nature of mind, one represented by the *sūtra* literature of ŚDS and *Laṅkāvatāra*, the other by the *śāstra* literature of Vasubandhu, Asaṅga, and at least occasionally, the tradition from which Sthiramati arose.

The CSL diverges so substantially from Sthiramati's *Triṃśikā-vijñapti-bhāṣya* that it may have been, in effect, an original exegesis by Paramārtha himself of Vasubandhu's *Triṃśikā-kārikas*, perhaps representing only a relatively new expansion of Vasubandhu's verses. In other words, perhaps no commentary on the verses had been produced by the time Paramārtha left India for Canton, and therefore he composed his exegesis on the verses on the basis of his own analysis of Vasubandhu's ideas or of ideas current at the time he left India for his missionary activities. In any event, we can no longer assume that Paramārtha's CSL is simply a translation of the *Triṃśikā-kārikās* or that his line of transmission of Yogācāra is closely aligned with Sthiramati. We are left with the impression that the CSL is a textual exegesis on the *Triṃśikā-kārikās* that hints at views similar to those in Sthiramati's commentary and sometimes suggests idiosyncrasies that are not to be found even in Paramārtha's other major works.

Translation

Chuan shih lun

The Evolution of Consciousness

[*A. Objective Content of Cognitive Acts*]

[Verse Ia:] Consciousness evolves (*pravartate*)[1] in two ways: (1) it evolves into selves (*ātman*); (2) it evolves into things (*dharma*).

[Exegesis:] Everything perceived [or cognized][2] is included in these two objects [of cognition]. These two really do not exist, but consciousness evolves into these two [false] representations.

[*B. Subjective Content of Cognitive Acts*]

[Verse Ib:] Next, we shall explain the three kinds of perceiver [or cognizer; also termed *vijñāna-pariṇāma*]:[3]

[Verse II:] (1) the retributive (*vipāka*) consciousness, namely, the *ālaya-vijñāna*; (2) the appropriating consciousness, namely, the *ādāna-vijñāna*;[4] (3) the consciousness of sense data, namely, the six [sense] consciousnesses (*vijñaptir viṣayasya*).[5]

[1. Retributive or Karmic Consciousness (61c5)]

[Exegesis:] The retributive consciousness is called "retributive" because it is derived from defilement and *karma*. It is also called the "fundamental" consciousness[6] because all seeds[7] of conditioned phenomena are dependent upon it and [called] the "abode" consciousness because it is the place where all seeds rest.

[Verse IIIa:] It is also called the "storehouse" consciousness because it is the place (*sthāna*) where all seeds are concealed.

[Exegesis:] Q: What kind of aspects (*ākāra*) and objects (*ālambana*) does this consciousness [*ālaya*] have?

[Verse IIIb:] A: Its aspects and objects cannot be [clearly] discriminated (*asaṃviditaka*) because they are identical and are not different [from the *ālaya-vijñāna*].

Q: If that is so, how do we know that it [*ālaya*] exists?

A: Because of its processes, we know that this consciousness exists. This consciousness can produce all defilement, *karma*, and retribution. Take ignorance, for example. It [*ālaya*] must generate ignorance.

(61c11)

Is it possible to discriminate [clearly] between its aspects and its objects [while in a state of ignorance]? If they can be discriminated from each other, then we do not refer to this state as ignorance ["devoid of knowledge"].[8] If they cannot be discriminated from each other, then you might deny the existence [of ignorance]. Yet we do affirm the existence [of both ignorance and knowledge] and deny their nonexistence. Because of the existence of hate, greed, [delusion], and other processes, we know that ignorance exists. The fundamental consciousness is also similar in that its aspects and objects are not distinguished from each other (*aparichinna*?). But because of its processes, we know that it [fundamental consciousness] exists.[9]

(62a4)

There are eight different names for this consciousness:[10] (1) basis,[11] [(2) insubmersible,[12] (3) storehouse,[13] (4) sacred,[14] (5) supreme,[15] (6) pure,[16] (7) true,[17] (8) Suchness,[18]] which are explained in the "Chapter on the Meaning of the Nine Consciousnesses."[19] Also, it [*ālaya-vijñāna*] is associated with five kinds of mental states (*citta-samprayukta-saṃskāra-dharma*):[20]

[Verse IIIc:] (1) [sensory] contact (*sparśa*), (2) attention (*manaskāra*),[21] (3) sensation (*vedanā*), (4) volition (*cetanā*), (5) conceptualization (*samjñā*).

(62a6)

[Exegesis:] Three variables—sense organs, sense data, and consciousness—combine to produce [sensory] contact.[22] When the mind is continually active, then it is called attentive.

[Verse IVa:] Sensation is only neutrality (*upekṣā*).[23]

[Exegesis:] Volition calculates what can and cannot be done, urging the mind to be correct or incorrect. This is called volition. Attention is like a galloping horse and volition is like the rider. A horse only gallops straight ahead but cannot avoid a wrong place or head toward the right place. Because of the rider, a horse can avoid the wrong and head toward the right place. Volition [like a rider] thus can enable one's attention to avoid reckless actions.

[Verse IVb:] This consciousness and its mental states are indeterminate (*avyākṛta*) in nature. It constantly flows, moment by moment, like the current and waves in a river;

(62a12)

[Exegesis:] The fundamental consciousness is like the current and the five [mental] states are like the waves[24]

[Verse Va:] until the attainment of Arhatship.[25]

[Exegesis:] The current and waves of the [mental] states are not eliminated. This is called the "first [evolution of] consciousness" (*ālaya-vijñāna*).

[2. Appropriating Consciousness or Ego (62a13)]

[Verse Vb:] Contingent upon this consciousness [and having it as its object],[26] there is the second [evolution], the "appropriating consciousness" (*ādāna*).

[Exegesis:] Appropriating is its essence.

[Verse VIa:] This [appropriating] consciousness is associated with four defilements (*kleśa*):[27] (1) ignorance (*ātma-moha*),[28] (2) views of self (*ātma-dṛṣṭi*), (3) conceit ("self-pride") (*ātma-māna*), (4) self-love (*ātma-sneha*).

[Verse VIb:] This consciousness is called "hidden [because of defilement] but indeterminate" (*nivṛtāvyākṛta*).[29]

[Exegesis:] There are also five kinds of associated mental states that have the same names as the above [namely, sensation and so forth] but are more coarse.

[Verse VII:] This consciousness and its associated [mental] states are eliminated in the Arhat stage, being ultimately eliminated upon entering cessation-meditation (*nirodha-samāpatti*).[30]

[Exegesis:] When the path of insight (*darśana-mārga*)[31] destroys the defiled consciousness and its mental states and when there is the attainment of the transcendent path (*lokottara-mārga*)[32] of the sixteen practices [of meditation on the Four Noble Truths], then it [defiled consciousness] is ultimately eliminated. The residual [defilement] that has not been eliminated belongs only to [the category of] volition.

[Verse VIIIa:] This is called the "second [evolution of] consciousness."

[3. Sense Consciousnesses (62a20)]

[Exegesis:] The "third" [evolution of consciousness]

[Verse VIIIb:] or consciousness of sense data [or matter] is the evolution of consciousness that appears as sense data [or matter],[33] developing into six kinds [of sense objects].

[Exegesis:] The evolution of consciousness appearing as sense data was mentioned above [in verse II].

[Verse VIIIc:] Their essence is connected with the three qualities [pleasant, unpleasant, and neutral]

[Verse IX:] and is associated with ten mental states,[34] ten kinds of good and bad actions, together with major (*kleśa*) and minor forms[35] (*upakleśa*) of defilement. All are composed of three types of sensation [pleasant, unpleasant, and neutral].

[4. Mental States (62a23)]

The ten kinds of mental states are the previously mentioned five—

[Verse Xa:] [sensory] contact, etc.—which are only the most coarse forms. The latter five are: (6) desire (*chanda*), (7) understanding (*adhimokṣa*), (8) mindfulness (*smṛti*), (9) meditation (*samādhi*), (10) wisdom (*dhī*).[36]

[a. Good Mental States (62a35)]

[Exegesis:] Among these, "understanding," as traditionally explained, is "resolve."

[Verse Xb:] The ten good acts are: (1) faith (*śraddhā*), (2) humility (*hrī*), (3) modesty (*apatrapa*),

[Verse XI:] (4) lack of greed (*alobha*), (5) lack of hatred (*adveṣa*), (6) stamina (*vīrya*), (7) reliance (*praśrabdhi*), (8) carefulness (*apramāda*), (9) noninjury (*ahiṃsā*), (10) equanimity (*upekṣā*).

[Exegesis:] These ten pervade the mind of the triple world [of desire, matter, and spirit] and the mind [in the realm] without outflows[37] [from defilement] and are classified as the great mental elements. Their nature is intrinsically good.

[b. Bad Mental States (62a29)]

The opposite of these ten are the intrinsically evil [mental states]. There are ten kinds of major defilements (*kleśa*): (1) greed (*rāga*), (2) hatred (*pratigha*), (3) delusion (*mūḍha*),

[Verse XIIa:] (4) pride (*māna*), (5)-(9) the five [false] views (*dṛṣṭi*) [of self; of the extreme metaphysical positions of nihilism and eternalism; of negation of anything real; of esteeming evil as good; of misguided moral disciplines], (10) skepticism (*vicikitsā*).

[Exegesis:] There are twenty-four kinds of minor defilements (*upakleśa*):

[Verse XIIb:] (1) bitterness (*krodha*), (2) blinding hatred (*upanāha*), (3) secretiveness (*mrakṣa*), (4) nonabandonment of evil ways (*pradāsa*), (5) jealousy (*īrṣyā*), (6) miserliness (*mātsarya*), (7) deceit (*māyā*),[38] (8) illusion (*śāthya*),

[Verse XIII:] (9) intoxication (*mada*), (10) aggression (*vihiṃsā*), (11) shamelessness (*āhrīkya*), (12) remorselessness (*anapatrāpya*), (13) without [self-]reliance (*styāna*), (14) frivolity (*auddhatya*), (15) faithlessness (*āśraddha*), (16) sloth (*kausīdya*), (17) carelessness (*pramāda*), (18) forgetfulness (*muṣitasmṛtitā*),

[Verse XIV:] (19) distraction (*vikṣepa*), (20) misunderstanding (*asamprajñā*), (21) depression (*kaukṛtya*), (22) drowsiness (*middha*), (23) reflection (*vitarka*), (24) investigation (*vicāra*).

(62b8)

[Exegesis:] There are two types within these minor defilements: (1) universal mental states [associated with all eight states of consciousness:] (*sarva-tragaiś caitaśaiḥ*); (2) restricted mental states [associated with only some states of consciousness:] (*viniyataiś caitaśaiḥ*).[39]

[C. *Relationship between Subjective and Objective Sides of Conscious Acts (62b8)*]

[Verse XVa:] The five [sense] consciousnesses

[Exegesis:] [subsumed] in the sixth consciousness—the intellect,

[Verse XVb:] the fundamental consciousness,[40]

[Exegesis:] and the appropriating consciousness[41]—these three [groups of] faculties

[Verse XVc:] ensue from causes and conditions. They occur either simultaneously or sequentially.

[Exegesis:] Having attention as the [immediate] cause; and external sense data (*viṣaya*) [or matter] as the [secondary] condition, consciousness occurs. If one's attention, at first, desires to apprehend the two sense data of form (lit. "color") (*rūpa*) and sound, then vision and hearing occur simultaneously and there will be two types of sense data [imputed on to an "external" object]. If one's attention is directed toward a certain locus, to see forms, hear sounds, and to smell odors, then these three [vision, hearing, and smell] occur simultaneously and there will be three types of sense data [imputed on to an "external" object] and so on; all the five [sense] consciousnesses may occur simultaneously or sequentially in a similar fashion. When there is the occurrence of only a single [sense] consciousness, there will be a single sense datum. They ensue from causes and conditions. Therefore, they [sequential and simultaneous consciousness/sense data series] are not the same. The seven consciousnesses occur in interaction with each other in the *ālaya-vijñāna*, just as groups of forms and images are reflected together in a mirror, or

[Verse XVd:] just as many waves are all in one body of water.

(62b17)

Q: On what occasions does this intellect (*mano-vijñāna*) not arise?

[Verse XVI:] A: Except for these six states—[cessation] meditation without conceptualization (*nirodha-samāpatti*), [meditation associated with the third level or *dhyāna* in] heavens without conceptualization (*asamjñi-samāpatti*), dreamless sleep, drunken stupor, unconsciousness, or a coma—the others always have it [intellect].

(62b20)

[Verse XVIIa:] The evolution of consciousness is

[Exegesis:] not separate from two principles:

[Verse XVIIb:] (1) the discriminator (*vikalpa*); (2) the discriminated [object] (*yad vikalpyate*). Since the discriminated [object] does not exist,

(62b21)

[Exegesis:] the discriminator also does not exist. Without a sense object to be grasped, consciousness cannot occur.[42]

[Verse XVIIc:] Therefore, the principle of Consciousness-Only can be upheld.

[*D. Definition of Consciousness-Only (62b22)*]

[Exegesis:] What does it mean to establish the principle of Consciousness-Only?

The meaning [of Consciousness-Only], fundamentally, is to dispense with sense objects and to dispense with the mind. Now if the objective world does not exist, Consciousness-Only would also be destroyed. This is what I mean by "the principle of Consciousness-Only is upheld." This is called the pure component [of consciousness] because both defilements and the objective world do not exist [in the system of Consciousness-Only].

Moreover, when I explain that the principle of Consciousness-Only is upheld, I mean that:

[Verse XVIII:] As for the consciousness containing the seeds of all phenomena [namely, the *ālaya-vijñāna*], it creates and evolves from one to another [form], evolving from each other onward and onward into varieties of discriminations and discriminated objects through mutual interaction [of the *ālaya* with other states of consciousness].

[Exegesis:] For this reason, outside of consciousness no events can take place. This is why it is called the impure component, for only the prior sense object is dispensed with but not consciousness itself.

Commentary (62b29) [on specific lines from verse XVIII:][43]

"As for the consciousness containing the seeds of all phenomena" this refers to the *ālaya-vijñāna*, which, with all its seeds of phenomena and seeds from the other seven consciousnesses, produces various sorts of unlimited phenomena according to their respective types. Thus, it is called "the consciousness containing seeds of all phenomena."[44]

"Onward and onward" means that, because of these consciousnesses, one can evolve and produce unlimited phenomena.[45] Some evolve into the sense organs and some evolve into sense data. Some evolve into an ego; others into consciousness. Such a variety of dissimilar kinds are the products of Consciousness-Only. Thus, it is said that: "It creates and evolves onward and onward."

"From one [form] to another . . . through mutual interaction" [of the *ālaya* with the other states of consciousness]:[46] "From one" means the five aggregates (*skandhas*) [that comprise an individual] evolve, [namely] from form to consciousness inclusive. "To another" means that friends, enemies, and acquaintances evolve, a variety of different kinds [of people]. From the perspective of one's own five (psychophysical) aggregates [called oneself] one calls them "other." Thus, "from one [form] to another, evolving from each other" means consecutive moments are not the same. Therefore, one says "through mutual interaction." All the various constructs are [evolved from] consciousness without an objective world. "Into varieties of discriminations" means that in each single [act of] consciousness there is both a discriminator and a discriminated object. The discriminator is identical to consciousness and the discriminated [object] is identical to the sense object. The discriminator is the nature of dependence (*paratantra-svabhāva*), and the discriminated is the nature of being discriminated (*parikalpita-svabhāva*). Therefore, one says "into varieties of discriminations and discriminated objects."[47] For this reason, outside of consciousness, there are no other sense objects. But only the existence of consciousness is maintained. Since dispensing with consciousness has not been explained yet, delusions and confusion have not yet been eliminated. Therefore, it is called the "impure" component [of consciousness].

Q: If one dispenses with sense objects but retains consciousness, then one can say that there is a principle of Consciousness-Only. But if both the sense object and consciousness are to be dispensed with, how can consciousness [of any kind] be maintained?

(62c16)

A: One establishes that Consciousness-Only temporarily dispenses with the sense object but retains the [existence of] mind. In the final analysis, however, one dispenses with sense objects in order to empty the mind. This is the correct meaning. Therefore, [when] both the sense object and consciousness are dissolved, this principle is upheld. [When] both the sense object and consciousness are dissolved, this [state] is identical to the true nature [*tattva* or *tathatā*]. The true nature is identical to Pure Consciousness (*amala-vijñāna*).[48] Additionally, we can say in the final analysis that this is Pure Consciousness.

[*E. Causes for Positing a Discriminating Subject versus a Discriminated Object*]

(62c20)

[Verse XIX:] The text says:[49] two kinds of latent impressions from past *karma*[50] and two kinds of latent forces can become the origin [of suffering by producing future retribution] bringing about birth and death [in a future rebirth].

(62c21)

[Exegesis:] The two kinds of latent impressions from past *karma* are identical to the "seeds" of *karma*: (1) latent impressions from past *karma*; (2) attachment to the latent impressions from past *karma*. Latent impressions from past *karma* are identical to the discriminated [object] and are discriminated in nature. Attachment to the influences from past *karma* is identical to the discriminator and is dependent in nature. The [discriminated] object is the sense object; the discriminator is consciousness. These two kinds of *karma* are called "the conventional truth of the origin [of suffering]," bringing about the production of the five *skandhas* [and notions of individuality or personhood].

The two kinds of latent forces are defilement: (1) latent force of aspects; (2) the primitive [or gross] latent force. The aspects are the essence of defilement that is dependent in nature and can include previous representations [of the object].

(62c28)

The primitive [latent forces] are defilement that is discriminated in nature, being the gross manifestation of an objective world. These two defilements are called the absolute truth [of the origin of suffering] because they can accumulate and direct the future five *skandhas* [in another rebirth]. From these [latent impressions from past *karma* and the latent forces], there are both kinds of truth of the origin [of suffering], the conventional truth and the absolute truth. If past *karma* has already been extinguished, but one still receives other [future] retribution, then one is still firmly positioned in life and death [in a future rebirth].

Commentary (63a2) [on specific lines from verse XIX:]

As for "the two kinds of latent impressions from past *karma*," each impression has two principles: (1) the object [discriminated], which is the latent impressions from past *karma*; (2) the discriminator, which is the attachment to the latent impressions from past *karma*. The object is the nature of discrimination that can produce a panorama of phenomena generated from seeds [in the *ālaya-vijñāna*]. This panorama of phenomena is called the latent impression from past *karma*. It has a name but no essence. The discriminator is the nature of dependence. It is the seed that generates *karma* and is called the attachment to latent impressions from past *karma*. It has an essence but is not absolute. "The two kinds of latent forces" are also similar [in having a discriminating subject and a discriminated object].

(63a7)

Every single defilement has two principles. (1) Discriminated [objects] are the primitive latent forces that produce the panorama of phenomena generated from defilement. They have names but no essence. (2) The discriminator is the essence of defilement. It also exists but is not absolute. It is the nature of dependence. However, what we have explained here as the discriminated [nature] and [the nature of] dependence are named differently in [the *Treatise on*] *the Three States of Insubstantiality* (SWHL). The nature of discrimination is called "the categories for aspects," and the nature of dependence is called "the primitive [delusions]."[51] If one considers the nature of discrimination as having an essence, having categories for aspects, and producing the panorama of phenomena of all defilements, we say that this is called defilement. The nature of dependence is the essence of defilement. Because it can bring about the retribution of life and death [propelling one into a future existence,] it is called primitive. Now because we explain here the nature of discrimination as the categories of aspects and the primitive manifestation [of an object world], we call it primitive.

(63a15)

The nature of dependence can be attached to the previous category of aspects and is thus called "aspects." Each [of these two categories] has its own meaning. If one wishes to turn to these meanings, [the *Treatise on*] *the Three States of Insubstantiality* has acceptable terminology.

[*F. Theory of Three Natures (63a17)*]

The text says: [Verse XX:] "Whatever is discrimination: if one discriminates this or that kind of thing, these kinds of things are called the nature of discrimination."

[Exegesis:] These only have names, but the essence [of a thing] that the name indicates does not really exist.[52]

[Verse XXI:] The essence [of a thing] that is indicated [by a name] does not really exist; this discrimination is generated contingent upon others.[53] Therefore it is called the nature of dependence. Both natures are inseparable; this is identical to the nature of the absolute.

[Exegesis:] If they were separable from each other, then the principle of Consciousness-Only would not be upheld, because sense objects would be different from consciousness. Because they are inseparable, there is Consciousness-Only without an objective world. Because there is no objective world, consciousness also does not exist. Because the sense object does not exist, and neither does consciousness, the principle of Consciousness-Only is established.

[Verse XXIIa:] This being then established, therefore the former nature (discrimination) and the latter nature (dependence) are neither identical to nor different from each other.

[Exegesis:] If one posits their identity or difference, then there is an error. Why? If the nature of discrimination is posited as identical to the nature of dependence, then the nature of discrimination would never exist nor could it include the five sets [of phenomena].[54] The nature of dependence could never exist either. If this were the case, then there could be no life or death, liberation, good or evil, morality or discipline. This cannot be. Therefore, since this is not the case, the nature of discrimination and the nature of dependence are not to be posited as identical.

(63a28)

If one posits that they are different, then given the nature of discrimination, one could not dispense with the nature of dependence. This follows because, if we view the nature of discrimination as devoid of existence, then and only then will we see that the nature of dependence is also devoid of existence. Therefore, we are not to posit that they are different.

Moreover, if the nature of discrimination is posited as being different from the nature of dependence, then the essence of the nature of discrimination should be posited as existing, and one should not say that it never exists. Existence can be differentiated from nonexistence, but how can we discuss the difference? Therefore, we only say that they are neither identical nor different and cannot posit either identity or difference [in regard to the two natures of discrimination and dependence].[55]

[Verse XXIIb:] It is like impermanence

[Exegesis:] and conditioned phenomena. We also cannot posit that they are either identical or different. Impermanence means not existing either in the previous or in the succeeding moment. The five aggregates are conditioned phenomena. If impermanence and conditioned phenomena were posited as being identical, then if impermanence did not exist, all phenomena would not exist. Since they both [impermanence and all phenomena] are not nonexistent, they are not to be posited as identical.

(63b8)

If they are posited as different, then when one views the impermanent, one should not understand conditioned phenomena. Because they are understood, they are not to be posited as different. Thus, they are neither identical nor different. Thus, all phenomena are like this: the form ["color"] and the pot are neither identical nor different. If the form and the pot were posited as identical, then the form could not be a pot, but if the pot were truly real and if the form is maintained as different from the pot, then when one sees form one should not apprehend the pot. Therefore, they are not maintained as identical or different. These two sets of explanations [on the relationship between identity and difference] are similar in that

[Verse XXIIc:] if one does not view the nature of discrimination, then one does not view the nature of dependence.[56]

[Exegesis:] Therefore, they are neither identical nor different. However, all phenomena have only three natures and are entirely included in these [three natures].

[*G. Theory of Three States of Insubstantiality or Naturelessnesses (63b15)*]

[Verse XXIII:] The Tathāgata, for the benefit of living beings, explained that all phenomena are devoid of a substantial nature. There are three kinds. The three natures were previously explained.[57]

[Exegesis:] The first two are conventional truth. The third one is absolute truth. All phenomena are included in the two truths, conventional and absolute.

The three states devoid of substantial natures are inseparable from the previously mentioned three natures.

[Verse XXIV:] The nature of discrimination is called the state devoid of a substantial nature with respect to characteristics [imputed on to a thing][58] because its characteristics have no essence. The nature of dependence is called the "state devoid of a substantial nature with respect to production" [of a thing as self-caused][59] because its essence with relation to causation does not exist [as a self-caused entity].

[Exegesis:] The essence [of an object in consciousness] appears as the aspect of matter. Matter is the nature of discrimination. Since discrimination does not exist, the essence [of an object] does not exist.[60] Since the causes do not exist either, the sense object, being derived from the nature of discrimination, can bring about effects on consciousness. If an objective world does not exist, what produces any effects? For example, seeds can produce a sprout. If the seed does not exist, how can a sprout emerge? Therefore, there is no production [of effects].[61]

[Verse XXVa:] The nature of the absolute is called "the state devoid of any substantial nature" with respect to the nature [imputed on to a thing][62]

[Exegesis:] because it neither exists nor does not exist [as some sort of substantial entity].

(63b24)

With reference to persons and phenomena, they are devoid of any substantial nature as existent things. With reference to these two Emptinesses [of self and things or persons and phenomena], they are devoid of any substantial nature as nonexistent things. Therefore, we deny both "the substantial nature of existence" and that of nonexistence and reiterate that this is referred to as "the state devoid of any substantial nature with respect to any nature" [imputed on to a thing].

[Verse XXVb:] These three states devoid of substantial natures are the absolute reality[63] in all phenomena.

[Exegesis:] Because these are separate from existence, they are called permanent. In order to indicate these three states devoid of substantial natures, we explain the principle of Consciousness-Only.

[*H. Supreme Knowledge (63b27)*]

[Verse XXVI:] Someone who cultivates the path to wisdom[64] but does not abide in the principle of Consciousness-Only has defilements produced by the propensities (*anuśaya*) of the twofold attachment [to perceiver and perceived][65] that have not been eliminated,

[Exegesis:] nor have their roots been eliminated. For this reason, one establishes the One Vehicle in which all are able to learn the Bodhisattva path.

(63c1)

[Verse XXVII:] If one says: "there is only the existence of consciousness" based upon attachment to what is presented before him [as an object], then since he has not yet eliminated this attachment [to dualistic perceptions], he does not enter Consciousness-Only.[66]

[Verse XXVIII:] If the cognizer (*vijñāna*) does not apprehend (*upalabhate*) the objects (*ālambanam*), the two [attachments to objects and to consciousness that grasps the object] are not manifested.[67] At that time the practitioner says: "I am entering Consciousness-Only."

[Exegesis:] Why? Because, by cultivating insight, I have eliminated all disorienting attachments [to an object].

[Verse XXIXa:] This is called "nonapprehension[68] [of an object as a substantial thing] that is neither thought[69] nor sense object." This wisdom is called "the transcendent[70] wisdom devoid of [false] discrimination"

[Exegesis:] which means there is no differentiating between cognizer and sense objects. It is called the "wisdom of Suchness" and

[Verse XXIXb:] also called "the transformation [termination] of the basis" (*āśraya-parāvṛtti*).

[Exegesis:] Therefore, one abandons the basis of life and death, based only upon the principle [of Consciousness-Only].

[Verse XXIXc:] Therefore, primitive [delusions] and the two attachments are simultaneously ended.

[Exegesis:] Gross [delusions] are the nature of discrimination, and the attachments [to them] are the nature of dependence. These two kinds [of natures] are both ended.

[Verse XXX:] This is called the "realm devoid of outflows [from defilement]" (*anāsrava-dhātu*). This is called "the inconceivable."[71] This is called "the absolutely real and good."[72] This is called "the fruit that permanently abides."[73] This is called "transcendent bliss,"[74] "the body of liberation,"[75] and the Dharma-body within the three bodies [of the Buddha].

Commentary (63c10) [on specific lines in verse XXVI:]

"The defilements produced by the propensities of the twofold attachment [to perceiver and perceived] that have not been eliminated."—This signifies the defilements [produced by] the propensities of the two attachments [to consciousness and its objects that are eliminated by the Path] of Insight and by [the Path of] Development, which can create seeds and produce unlimited defilements onto the mind;[76] all take the fundamental consciousness [*ālaya*] for their foundation. If the foundation is not yet eliminated, the branches will not end either.

As the *Śrīmālādevī-sūtra* explains: "If the stage of ignorance is not absolutely eliminated, then the limitless four stages of abiding will not be absolutely eliminated."[77]

[Commentary (63c14) on specific lines in verse XXVIII:]

"If the cognizer does not apprehend the object, the two [attachments to objects and to consciousness that grasps the object] are not manifested." The "sense objects" are the objects of Consciousness-Only; this is confusion concerning Consciousness-Only. Because there are no objects, there is [also] no consciousness. Since consciousness does not exist, the mind that apprehends Consciousness-Only as an object also does not exist. Therefore, it is said that "the two are not manifested." These two [sense objects and consciousness] only refer to two [processes of] consciousnesses presented with a sense object before them, but the sense object [presented] before consciousness is already nonexistent. This is the culmination of the "Evolution of Consciousness."[78]

Appendixes

APPENDIX A

Chronology of Paramārtha's Life

499

Born to a Brahman family of the Bhāradvāja *gotra* in Ujjain, Malwa province, northwest India.

545 (Liang dynasty: 11th yr Ta-t'ung)

Missionary activity in Funan (Southeast Asia).

Summoned to China by Emperor Wu of Liang, accompanied by Rear Guard Chang Fan (or Chang Szu).

546 (1st yr Chung Ta-t'ung; 12th yr Ta-t'ung)

(47 years old)

September 25: Arrived in Canton.

548 (2nd yr T'ai-ch'ing)

Intercalary month (August 20-September 17): Arrived in the capital city of Nanking and had an audience with Emperor Wu in the Pao-yün temple quarters.

549 (3rd yr T'ai-ch'ing)

(50 years old)

[April 24: Hou Ching seized Nanking.]

[June 12: Death of Emperor Wu.]

550 (4th yr T'ai-ch'ing)

Tenth month (October 26-November 25): Fled to Fu-ch'un, 150 miles southeast of Nanking; received sponsorship of Governor Lu Yüan-che and resumed translation activity.

Translated *Shih-ch'i-ti-lun* (Treatise on the Seventeen Bodhisattva

Stages) in 5 *ch.*, assisted by twenty-one monks including Pao-ch'iung; translation abruptly ended.

552 (3rd yr Ta-pao [T'ien-pao]; 1st yr Ch'eng-sheng)
(53 years old)
[January 1: Hou Ching proclaimed himself emperor.]
Returned to Nanking at invitation of Hou Ching.
[April 28: Hou Ching forced by Wang Seng-pien and Ch'en Pa-hsien to flee Nanking.]
[May 26: General Wang Seng-pien received the corpse of Hou Ching in Nanking.]
[December 13: Hsiao I proclaimed emperor (Yüan) and capital moved to Chiang-ling.]

552-53 (1st-2nd yr Ch'eng-sheng)
Pursued translation activities under the reign of Emperor Yüan at the Cheng-kuan temple in Nanking. Translated the *Suvarṇa-prabhāsa-sūtra* (*Chin kuang-ming ching*) with over twenty monks, including Yüan-ch'an, at the Cheng-kuan temple and at Yang Hsiung's residence in the Ch'ang-fan region of Nanking.

554 (3rd yr Ch'eng-sheng)
(55 years old)
Second month (March 19-April 17): Traveled to Yüchang and visited the Pao-t'ien temple where he met Ching-shao.
Translated the *Mi-lo hsia sheng ching* (Sūtra of Maitreya's Descent [from Heaven]) and the *Jen wang pan-jo ching* (Sūtra of the Perfection of Wisdom of the Benevolent King) at the Pao-t'ien temple, assisted by eleven monks, including Hui-hsien.
Moved to the Mei-yeh temple in Hsin-wu.
Translated the *Chiu shih i-chi* (Commentary on the Theory of Nine Consciousnesses) in 2 *ch.* at the Mei-yeh temple.
Moved to Shih-hsing where he allegedly translated the *Ta-sheng ch'i hsin lun* (but this text was allegedly translated in 553-54 according to the colophon and in 550 according to the LTSPC and the KYL).

555 (4th yr Ch'eng-sheng; 1st yr Chao-t'ai; 1st yr Ta-ting)
[February 7: Death of Hsiao I. Hsiao Ch'a proclaimed emperor.]
Translated the *Sui-hsiang lun chung shih-liu li shu* (a commentary on the *Abhidharma-kośa* attributed to Guṇamati) in 555-56.
[November: Death of Wang Seng-pien. Hsiao Fang-chih proclaimed emperor.]

557 (Ch'en dynasty: 1st yr Yung-ting; 3rd yr Chao-t'ai)
(58 years old)

Probably escorted to Nan-k'ang in Kiangsi by Hsiao Po before the third month (April 15-May 13) when Hsiao Po was killed.

October 16: Completed the translation of *Wu-shang i ching* (*Anuttarāśraya-sūtra*)(Supreme Foundation Sūtra) at the Ching-t'u temple in Nan-k'ang, sponsored by Governor Liu Wen-t'o.

[November 16: Ch'en Pa-hsien proclaimed emperor.]

558 (2nd yr Yung-ting)

(59 years old)

Seventh month (July 31-August 29): Returned to Yüchang.

Translated the *Shih-pa k'ung lun* at the Hsi-yin temple in Yüchang.

Visited Lin-ch'uan (Kiangsi) and Chin-an (Fukien).

At Lin-ch'uan, translated the *Madhyānta-vibhāga* and perhaps also the *Wei-shih lun* (Treatise on Consciousness-Only).

At Chin-an, probably met Seng-tsung, Fa-chun, Chih-wen, Hui-jen, Hui-k'ai, Fa-jen, Hui-kuang, and Fa-t'ai (or at Liang-an in 563).

Translated the *Ch'eng lun shih i* (An Explanation of Correct Doctrines) at the Fo-li temple in Chin-an.

559 (3rd yr Yung-ting)

(60 years old)

Desired to set sail for Malaysia but was dissuaded by disciples.

561 (2nd yr T'ien-chia)

(62 years old)

Translated the *Saṃdhinirmocana* either at the Chien-tsao temple or at the Ssu-t'ien-wang temple in Liang-an.

Probably began translating the *Mahāyāna-saṃgraha* at the Chien-tsao temple under the patronage of Governor Wang Fang-she.

562 (3rd yr T'ien-chia)

Continued translating the *Mahāyāna-saṃgraha*.

Ninth month (September 17-October 16) or November 7 (Ui): Set sail for India from Liang-an.

563 (4th yr T'ien-chia)

Twelfth month (January 10-February 9): Boat driven back to south China.

Resided at the Chih-chih temple in Governor Ouyang Wei's residence at Kwangchow.

Completed the translation of the *Mahāyāna-saṃgraha* under Governor Ouyang Wei's patronage, assisted by Hui-k'ai and Seng-jen.

Probably began translating the *Wei-shih lun* or revised it at this time.

After death of Ouyang Wei, received sponsorship of his son Ouyang Ho.

564-68 (5th yr T'ien-chia to 2nd yr Kuang-ta)

Active translation period at the Chih-chih temple: *Vajracchedikā*, *Kuang-i fa-men ching*, *Lu erh shih erh ming liao lun* (a treatise composed by the Sammitiya Vinaya master Buddhatrāta), *Wu-hsiang lun* (*Chuan shih lun*, *San wu-hsing lun*, and *Hsien-shih lun*), the *Abhidharma-kośa*, and Vasubandhu's biography.

568 (2nd yr Kuang-ta)

Sixth month (July 10-August 8): Attempted suicide in mountains north of Canton but was restrained by his disciples and Ouyang Ho's guards.

Resided at Wang-yüan temple in Kwangchow, though urged by his disciples to return to Nanking for security.

Refused invitation to court by Emperor Wen. Court monks memorialized that his teachings were dangerous to the government.

September 18: Death of favorite disciple, Hui-kai (518-68).

Continued translation of the *Abhidharma-kośa*.

Became very ill.

569 (1st yr T'ai-chien)

February 12: Death of Paramārtha at the age of seventy.

February 13: Cremated. Stūpa constructed at Ch'ao-ting near Canton.

February 15: Seng-tsung, Fa-chun, and other disciples returned to Mount Lu in Kiangsi to disseminate his work.

APPENDIX B

Major Works Attributed to Paramārtha

1. *Shih ch'i ti-lun*: HKSC; KYL 538b11-12; NTL 266a24; LTSPC 99a4; KC 36412-14. Date: 550, HKSC, LTSPC, KYL, NTL; 548-54, KC. No. of *chüan*: 5. Place: Fu-ch'un, HKSC, LTSPC, KYL, NTL; Ch'eng-kuan temple, KC. Patron: Lu Yüan-che. Other information: Translated with Pao-ch'iung and 20 others.

2. *Chin-kuang ming ching* (*Suvarṇa-prabhāsa-sūtra*): HKSC; KC 364c13; KYL 538a27; NTL 266a22 and 314b4-5; FC 115a18. Date: 552-54, HKSC; 552, LTSPC; 554, KC; 553, Pao-kuei; Ch'en, FC, NTL. No. of *chüan*: 7, FC, NTL, KC, KYL; 6, CT. Place: Cheng-kuan temple (Nanking), HKSC, NTL, KC, KYL, KSC; Yang Hsiung's house, NTL, KYL. Other information: Translated with Yüan-ch'an and 20 others.

3. *She ta-sheng lun* (*Mahāyāna-saṃgraha*), T.1593.31: HKSC; LTSPC 87c21; FC 141c6-7 and 141c12-13; NTL 273b8 and 294c10-13; KYL 545b24; KC 364c21-27. Date: 563, LTSPC, HKSC, NTL, KYL; Ch'en, FC, NTL. No. of *chüan*: 3. Place: Kuangchou, NTL, FC, YT, CT; Chih-chih temple, NTL. Patron: Ouyang Ho. Other information:—*shih lun*, 12 *chüan*, text, FC, CT, YT (and 10 and 15 *chüan* are listed); 15 *chüan*, NTL, KYL.

4. *Kuang i fa-men ching*, T.97.1: HKSC; LTSPC 87c17; FC 116b22; KYL 545c10. Date: 562-63, HKSC; Ch'en, NTL; 563, KYL. No. of *chüan*: 1. Place: Chih-chih temple, HKSC, KYL; Chin-an-fo-li temple, FC, CT. Patron: Ouyang Wei.

5. *Wei-shih lun*, T.1589.31: HKSC; FC 141c16; LTSPC 88a12; NTL 27c7; KYL 545c5; KC 365a5. Date: 562-63, HKSC; Ch'en, FC. No. of *chüan*: 1. Place: Chih-chih temple. Patron: Ouyang Wei. Other information:—*wen-i-ho*, LTSPC, NTL. LTSPC cites it as 1 *chüan*.

6. *Chü-she lun* (*Abhidharma-kośa*), T.1559.29: HKSC; LTSPC 87c19 and 88a4, a15; FC 142b6; NTL 273b6-7, 17; KYL 545c16-18; KC 364c24. Date:

564, KYL; Ch'en, FC. No. of *chüan*: 16, LTSPC, NTL, KC, KYL; 22, FC, YT, CT. Place: Chih-chih temple, HKSC; Lin-chuan, LTSPC, KYL. Patron: Ouyang Ho.

7. *Chin-kang po-jo po-lo-mi ching* (*Vajracchedikā-prajñāpāramitā-sūtra*), T.237.8: LTSPC 87c15 and 88a4, a16, 88b7-8; NTL 273b2, 274a6; KC 364c23, c29; KYL 545b20, 546a1, and 546c1-3. Date: 562, Ui; Ch'en, KC, KYL. No. of *chüan*: 1. Other information:—*shu-ho*, 11 *chüan*, LTSPC, NTL.—*lun*, 1 *chüan*, KYL, KC, LTSPC. NTL does not give the number of *chüan*.

8. *Wu-shang i ching*, T.669.16: LTSPC 87c13 and 88a18 (commentary); FC 115c5; NTL 273a29; KC 364c22; KYL 538b1-2. Date: 558, LTSPC, NTL; Ch'en, KC; 557, KYL (based on colophon). No. of *chüan*: 2. Place: Ching-t'u temple (Nank'ang), LTSPC, NTL; Kuangchou, FC; P'ing-ku prefecture, KYL. Patron: Liu Wen-t'o. Other information:—*shu*, 4 *chüan*, LTSPC.

9. *Chieh-chieh ching*, T.677.16: LTSPC 87c14 and 88a17 (commentary); FC 120a17; NTL 273b1; KC 364c23; KYL 545b21. Date: 561, LTSPC; Ch'en, FC, NTL, KC. No. of *chüan*: 1. Place: Chien-tsao temple in Liang-an. Other information:—*shu* in 4 *chüan*, LTSPC, NTL.

10. *Lü erh shih erh ming liao lun*, T.1461.24, composed by Sammitiya Vinaya master Buddhatrāta: LTSPC 88a5; FC 140a15 and 142b9; NTL 273b19; KYL 545c14-15. Date: Ch'en. No. of *chüan*: 1. Other information: Also called *Ming-liao-lun*, HKSC, LTSPC, NTL, KYL, YT.

11. *A p'i t'an ching*, T.1482.24.458. Date: Ch'en. No. of *chüan*: 9, LTSPC, NTL, KC; 2, KYL, FC, YT. Other information:—*lun*, 2 *chüan*, written in Ch'en, FC, YT, NTL.

12. *Nieh-pan ching pen yu chin wu ke lun*, T.1528.26, composed by Vasubandhu: LTSPC 99a7; KC 364c16; NTL 266a28, 273b20, and 295b28-c1; FC 141a14; KYL 538b3 and 546a2. Date: 550, KYL; 548-54, KC; Ch'en, FC, NTL. No. of *chüan*: 1. Place: Kuangchou. Other information: *Pen yu chin we lun*: LTSPC; *Ta nieh-pan ching lun*: FC, CT (1 *ch*.), NTL, KYL (1 *ch*.); *Pen yu wu lun*: KYL (*Liang*); *Nieh-pan pen yu chin wu lun*: NTL (Ch'en).

13. *I chiao ching lun*, T.1529.26, composed by Vasubandhu: LTSPC 88a6, 115a4, and 120a7; KYL 545b2; FC 143c25; NTL 273b21 and 336a12; KC 365a1. Date: Ch'en. No. of *chüan*: 1. Other information: Listed as an "apocryphal" text, NTL.

14. *Chüeh ting tsang lun*, T.1548.30, part of *Yogācārabhūmi* by Asaṅga: KYL 538b5. Date: Liang. No. of *chüan*: 3.

15. *Chuan shih lun*, T.1587.31, translation and exegesis of Vasubandhu's *Triṃśikā-kārikās*: KYL 545c4. Date: Ch'en. No. of *chüan*: 1. Other information: Published together with the *Hsien-shih-lun* and extracted from the WHL, KYL.

16. *Chung pien fen-pieh lun*, T.1599.31, *Madhyānta-vibhāga* by Vasubandhu: LTSPC 88a3; FC 141b3; NTL 273b15; KC 364c28. Date: Ch'en.

No. of *chüan*: 3, LTSPC, FC, YT, NTL, KC, KYL; 2 , CT. Place: Lin-ch'uan. Other information:—*shu* in 3 *chüan*, NTL.

17. *Fo-hsing lun*, T.1610.31: LTSPC 87c22 and 88a14; NTL 273b10, c9 and 295a11; KC 364c26; KYL 545c1. Date: Ch'en, LTSPC, NTL, KYL, KC. No. of *chüan*: 4, LTSPC, NTL, KC, KYL. Other information:—*i* in 3 *chüan*, LTSPC, NTL.

18. *Shih pa k'ung lun*, T.1616.31, attributed to Nāgārjuna: NTL 273b14; KC 365a3; KYL 545b23. Date: Ch'en. No. of *chüan*: 1, YT, CT, KC, KYL; 3, NTL. Other information: LTSPC: *Ta k'ung lun*, 3 *chüan*; translated at Yü-chang, Hsi-yin temple.

19. *San wu-hsing lun*, T.1617.31.867: LTSPC 88a7; FC 141b10; NTL 273b22; KC 365a1; KYL 545c7; TCL 406c13. Date: Ch'en. No. of *chüan*: 1, LTSPC; 2, KC, KYL. Other information: KYL: extracted from the WHL. See also no. 15, *Chuan shih lun*, above.

20. *Hsien shih lun*, T.1618.31: KYL 545c3; TCL 407b2. Date: not known. Other information: Does not appear in LTSPC, FC, YT, CT, NTL, KC, or HKSC. KYL: An excerpt from the WHL; became a separate text during Ch'en. TCL: Misidentifies translator as Hsüan-tsang. See nos. 15 and 19 above.

21. *Wu hsiang ssu ch'en lun*, T.1619.31: NTL 273c6, 295b19-21, and 321b7; KC 365a4; KYL 545c8. Date: Ch'en. No. of *chüan*: 1. Other information: *Kuan so yüan lun*: NTL, KYL.

22. *Chieh chüan lun*, T.1620.31: NTL 273c5, 295c23, and 321c6; KC 365a4; KYL 545c9. Date: Ch'en. No. of *chüan*: 1.

23. *Ju shih lun*, T.1633.32: LTSPC 88a18 (commentary); FC 141b12; NTL 266a27, b1; KC 364c15. Date: Ch'en, LTSPC, FC, YT, NTL; 548-54, KC; 550, Ui. No. of *chüan*: 1, YT, KYL; 2, FC. Place: Fu-ch'un. Patron: Lu Yüan-che. Other information: *Fan chih lun*, CT says Ch'en, 1 *chüan*. NTL:—*shu*, Ch'en, 3 *chüan*.

24. *Sui hsiang lun*, T.1641.32, *Lakṣaṇānusāra-śāstra*, a commentary on the *Abhidharma-kośa*, attributed to Guṇamati: LTSPC 88a8, a20; FC 141b18; NTL 273b25, c19; KC 365a2; KYL 545c19. Date: Ch'en. No. of *chüan*: 1, LTSPC, KC, KYL; 2, CT. Place: Shih-hsing. Other information: LTSPC, NTL: both list —*chung-shih-liu-ti-shu*. LTSPC, NTL, KC: list —*ch'iu-na*. Ui: Tibetan text by the same title is attributed to Pūrṇavardhana; attribution to Guṇamati is wrong.

25. *Fo shuo li shih a-pi-t'an lun*, *Loka-utsthanābhidharma-śāstra*, T.1644.32. Date: 559, LTSPC, KYL; Ch'en, YT, CT; 558, NTL. No. of *chüan*: 10. Other information: LTSPC, NTL: omit the final word, *lun*.

26. *Ssu ti lun*, T.1647.32: LTSPC 87c22 and 88a19; FC 142b8; NTL 273b11, c17; KC 364c26; KYL 545c22. Date: Ch'en. No. of *chüan*: 4. Place: Nan-k'ang, Kuangchou. Other information: *shu* in 3 *chüan*, NTL. "Composed by Vasuvarman," KYL.

27. *Pao-hsing wang cheng lun*, T.1656.32: LTSPC 88a9; FC 141b23; NTL

273b26; KC 365a3; KYL 545c6. Date: Ch'en, LTSPC, FC, CT, NTL, KYL. No. of *chüan*: 1, LTSPC, FC, CT, KC, KYL. Other information: Sanskrit title, *Ārya-ratnāvalī*, attributed to Nāgārjuna.

28. *Ta tsung ti hsüan wen pen lun*, T.1669.32. Date: not known. Not listed in any catalogue or index. Perhaps wrongly attributed to Paramārtha.

29. *Shih-pa pu lun*, T.2032.49: LTSPC 99a7 and 88a17 (commentary); NTL 266a28 and 273c2; KC 364c15-16 and 365a5; KYL 545c23. Date: 550, LTSPC, NTL; Ch'en, KC, KYL. No. of *chüan*: 1. Place: Fu-ch'un. Patron: Lu Yüan-che. Other information: May be the same text as the *Pu chih i lun*, no. 30 below.

30. *Pu chih i lun*, T.2032.49. See no. 29 above. LTSPC lists *Chih-pu-lun*.

31. *P'o-sou-p'an-tou fa-shih chuan*, T.2049.50: LTSPC 88a21; NTL 273c20; KC 365a6-7; KYL 545c24. Date: Ch'en. No. of *chüan*: 1. Other information: Biography of Vasubandhu.

32. *Chin ch'i shih lun*, T.2137.54.1245, *Suvarṇa-saptiti* of the *Sāṃkhya-kārikā* composed by Iśvarakṛṣṇa: LTSPC 88a3; NTL 273b16; KC 364c28; KYL 545c25-26. Date: Ch'en. No. of *chüan*: 2, LTSPC, KC, KYL; 3, YT, NTL. Other information: NTL and KC list another title, *Seng-ch'ü-lun*, in 3 *chüan*.

APPENDIX C

She-lun and Ti-lun Lineage

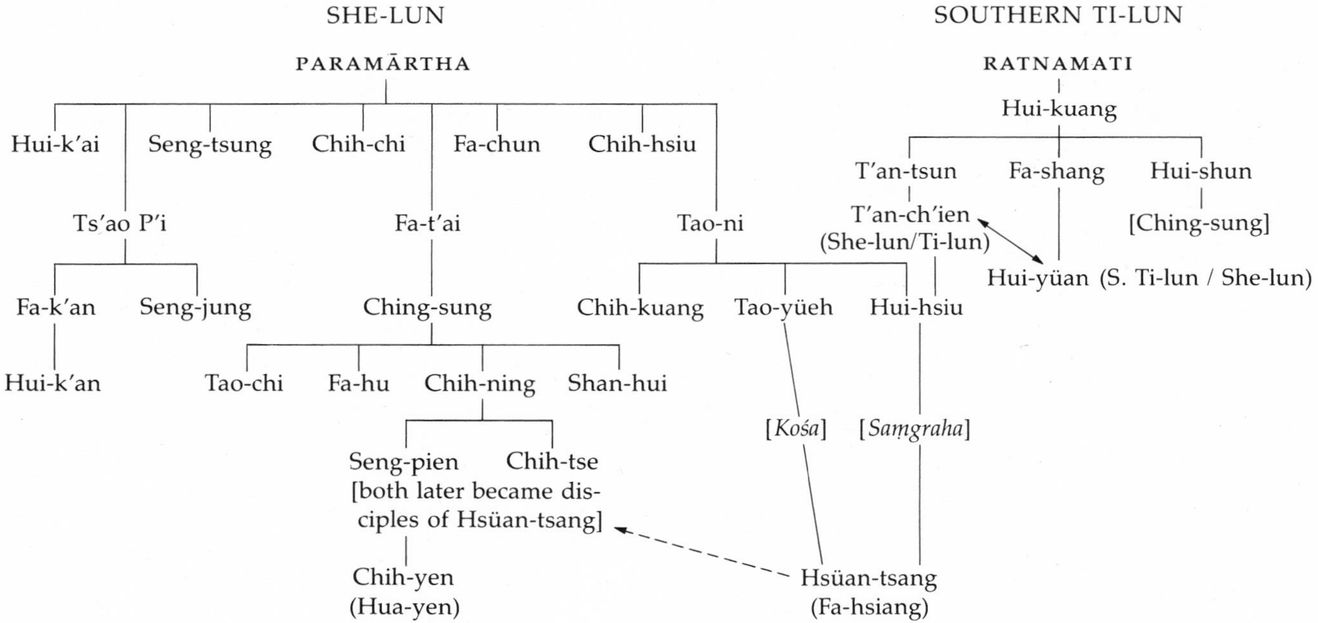

Reference Matter

Abbreviations

AFM	*The Awakening of Faith in Mahāyāna* (Ta-sheng ch'i hsin lun)
CCC	*Chieh-chieh ching*
CSL	*Chuan shih lun*
CTTL	*Chüeh ting tsang lun*
CWSL	*Ch'eng wei-shih lun*
FC	*(Fa-ching) Chung ching mu-lu*
HKSC	*Hsü kao seng chuan*
HSL	*Hsien shih lun*
HYSCL	*Hsien-yang sheng-chiao lun*
KC	*Ku-chin i ching t'u chi*
KSC	*Kao seng chuan*
KYL	*K'ai-yüan shih chiao mu-lu*
LTSPC	*Li-tai san-pao chi*
NTL	*Ta t'ang nei tien lu*
ŚDS	*Śrīmālādevī-sūtra*
SPKL	*Shih-pa k'ung lun*
SWHL	*San wu-hsing lun*
T	*Taishō shinshū daizōkyō*
TCL	*Ta-chou k'an ting chung-ching mu-lu*
WHL	*Wu-hsiang lun*
YT	*(Yen-tsung) Chung ching mu-lu*
ZZ	*Dai nihon zokuzōkyō*

Notes

Introduction

1. O'Brien, "A Chapter on Reality from the *Madhyāntavibhāgaśāstra,*" p. 283.

Chapter 1

1. Reynolds and Capps, eds., *The Biographical Process*, p. 3.

2. *Kao seng chuan* (KSC) and *Hsü kao seng chuan* (HKSC), T.2059.50 and T.2060.50, respectively. The KSC was compiled by Hui-chao (497-554) of the Liang dynasty in approximately A.D. 530. It is a record of approximately 257 eminent monks and 243 of their assistants or disciples for the years A.D. 67 to 519. This collection of biographies served as a model for all subsequent biographical collections. The HKSC, its immediate successor, was compiled by Tao-hsüan (596-667) of the T'ang dynasty in approximately 645. It is a record of 340 eminent monks and 60 of their assistants from A.D. 520 to 641. Paramārtha's biography is included in HKSC.

3. Yūki Reimon, *Seshin yuishiki no kenkyū*, p. 9, says that by the end of Sui and beginning of T'ang, the She-lun school of Buddhism founded by Paramārtha had been completely transformed into Hua-yen.

4. Chattopadhyaya, *Early History of North India*, pp. 227-28.

5. The name Mihirakula is equivalent to the Iranian name Mithra (Sanskrit: Mitra). He may have been the first of the Maitraka dynasty, which ruled Valabhī from the early sixth century. Much of Mihirakula's life and political activities remains obscure. In both Mandasor stone inscriptions Yaśodharman is described as the supreme sovereign over lands that even the Hūṇas and Gupta rulers could not conquer and the one to whom Mihirakula paid homage, dated A.D. 533-34 (Fleet, *Corpus*

Inscriptionum, 3: 142-58). The Gwalior inscription mentions the fifteenth year of Mihirakula's reign.

6. Watters, trans., *On Yuan Chwang's Travels in India*, 1: 289.

7. If the fifteenth year of Mihirakula's reign is 526-27 and he is said to have paid homage to Yaśodharman in 533, then his reign must have ended some time between 526-27 and 533.

8. Filliozat, *Political History of India*, trans. Spratt, pp. 180-81. Yaśodharman may have participated in the war against Mihirakula as a vassal of Bālāditya II. On a separate occasion in 517 Bālāditya II may have attempted to wage war against Mihirakula while the latter was in a confrontation in Kashmir. Unsuccessful at that time, Bālāditya may have attempted a later attack in Magadha after Yaśodharman's victory. Some historians deny that there were two defeats of Mihirakula. See Goyal, *A History of the Imperial Guptas*, pp. 350-53.

9. Filliozat, p. 176.

10. "Funan" is the modern Peking alteration of the Middle Chinese Bu-nam, reproducing the Old Khmer Bnam, and means "mountain," referring to the kings' pretensions that they were *śaila-rāja*, "kings of the mountain" or divine rulers of the mythical Mount Sumeru. See Coedès, *Les États Hindouisés d'Indochine*, 2nd ed., p. 74.

11. The monks Mandra and Saṃghapāla have translations listed in the *Ku-chin i ching t'u chi* (KC), T.2151.55.364b14-20 and 364b21-c6 respectively. Mandra translated three texts: the *Pao-yün ching*, the *Fa-chieh ti hsing wu fen-pieh ching*, and the *Wen-shu-shih-li shuo pan-jo po-lo-mo ching*, totaling eleven *chüan*. Saṃghapāla translated eleven texts, including the *A-yü-wang ching* (Sūtra on King Aśoka), the *P'u-sa tsang ching*, and the *Wen-shu-shih-li shuo pan-jo po-lo-mi ching* (perhaps a collaboration with his compatriot Mandra). At the end of Paramārtha's biography (HKSC 2060.50.431a4-6) is appended a note on a Ch'en translation of the *Ta-sheng pao-yün ching* in eight *chüan* by a Funan monk named Subodhi, mentioning that Subodhi's text is slightly different from the Liang translation by Mandra in seven *chüan*. Subodhi's translation is also listed in the KC, 365c2-5. In Saṃghapāla's biography (HKSC 426a3-b12) it says that the monks Mandra and Saṃghapāla collaborated on all three of the texts that the KC attributes to Mandra. There is no separate biography for Mandra in HKSC.

12. King Jayavarman and his son Rudravarman, who was the last king of Funan, are mentioned in the *Liang shu* (Peking, 1972), *ch.* 54, pp. 789-90. See Coedès, *Les États Hindouisés d'Indochine*, pp. 104-5, for the details of the rise and decline of Rudravarman's power. See also Malleret, *La Culture du Fou-nan*, p. 369, and Majumdar, *Kambuja-deśa*, p. 34.

13. HKSC 2060.50.429c11-12, 20-21.

14. See Strickmann, "On the Alchemy of T'ao Hung-ching," esp. pp.

155-58. Wu also supported the great Taoist scholar T'ao Hung-ching who was reconstructing and editing the Taoist canon at Mao Shan.

15. The practice of "abandoning the body" (*she-shen*) was popular among the ruling class from the time of Southern Ch'i, but Wu of Liang was the first emperor to engage in it. Wu first "abandoned his body" in 527, when he was sixty-four years of age; for four days he acted as a servant at the T'ung-t'ai temple and granted amnesty to prisoners. In 529 he again performed this practice at the T'ung-t'ai temple, this time as a temple craftsman in a commoner's garment. He lectured on the *Nirvāṇa-sūtra* and ransomed himself for one million copper cash. This period lasted seventeen days. The third "abandonment of the body" took place in 546 at both the Fa-chia and T'ung-t'ai temples, lasting thirty-seven days. The last occurrence of this practice took place a year later (547) and lasted forty-three days. Wu was criticized: "In the first year of T'ai-ch'ing, Emperor Wu, by abandoning his body . . . forgot he was Emperor under Heaven." See Mori Mikisaburō, *Ryō no butei*, pp. 144-48, 166-69, for further discussion of Emperor Wu's zeal in undertaking this practice and aristocratic opposition to Wu's actions. The idea of this practice was given to Wu from Saṃghapāla's translation of the *Sūtra on King Aśoka* (T.2043.50).

16. Ch'en, *Buddhism in China*, p. 126.

17. See Miyakawa Hisayuki, *Rikuchōshi kenkyū*, pp. 138-43, for an analysis of the downfall of the Liang and the rise to power of Ch'en Pa-hsien.

18. See Kawakatsu Yoshio, "La décadence de l'aristocratie chinoise sous les Dynasties du Sud."

19. See Hou Ching's biography, *Liang shu, ch.* 56, pp. 833-67; *Nan shih* (Peking, 1975), *ch.* 80, pp. 1993-2018.

20. Miyakawa, *Rikuchōshi kenkyū*, p. 147.

21. For an analysis of the conditions contributing to Hou Ching's uprising see two articles by Kawakatsu Yoshio: "Kokei no ran to Nanchō no kahei keizai" and the previously cited "La décadence de l'aristocratie chinoise."

22. According to Yen Chih-t'ui, the death of Hsiao T'ung, heir-apparent to Emperor Wu, in 531 sowed the seeds of trouble for the Liang. Because the line of succession was interrupted, all the sons felt equally entitled to the throne. See Dien, *Pei ch'i shu 45: Biography of Yen Chih-t'ui*, p. 6.

23. *Nan shih, ch.* 80, p. 2016.

24. See Wang Seng-pien's biography in *Liang shu, ch.* 45, pp. 623-37; and Ch'en Pa-hsien's biography, *Ch'en shu* (Peking, 1972), pp. 1-43. For the campaign, see *Liang shu, ch.* 56, p. 861, in which Hou Ching's defeat is described, and *ch.* 45, pp. 627-29; also *Ch'en shu, ch.* 1, pp. 3-6.

25. Both *Liang shu, ch.* 56, p. 862, and *Nan shih, ch.* 80, p. 2016, con-

tain vivid descriptions of Hou Ching's death and the destruction of his corpse; also see *Liang shu, ch.* 5, p. 125.

26. For the date see *Liang shu, ch.* 5, p. 131.

27. See Kawakatsu, "La décadence de l'aristocratie chinoise," p. 18.

28. *Liang shu, ch.* 5, p. 133.

29. *Chou shu,* compiled by Ling-hu Te-fen (583-666) in 50 *ch.* (Peking, 1971), esp. *ch.* 2, p. 36; *Liang shu, ch.* 5, p. 135.

30. *Liang shu, ch.* 6, pp. 143-44.

31. HKSC 2060.50.429c6-431a6. All biographical data presented on the figure of Paramārtha are based upon this account, unless otherwise noted. At one time there were three biographies of Paramārtha, one also by Seng-tsung and one by Chiu-hsiu; only Ts'ao P'i's fragments remain and form the basis for the account given in the HKSC. See HKSC 2060.50.430b16 and 432a4 for the acknowledgment of the other lost biographies. Ui Hakujū has analyzed Paramārtha's biography in great detail (*Indo tetsugaku kenkyū,* 6: 5-130); and his work is the single most important secondary source in my analysis of the HKSC. For a partial French translation see Takakusu Junjiro, "La Sāṃkhya-kārikā."

32. Ujjain, in Malwa province (present-day Madhya Pradesh), is twenty miles west of the Chambal River and approximately 250 miles west of Valabhī. See the preface to *She ta-sheng lun,* T.1593.31.112c4, for the Bhāradvāja designation of Paramārtha's *gotra.*

33. HKSC 2060.50.429c10-11.

34. HKSC 2060.50.429c12-13. The imperial escort of the Funan ambassador back to his own country probably took place early in the Ta-t'ung era. See *Liang shu, ch.* 3, p. 79 (Peking; Chung-hua shu-chü, 1972), where a Funan envoy is mentioned as having brought tribute to the emperor in the autumn, seventh month, of the first year Ta-t'ung (535). The date of Paramārtha's arrival in Nanking, 546, is at the end of the Ta-t'ung reign.

35. HKSC 2060.50.429c12-16.

36. *Li-tai san-pao chi* (LTSPC), 2034.49.106a3-12.

37. See note 34 for tentative dating.

38. *Ta-sheng ch'i-hsin lun* (CHL), T.1666.32.575a17-22. The CHL and its colophon, allegedly by Chih-k'ai (also known as Hui-k'ai), are probably an apocryphal text, not translated by Paramārtha. The debate on the authorship and translator of the *Ta-sheng ch'i-hsin lun* has continued for almost fifty years among Japanese Buddhologists. Mochizuki Shinkō, in one of the classic studies, "Daijō kishinron" (1934), gives the documental discrepancies among historical sources on the *Ch'i-hsin lun,* namely, that the colophon attributed to Hui-k'ai is a forgery, that the translation style does not agree with Paramārtha's, and that Fa-ching's catalogue (compiled in 594) already doubted the authenticity of the text. Fa-ching remarks that it is not listed in Paramārtha's collection of

works. Mochizuki suggests that the *Ch'i-hsin lun* may be a synthesis of both Northern and Southern Ti-lun and therefore in its text a compromise on the issue of a pure or impure *ālaya*. Ui (*Indo tetsugaku*, 6: 62-64) gives additional arguments for doubting Paramārtha as the translator. According to Ui, the colophon to the *Ch'i-hsin lun* attributed to Hui-k'ai could not have been written by him in the third year, Ch'eng-sheng (554), because Hui-k'ai did not become Paramārtha's disciple until the fourth year, T'ien chia (563). Furthermore, the colophon dates the translation of the *Ch'i-hsin lun* as third and fourth years of Ch'eng-sheng, but the LTSPC and *K'ai-yuan shih chiao mu-lu* (KYL) give fourth year, T'ai-ching (550). In addition, the *Ssu lun hsüan-i* states that the text was composed by a Northern Ti-lun master. On the other hand, Tokiwa Daijō, *Shina bukkyō no kenkyū*, 2: 38, thinks the *Ch'i-hsin lun* does express Paramārtha's ideas, viewing the She-lun and Northern Ti-lun schools as similar in content (2nd ed., p. 104); Mochizuki thinks that She-lun, Southern Ti-lun, and the *Ch'i-hsin lun* share doctrinal affinity.

39. KYL 2154.55.538b24-27.

40. LTSPC, citing Pao-kuei's introduction to the *Suvarṇaprabhāsa*, gives the date, "the first year of T'ai-ch'ing," 547. Cf. T.2034.49.106a10. According to Ui, *Indo tetsugaku*, 6: 13, this must be a scribe's error since all other sources give "the second year of T'ai-ch'ing."

41. The only citation for *Pao-yün tien* in the palace of Emperor Wu of Liang is in Paramārtha's biography. However, a *Chung-yün tien* is mentioned in the biographies of T'an-luan (HKSC 2060.50.470a29), Pao-ch'iung (479a20), Seng-ta (553a7), and Hui-yün (650b17) as the place where Emperor Wu of Liang invited them to lecture on Buddhist doctrine. In Seng-ming's biography (693b et passim) miraculous Buddhist statues are housed in the *Chung-yün tien*. The *Pao-yün tien* may be a scribe's error for *Chung-yün tien*, or the name of the palace temple may have been changed during the Late Liang to *Pao-yün*, perhaps in commemoration of the *sūtra* translated by Mandra and Saṃghapāla of Liang. The emperor himself lectured on *sūtras*, and eminent monks attended his sermons at the *Chung-yün tien*. Cf. *Liang shu, ch.* 3, p. 96.

42. The biography of Pao-ch'iung is recorded in the HKSC (478c6-479c20), but it does not mention the *Shih-ch'i ti-lun* or Paramārtha.

43. The *Treatise on the Seventeen Bodhisattva Stages* (*Shih-ch'i ti-lun*) was a commentary on a *sūtra* by the same name, consisting of part of the *Bodhisattvabhūmi*. The *Yogācārabhūmi*, of which the *Bodhisattvabhūmi* is a part, discusses seventeen stages to Nirvāṇa, including the stages of Pratyeka-buddha and Śrāvaka (seventeen stages altogether). Sakaino claims that Paramārtha's translation could not have been complete if one looks at the number of *chüan* corresponding to that part of the *Bodhisattvabhūmi* in Hsüan-tsang's translation (Sakaino, *Shina bukkyō seishi*, 2nd. ed., 1972, p. 707). The date of Paramārtha's move to Fu-

ch'un is given in the *Yü-chia lun chi* (T.1828.42.311b28) by Tun-lun. According to Paramārtha's biography of the Yogācārin master, Vasubandhu (T.2049.50.188c13-16), Maitreya descended from the Tuṣita heaven and lectured on the *Sūtra of the Seventeen Bodhisattva Stages* for Asaṅga's edification. Prabhākāramitra's biography mentions that Śīlabhadra transmitted a text titled *Shih-ch'i ti-lun* (HKSC 2060.50.440a3). In K'uei-chi's biography of Hsüan-tsang (*Ta-tzu-en ssu san-tsang fa-shih chuan*) (T.2053.50.222c4-6) it is also said that K'uei-chi and Hsüan-tsang vowed to travel west, taking the *Shih-ch'i ti-lun* with them, in order to interpret points of controversy.

44. KYL 2154.55.538b11-14.

45. HKSC 2060.50.429c25.

46. *Ta t'ang nei tien lu* (NTL), 2149.55.266a24-25, and LTSPC 2034.49.99a4. The LTSPC also gives the same date and place of translation for *Ta-sheng ch'i-hsin lun*, though this is almost certainly not one of Paramārtha's translations. The KC also lists this text (364c12-14).

47. In the year 552 Liang was in the first year of Ch'eng-sheng, but the HKSC is using Northern Ch'i's Dynastic regnal titles. Some manuscripts noted in the *Taishō* (p. 429) use T'ai-pao or Ta-pao, but Ta-pao lasted only one year. If it had continued, the year 552 would have corresponded to the third year of Ta-pao.

48. HKSC 2060.50.429c26-27.

49. There is a story of a monk who starved for over a year to the point of impending death. This period of ruin and shortage of food was the time at the end of Liang when Hou Ching set out to take over south China. Even when someone offered him a bowl of rice with just the slightest trace of pork hidden in it, he would not eat it and go against the laws of vegetarianism, although "his stomach burned like fire" (HKSC 2060.50.481a4-7).

50. Seng-ta's biography (HKSC 2060.50.553a12) says that Hou Ching built two temples on a mountain named T'ien-kuan, but these two temples are not mentioned elsewhere in the HKSC. In T'an-yin's biography (608c6-10) Hou Ching is said to have built two temples, one to the spirits (*shen-hsien*) and later, after his insurrection, the Ta-yen temple, in Yeh-tung. Seng-ming's biography contains a wealth of information on Hou Ching's revolt (especially 692b21-693b24), involving miraculous Buddhist statues with halos and fortune-telling powers. These miracles also occur in the *Chung-yün* quarters during Late Liang and early Ch'en after the death of Hou Ching.

51. *Nan Shih, ch.* 80, p. 2011, relates an interesting story about how a Buddhist monk, before Emperor Wu's overthrow, foretold Hou Ching's violent death. Emperor Wu is then said to have analyzed the name Hou Ching by breaking the two Chinese characters into six characters meaning: "a petty man who will be emperor for one hundred days."

52. LTSPC 2034.49.98c22. Another monk who did translation work at the Cheng-kuan temple was Saṃghapāla, a monk from Funan who was invited to China by Wu of Liang (HKSC 2060.50.426a13).

53. NTL 2149.55.266a22; KYL 2154.55.538a27.

54. KC 2151.55.364c13.

55. Ui cites a Tunhuang manuscript of the composite translation of the *Suvarṇaprabhāsa* (T.664) by Pao-kuei. See *Indo tetsugaku*, 6: 16-18. Other *sūtra* catalogues claim that the *Suvarṇaprabhāsa* was translated by Paramārtha during the Ch'en dynasty; for example, Fa-ching's catalogue (T.2146.55.115a18) and Ching-t'ai's catalogue (T.2148.55.182b6).

56. Ui, *Indo tetsugaku*, 6: 18. Hsüan-tsang's rate of translation was calculated by one Japanese Buddhologist as three *chüan* per week, a rate Paramārtha would have had to match for the above-mentioned translation dates to be correct. See Fukaura Shōbun, "Genjō sanzō zehiron," p. 12.

57. Ui, *Indo tetsugaku*, 6: 19, but no reference is given for this information. See Ching-shao's biography, HKSC 2060.50.480a7-9. Ching-shao met Paramārtha in Yüchang, but it is not clear which trip to Yüchang is meant. Ui says that Ching-shao was forty-seven years old and Paramārtha fifty-six years old (according to the Chinese way of calculating age), which would indicate that Paramārtha met Ching-shao in 554.

58. Ui, *Indo tetsugaku*, 6: 19.

59. T'ang Yung-t'ung, *Han Wei Liang-chin Nan-pei-ch'ao Fo-chiao shih*, pp. 855-67.

60. LTSPC 2034.49.98c24-99a3,a10. The HKSC does not list either the *Mi-lo hsia sheng ching* or the *Jen wang po-jo ching* and its commentary.

61. Ching-shao's biography is listed in the HKSC 2060.50.479c21-480c1. Ching-shao enjoyed the patronage of Emperor Chien-wen and the princes of Shao-ling and Yüeh-yang.

62. See LTSPC 2034.49.99a10; NTL 2149.55.266b3.

63. The *Chiu shih i-chi* is listed in LTSPC 2034.49.99a11, as a translation in the third year, T'ai-ch'ing (549), but this date seems unlikely, because of Hou Ching's rebellion during that year and Paramārtha's flight to Fu-ch'un. If a commentary by that name ever existed, it was probably made in 554 after Paramārtha left Yüchang. Although this commentary is also listed in NTL (2149.55.266b6) with information identical to LTSPC, it is not listed in the HKSC or KYL. The LTSPC must be in error. See Katsumata Shunkyō, *Bukkyō ni okeru shinshikisetsu no kenkyū*, p. 691; Yūki Reimon, "Shina yuishiki shijō ni okeru Ryōga-shi no chii," p. 38.

64. See *Liang shu, ch.* 6, p. 147. Hsiao Po is given the title Grand Guardian in the twelfth month of 556; *Ch'en shu, ch.* 9, p. 158.

65. Ouyang Wei's biography, *Ch'en shu, ch.* 9, pp. 157-59, gives details on the relationship between Ouyang Wei and Hsiao Po.

66. *Liang shu, ch.* 6, p. 148.

67. HKSC 2060.50.430a1-2.

68. This text is listed in LTSPC 2034.49.88a20, without any translation date or attribution to Guṇamati. Another text, entitled *Sui-hsiang lun*, attributed to Guṇamati, is listed in the LTSPC (88a8). Both are catalogued under Ch'en dynastic translations. Either the *Commentary on the Sixteen Truths* was translated earlier than the Ch'en in Shih-hsing, that is, in 555 or 556, or the place of translation is incorrect. The NTL, KC, and KYL all give Guṇamati's *Sui-hsiang lun* as a Ch'en translation (2149.55.273b25; 2151.365a2; 2154.545c19). Probably the *Commentary on the Sixteen Truths* corresponds to the extant translation in the *Taishō*, which is entitled simply the *Sui-hsiang lun*. This text would not be the same as Guṇamati's, which is lost. Ui (*Indo tetsugaku*, 6: 97) does not take a position on whether the two texts *Sui-hsiang lun* and *Sui-hsiang lun chung shih liu ti shu* were translated in Ch'en or in Liang, the latter at Shih-hsing. Probably the text now listed in the *Taishō* is the Late Liang translation at Shih-hsing. The text, now lost, attributed to Guṇamati, was the referred text from the Ch'en dynasty.

69. The *Wu-shang i ching* is a Liang translation even though the LTSPC (T.2034.49.87c13) states it is a Ch'en translation, completed during the second year of Yung-ting. The KYL criticizes the LTSPC dating since there was no third year of Chao-t'ai during the second year of Yung-ting. This regnal date would be equivalent to second year T'ai-p'ing and *first* year Yung-ting. However, on the eighth day, ninth month, of Chao-t'ai, Yung-ting had not been established yet, and therefore neither had the Ch'en dynasty. See KYL 2154.55.538b1-2, 546c25, 596c22-27 (citation from *Wu-shang i ching* colophon).

70. KYL 2154.55.538b1-2. The LTSPC claims the text is a Ch'en translation, completed in the second year Yung-ting (558), at the Ching-t'u temple in Nan-k'ang (2034.49.87c13). The NTL agrees with the LTSPC (2149.55.273a29). The colophon is preserved in part in the KYL (596c20-27). The KYL criticizes the dating methods of the LTSPC, which catalogues texts only up to the fifth year of Ch'eng-sheng (556), the year that Liang was coming to an end. The fifth year Ch'eng-sheng corresponds to the second year Chao-t'ai. In the ninth month of that year the reign was changed to T'ai-p'ing. In the tenth month of the following year (557), the Ch'en dynasty was established. Therefore, the KYL argues, October 16, 557, was still within the Liang dynasty. (Twenty-two days later Ch'en Pa-hsien established his reign, beginning the Yung-ting period.) According to Jikidō Takasaki, the *Wu-shang i ching* may be an adaptation of the *Ratnagotra-vibhāga*. See his essay, "Shindaiyaku Shōdaijōron seshinshaku ni okeru nyoraizō setsu."

71. KYL 2154.55.545c2,5. No translation dates are given, but since Paramārtha moved to Yüchang in the middle of 558 and then to Fukien in 561, these texts were translated within that period. Also see NTL

2149.55.273b15,c7 (lists *Wei-shih lun wen-i ho*), and LTSPC 2034.49.88a3-12 (same information as NTL).

72. Cf. Fa-t'ai's biography, HKSC 2060.50.431a9-12.
73. HKSC 2060.50.503b22-23.
74. HKSC 2060.50.609b19-21.
75. Ui, *Indo tetsugaku*, 6: 24-25.
76. LTSPC 2034.49.88a13; NTL 2149.55.273c8.
77. HKSC 2060.50.430a3.
78. *Chieh-shen-mi-ching shu*, ZZ 34.299b5-12.
79. Ui asserts that Hui-k'ai gives these dates in his colophon to the *She ta-sheng lun*, but no such information appears either in this colophon or in the colophon to the *Ta-sheng wei-shih lun* preserved in the *Taishō*. *Indo tetsugaku*, 6: 20-26.
80. Fa-t'ai's biography, HKSC 2060.50.431c7-9.
81. LTSPC 2034.49.87c21; NTL 2149.55.273b8; KYL 2154.55.545b24.
82. HKSC 2060.50.430a8-9.
83. HKSC 2060.50.430a18-19.
84. HKSC 2060.50.430a23-27.
85. HKSC 2060.50.430a27-b3.
86. HKSC 2060.50.430b4-7.
87. HKSC 2060.50.430b16-19.
88. Hui-k'ai's introduction to *She ta-sheng lun*, T.1593.31.112c22.
89. HKSC 2060.50.430c2-13.

Chapter 2

1. See Appendix B for a listing of all the texts believed to have been translated or composed by Paramārtha. The total number of works now extant in the canon consists of four *sūtras*, totaling five *chüan*; twenty-five *śāstras*, totaling 101 *chüan*. If one includes the *Ta-sheng ch'i hsin lun* then there are twenty-six commentaries totaling 102 *chüan*. In addition, Paramārtha wrote a biography on Vasubandhu in one *chüan* and translated a portion of Iśvarakṛṣṇa's *Sāṃkhya-kārikā* in three *chüan*.
2. The long controversy over the different forms of Yogācāra in China together with the disputes over accuracy in translations vis-a-vis Hsüan-tsang and Paramārtha has produced volumes in Buddhological research. Some of the studies I have found most useful in assessing Paramārtha's contribution to Buddhist thought are: Fukaura Shōbun, "Genjō sanzō zehiron," *Bukkyōgaku kenkyū* (January 1949), pp. 1-18; Ueda Yoshifumi, *Bukkyō shisōshi kenkyū*, esp. pp. 38-64; Yūki Reimon, *Seshin yuishiki no kenkyū*, esp. pp. 145-64; Paul Wilfred O'Brien, "A Chapter on Reality from the *Madhyāntavibhāga śāstra*," *Monumenta Nipponica* 9 (1953): 277-303; and especially Ui Hakujū, *Indo tetsugaku kenkyū*, vol. 6.
3. For discussion of the Yogācārin doctrines that contributed to the formative period of Hua-yen see Kamata Shigeo, *Chūgoku kegon shisōshi no kenkyū*.
4. Good discussions of She-lun and Ti-lun disciples and their lin-

eages are given in Tokiwa Daijō, *Shina bukkyō no kenkyū* (2nd. ed., 1978), 2: 37-44; Sasaki Gesshō, *Shōdaijōron*, pp. 36-52; Katsumata Shunkyō, *Bukkyō ni okeru shinshikisetsu no kenkyū*, pp. 639-89, 767-801.

5. Not all the principal disciples of Paramārtha's lineage are mentioned in this section. A useful chart of monks and references to the HKSC is given in Yoshida Dōkō, "Chūgoku nambokuchō Zui-Tō-sho no Jiron-Shōron no kenkyū shatatsu." Also see Katsumata, *Bukkyō ni okeru shinshikisetsu*, pp. 747-801.

6. HKSC 2060.50.430b10-12. Other monks did accompany Seng-tsung and Fa-chun to Canton, but they are not mentioned in Paramārtha's biography. Some of these others include Hui-k'ai, Fa-jen, Ching-shao, Chih-wen, and Hui-k'uang, who are mentioned in the succeeding section. To the best of my knowledge, no epigraphic data on the stele of Paramārtha exists today, nor could I locate Ch'ao-ting geographically in any of the sources I consulted.

7. HKSC 2060.50.430b8-9.

8. Fa-t'ai's biography: HKSC 2060.50.431a7-432a8.

9. Chih-wen's biography: HKSC 2060.50.609b7-c29.

10. Hui-k'uang's biography: HKSC 2060.50.503b15-c17. Hui-k'uang is said to have been a member of the Ts'ao clan although we do not know if he had any kinship relationship with Ts'ao P'i and Hui-k'ai, also belonging to a Ts'ao clan. Hui-k'uang met Paramārtha at the same time that Ts'ao P'i and Hui-k'ai were at the Chih-chih temple in Canton, after the long journey from Nanking, so a kinship is plausible.

11. HKSC 2060.50.431a19-21.

12. Ching-sung's biography (HKSC 2060.50.501b6-502a25) records his meeting with Fa-t'ai and his course of study, including Paramārtha's major works, *Fo-hsing lun*, *Madhyānta-vibhāga*, *Wu-hsiang lun*, and *Wei-shih lun* and the two compendia, *Mahāyāna-saṃgraha* and the *Abhidharma-kośa*.

13. Hui-shun's biography: HKSC 2060.50.484b3-23.

14. Hui-k'uang's biography, HKSC 2060.50.607b18-608b29.

15. HKSC 2060.50.502a2.

16. Fa-hu's biography (HKSC 2060.50.530b20-c27) mentions his meeting with Ching-sung and his accomplishments in his She-lun studies.

17. Chih-ning's biography (HKSC 2060.50.504c26-505a29) records a dialogue between the master Ching-sung and his disciple Chih-ning in which Chih-ning claims there is no time or reason for studying any other text than the *Saṃgraha*.

18. Tao-chi's biography (HKSC 2060.50.532b14-c27) does not give an account of his meeting with Ching-sung, but in Ching-sung's biography the intense grief of Tao-chi for his master is vividly described. Tao-chi was one of Hsüan-tsang's earliest instructors, while Hsüan-tsang was an adolescent. Cf. Hsüan-tsang's biography (HKSC 2060.50.446c24-27).

19. Shan-hui's biography is recorded in the HKSC 2060.50.688b7-c14. Shan-hui learned the philosophy of the *Saṃgraha* at the P'eng-ch'eng temple, presumably under Ching-sung although it is not indicated in his biography that Ching-sung was his teacher. He also had heard Chi-tsang lecture on the *Lotus sūtra*.

20. See Seng-pien's biography: HKSC 2060.50.540a24-c13. Seng-pien studied under Chih-ning at the Ch'an-ting temple, one of the great centers of She-lun scholarship. His understanding of the *Abhidharma-kośa* was so remarkable that Tao-yüeh (one of the students of Tao-ni, direct disciple of Paramārtha) requested that he lecture on the text. Seng-pien also wrote commentaries on some of Paramārtha's major works, including the *Samgraha, Wei-shih lun,* and *Wu-hsiang lun*. It is also claimed that Seng-pien became Hsüan-tsang's disciple on hearing him discuss the *Abhidharma-kośa* (HKSC 2060.50.447b6-9). This event is difficult to establish, however, since no mention of this meeting occurs in Seng-pien's own biography.

21. According to Chih-tse's biography (HKSC 2060.50.655a19-b6), he met the monk Chih-ning shortly after leaving home to become a monk, when he was twenty years of age. After hearing Chih-ning lecture on the *Saṃgraha*, he had no other aim in life but to continue his studies on the text.

22. See Chih-yen's biography: HKSC 2060.50.602a25-c7. Also see Robert M. Gimello, "Chih-yen and the Foundations of Hua-yen Buddhism" (unpublished Ph.D. dissertation, Columbia University, 1976), for a persuasive argument indicating a teacher-student relationship between Seng-pien and Chih-yen.

23. According to the HKSC, at the time of composition (c. 645), the Ta-ch'an-ting temple had changed its name to Ta-tsung-chih. See Tao-yüeh's biography (T.2060.50.527c13-14).

24. HKSC 2060.50.431b7-9.

25. This dating of Hui-k'ai's materials is according to Ui, *Indo tetsugaku*, 6: 5-6, who does not give the sources for his dates. The *Wei-shih lun* was translated some time after the twelfth month, third year, of T'ien-chia (that is, at the very end of the year 562). The *Saṃgraha* was translated in 563 and lectures on the treatise commenced in 564. The *Kośa* was translated in the fifth year of T'ien-chia or 564. Hence, Ui's series of dates for Hui-k'ai's introductions to these texts follows the order of translation. It is somewhat puzzling that Hui-k'ai allegedly wrote an introduction to the *Kośa* before the text was completely translated because Paramārtha's biography clearly states that Paramārtha continued to translate the *Kośa* after Hui-k'ai's death.

26. HKSC 2060.50.431b24-c2.

27. Fa-k'an's biography: HKSC 2060.50.513a19-c18, esp. 2060.50.513a29.

28. Hui-k'an's biography: HKSC 2060.50.652b11-c3. The biography says that Hui-k'an, after going south of the mountains (*Ling-nan*), that is, to Kwangtung, had a profound enlightenment experience (*shen-wu*) during meditation, after reading some of Paramārtha's writings.

29. See Fa-t'ai's biography: HKSC 2060.50.431c2-a8.

30. HKSC 2060.50.431c14-16.

31. HKSC 2060.50.431c27-28.

32. HKSC 2060.50.432a3-5.

33. Sasaki (*Shōdaijōron*, p. 40) postulates (though without giving textual evidence) that Tao-ni may have received instruction on the *Saṃgraha* from Hui-k'ai.

34. HKSC 2060.50.671b28-29 (Chih-kuang's biography).

35. HKSC 2060.50.527a13-528c3.

36. HKSC (2060.50.527b29) simply gives *Shih pa lun*. This is an allusion to Paramārtha's *Shih pa k'ung lun* (T.1616.31.861), falsely attributed to Nāgārjuna and corresponding to part of the *Madhyānta vibhāga-bhāṣya* by Vasubandhu.

37. The discourse is given in some detail in dialogue form between Tao-yüeh and a group of clerics in the HKSC 2060.50.527b12-c29. Fa-ch'ang's biography, HKSC 2060.50.540c14-541b23; Chih-shou's biography, HKSC 2060.50.614a1-615a24; Seng-pien's biography, HKSC 2060.50. 540a24-c13. Hui-ming has no separate biography but is mentioned in both Hsüan-tsang's and Prabhākāramitra's biographies (455a13 and 440a28-29, respectively).

38. HKSC 2060.50.528a24-b1. Katsumata (*Bukkyō ni okeru shinshikisetsu*), p. 776, gives the complete transliteration for Prabhākāramitra's name.

39. Hui-hsiu's biography, HKSC 2060.50.544b1-545b11.

40. T'an-ch'ien's biography is recorded in HKSC 2060.50.571b12-574b6. For his flight to Nanking see HKSC 572a8-9.

41. T'an-tsun's biography, HKSC 2060.50.484a11-b2. T'an-tsun is also known as Seng-tsun; his dates are not known.

42. HKSC 2060.50.572a26-27.

43. Tao-hsüan, compiler of the HKSC, considered T'an-ch'ien the first transmitter of She-lun thought to north China (HKSC 2060.50.572b14-20) and tradition follows suit, but it is in fact extremely difficult to assess who was the first transmitter of Paramārtha's ideas to north China.

44. Hui-tsang's biography: HKSC 2060.50.498a23-b29.

45. T'an-yen's biography: HKSC 2060.50.487b3-489c7.

46. HKSC 2060.50.574b3-4. The lost treatise on the "nine consciousnesses" may be further proof that a text on that subject, traditionally associated with the She-lun school, did, in fact, exist.

47. Hui-yüan's biography: HKSC 2060.50.489c26-492b1.

48. *Ta-sheng i chang*, T.1851.44, twenty-six *chüan*.

49. *P'u-sa ti-ch'ih ching*, T.1581.30; *P'u-sa shan chieh ching*, T.1582 and 1583.

50. The first translation of the *Daśabhūmika-sūtra* was by Dharmarakṣa, entitled *Chien pei i-ch'ieh chih te ching* (T.285), in 5 *ch*. It was completed on the eleventh day, eleventh month, of the seventh year of Yüan-k'ang, Western Chin (December 11, 297). See Yüan-chao's *Chen-yüan hsin ting shih chiao mu-lu*, T.2157.55.791a21. The second translation, *Shih chu ching* (T.286), in 4 *ch*., was made by Kumārajīva between the fourth and eleventh years of Hung-shih, Later Ch'in (402-9). See KC 2151.55.359a16, 359c1. The third translation, as the twenty-second chapter (*p'in*) of the *Avataṃsaka-sūtra*, was undertaken by Buddhabhadra under the title *Ta-fang kuang fo hua-yen ching* (T.279) between April 30, 418, and February 5, 422, according to Fa-ching's *Chung ching mu-lu*, T.2145.55.11c9. This translation was begun in 398 (second year, Lung-an, Chin dynasty) according to KC 2151.55.357a13.

51. Guṇabhadra's translation of the *Laṅkāvatāra-sūtra* under the title *Leng-chia-a-pa-to-lo pao ching* (T.670) in four *chüan* was in the twentieth year of Yüan-chia, Liu Sung dynasty (443). See NTL 2149.55.258c14, Ming-ch'üan's *Ta-chou k'an ting chung ching mu-lu*, T.2153.55.387b8.

52. HKSC 2059.50.344a5-345a23. Guṇabhadra, a Central Indian scholar who departed for Canton in 435 via Ceylon, brought the first Yogācāra literature with him, but it was largely overlooked until the Late Wei. Among the *sūtras* Guṇabhadra translated are the *Ta fa ku ching* (T.270), a Tathāgatagarbhan text, the *Saṃdhinirmocana* (T.678), and the *Laṅkāvatāra-sūtra* (T.670).

53. The *Shih-ti ching lun* (T.1522), 12 *ch*. See KYL 2154.55.541a8, c23-29; HKSC 2060.50.428c26-429a18 (Bodhiruci's biography).

54. LTSPC 2034.49.c15-16; see *Ju leng chia ching* (T.671), 10 *ch*.

55. For a brief historical summary of the schism between Northern and Southern Ti-lun see the two previously cited works by Yūki Reimon, "Shina yuishikigaku shijō," and *Seshin yuishiki no kenkyū*, pp. 7-12; Yūki's primary source materials are Hui-yüan's *Ta-sheng i chang* and Chih-i's (538-97) *Miao-fa lien-hua hsüan-i* (T.1716.33) and *Mo-ho chih-kuan* (T.1911.46). Also see Fukaura Shōbun, *Yuishikigaku kenkyū*, 1: 180-208. A thoroughly detailed study is given by Sakaino Kōyō, *Shina bukkyō seishi* (2nd. ed.), pp. 655-97. I quote from all these texts in my discussion on Ti-lun and She-lun. Yūki, in his article "Shina yuishikigako shijō" (p. 26), states that both the Northern Ti-lun and the *Laṅkāvatāra-sūtra* adhered to nine states of cognition; this position was originally shared by Southern Ti-lun before its departure from Bodhiruci's interpretation. Yūki hypothesizes that Hui-yüan's theory of nine consciousnesses derives from Fa-shang's research on the *Laṅkāvatāra-sūtra*, and denies that the early stages of She-lun Buddhism believed in

nine consciousnesses (pp. 28-31). To find a complete theory of nine states of cognition, Yūki maintains that one must look outside Paramārtha's corpus. However, this does not rule out, in my opinion, that his works were the textual foundation for this theory, and the tradition clearly attributes the source to Paramārtha as well as to the *Laṅkāvatāra-sūtra*. Yūki argues that the nine names given for the *ālaya* in the *Hsien shih lun* were incorrectly associated with a ninth consciousness known as the *amala* by later exegetes, but all the commentators who describe a ninth state of cognition explicitly designate it as the *amala*. From Paramārtha's extant corpus, it is clear that the *amala-vijñāna* is quite distinct from the eighth state or *ālaya-vijñāna*. Yūki is in error in this matter.

56. Fa-shang's biography: HKSC 2060.50.485a1-486a6.

57. For example, Mochizuki Shinkō in his article "Daijō kishinron" maintains that She-lun Buddhism was closer to Northern Ti-lun since the *ālaya* is false and the support for all *dharmas* in the latter school, though in his subsequent discussions he groups Southern Ti-lun and She-lun together. Sakaino (*Shina bukkyō seishi*, pp. 684-85) also considers Northern Ti-lun the closest in transmission of ideas to She-lun, claiming that the Northern Ti-lun believed in nine consciousnesses since the eighth was false; however, the textual source he cites to support this claim (*Fa-hua hsüan-i shih-ch'ien, ch.* 18, T.1717.33.942c21-22) merely says that the She-lun is in agreement with Northern Ti-lun's view of the *ālaya*, not that the northern branch posited nine consciousnesses. Sakaino does not give the complete citation but Katsumata does (*Bukkyō ni okeru shinshikisetsu*, p. 654).

58. Although I have found Yūki Reimon to be the most useful secondary source in formulating my own views on doctrinal representation of Ti-lun and She-lun thought, I should mention other Buddhological scholarship that has informed my own speculations: Yamada Ryōsen's article, "Yuishiki kyōgaku ni okeru manashiki no tokusei," Sasaki Gesshō's *Shōdaijōron*, especially chap. 5, and Katsumata Shunkyō's *Bukkyō ni okeru shinshikisetsu*, especially pp. 657-789.

59. T.2799.85.761-782b13.

60. T.2799.85.763c23-26.

61. T.2799.85.764b6-10.

62. T.2799.85.771c11.

63. T.2799.85.771b29-c3.

64. T.2799.85.764a8-9.

65. T.2799.85.773c2.

66. See Takemura Makio, "Jiron-shū Shōron-shū Hossō-shū," pp. 279, 289-92, for a discussion of the nonduality between *saṃskṛta* and *asaṃskṛta* in Tathāgatagarbha thought as contrasted to their duality in the Fa-hsiang school.

67. *Ju leng-chia ching* (Sanskrit: *Laṅkāvatāra-sūtra*), translated by Bodhiruci of Northern Wei, T.671.16.556b29-c1: "Mahāmati, the *ālaya-vijñāna* is called the Tathāgatagarbha when it coexists with the seven conscious modes in ignorance." "The Tathāgatagarbha does not reside

in the *ālaya-vijñāna* because the seven kinds of conscious states arise and cease but the Tathāgatagarbha does not arise and cease" (c11-12). This latter passage, asserting a separation between the Tathāgatagarbha and the *ālaya-vijñāna*, does not appear in either the Sanskrit or in Guṇabhadra's recension: "When there is no evolving (*chuan*) and no separation [from defilement] in what is called the Tathāgatagarbha/*ālaya-vijñāna* (*ju-lai-tsang shih-tsang*), then the seven consciousnesses evolve without end" (T.670.16.510b16-17). See Jikidō Takasaki, "Shōmangyō to Yuishiki shisō," for a discussion of this passage. Takasaki claims that since the six consciousnesses are momentarily extinguished, the seventh is considered mind itself in some of the early commentaries on the ŚDS.

68. Bodhiruci may have asserted only seven consciousnesses in his psychological model, probably preceding the postulating of an independent, defiled consciousness or *manas*. The seventh consciousness was the "seed consciousness," usually considered a synonym for the *ālaya*. The eighth was Suchness. See Katsumata, *Bukkyō ni okeru shinshikisetsu*, pp. 657-65.

69. Tsurumi Ryōdō in his article "Shōman hōkutsu no senjō ejisetsu" compares the *Śrīmālādevī-sūtra* with Chi-tsang's commentary on that text in which Chi-tsang asserts that *hsin-fa chih* or "knowledge of mental entities" represents the seventh consciousness and *tsang shih* or "storehouse consciousness" is the eighth consciousness, *ālaya-vijñāna* (p. 136). The ŚDS does not discuss the *ālaya* but only the Tathāgatagarbha. It does contain the same numbering pattern as the system of thought found in both Northern and Southern Ti-lun.

70. Yoshizu Yoshihide, in "Eon no Kishinron-shū o meguru shomondai," discusses the authorship of the *Ta-sheng ch'i hsin lun i-shu*, which many Japanese Buddhologists believe was composed after Hui-yüan's time. No one in the Chinese Buddhist tradition doubted the authorship of this commentary, however. Yoshizu suggests that the text represents the essential teachings of Hui-yüan found in his other works and was perhaps written by one of his students. Hirakawa Akira (*Daijō kishinron*, p. 399), agreeing with Yoshizu, concludes that the *Ta-sheng i chang* is therefore the earlier of the two texts. Whatever its authorship, the text accurately represents Hui-yüan's philosophical position. Though I find Yoshizu's arguments persuasive and agree with him on this issue, I have relied upon Hui-yüan's other writings as well in order to substantiate my conclusions.

71. Passages from the *Laṅkāvatāra*, Bodhiruci's recension, that are similar in meaning: "The mind (*hsin*) can accumulate *karma*, ideation (*i*) can examine sense fields, consciousness (*shih*) can completely comprehend objects of consciousness. The five [sense] consciousnesses can appear as discriminations" (T.671.16.523c4-5). "The fundamental con-

sciousness (*pen-shih*) is only this mind (*hsin*); ideation (*i*) can conceptualize (*nien*) an objective world and can grasp onto an objective world. Therefore, I say there is only mind" (T.671.16.567c14-15). Guṇabhadra's recension: "Mind (*hsin*) designates the collection of *karma*; ideation (*i*) designates an extensive collection [of concepts]; the [five] consciousnesses cognize the objects of consciousness; their appearances as objects are explained as of five types" (T.670.16.484b24-25).

72. ZZ 71.155ab.

73. ZZ 71.218b.

74. T.1843.44.179a21-22.

75. T.1843.44.179a26.

76. T.1843.44.179b8-9. The quotation from the ŚDS has been slightly altered. Guṇabhadra's recension uses the term *ju-lai-tsang* whereas the *Ch'i hsin lun i-shu* uses *tsang-shih* and changes the order of the phrases. The ŚDS, Guṇabhadra's recension, reads as follows: "O Lord, if there were no Tathāgatagarbha, there would be no revulsion toward suffering nor the aspiration to seek Nirvāṇa. Why? Because the seven (mental) phenomena—the six consciousnesses and the knowledge of (accompanying) mental phenomena—do not continue even momentarily and do not cause ('plant') the seeds of suffering, there cannot be revulsion from suffering nor the aspiration to seek Nirvāṇa [in these seven states]" (T.353.12.222b14-17). The *Ch'i hsin lun i-shu* (pp. 185c26-27) cites this same passage from the ŚDS in a form closer to the original.

77. T.1843.44.179c14.

78. T.1843.44.186c15.

79. T.1843.44.185c17-20.

80. T.1843.44.197c5-8.

81. One of the definitions given for *ādāna-vijñāna* in the Tunhuang manuscript entitled *She ta-sheng lun chang* is *wu-chieh shih*, "the unenlightened consciousness" or consciousness "that interacts with four delusions" (T.2807.85.1013b28). The *Ch'i-hsin lun i-shu* glosses *wu-chüeh* (unenlightened) and *wu-chieh* (an abbreviation perhaps for *wu chieh-t'o* or *nirmokṣa*) as equivalents (T.1843.44.182c19-22). Tao-chi's *She-lun chang*, cited in Gyōnen's *Kegon kumokushō hotsugoki*, lists seven names for the *ādāna*, including *wu-chieh*. See *Dainihon bukkyōzensho*, vol. 122, 75b-76a (pp. 393-94). Citations given by Katsumata (*Bukkyō ni okeru shinshikisetsu*, p. 726) suggest that all She-lun followers *always* regarded the *ādāna-vijñāna* as the seventh mode of cognition.

82. The description of the *ālaya* as *wu-mo* is not found in any of Paramārtha's extant writings although Fa-tsang (*Ta-sheng ch'i hsin lun i-chi*, T.1846.44.255c4-6) and others attribute this to Paramārtha. This term does occur in a Tunhuang manuscript, *She ta-sheng lun chang* (T.2807.-85.1013a27-b1) which may have been written by a She-lun disciple of Paramārtha. The association of the term *wu-mo* with Paramārtha's translation style is difficult to explain. Perhaps *wu-mo* was used in some of the lost works of this Indian master.

83. T.1851.44.524c7-525a1. Though in the *Mahāyāna-saṃgraha* the *ālaya-vijñāna* is a receptacle for seeds evolving in the mind, Hui-yüan

views the *ālaya* not as the reservoir for subconscious seeds but as the source of Suchness as well as ignorance, thus tempering the influence from the *Saṃgraha*.

84. T.1851.44.530c8-14; *Laṅkāvatāra* citation, T.671.16.565b24 (Bodhiruci). There is no section corresponding to the Sagāthakam in Guṇabhadra's version.

85. Paramārtha refers to the *amala-vijñāna* in the following texts: *Chuan shih lun*, T.1587.31.62c19-20; *Shih-pa k'ung lun*, T.1616.31.863b20-24, 864a26-28; *San wu-hsing lun*, T.1617.31.872a5-15; *Chüeh-ting tsang lun*, T.1584.30.1020b11-27, 1022a15-17, 1025c23-25, 1031a3-5. These passages will be discussed in chapter 5. Also note the use of this term in the *Ta-sheng chuang-yen ching lun (Mahāyānasūtrālaṃkāra)*, T.1604.31.623a9, attributed to Asaṅga and translated by Prabhākāramitra during the T'ang.

86. T.1851.44.530c9-16. Although Hui-yüan cites the *Laṅkāvatāra-sūtra* as his scriptural authority on the *ādāna-vijñāna*, that term for the seventh consciousness is not found in the *Laṅkā*. Katsumata (*Bukkyō ni okeru shinshikisetsu*, p. 668) suggests that the notion of *ādāna* developed late in Hui-yüan's work and illustrates Paramārtha's influence.

87. This is cited incorrectly in the *Taishō* as located in *chüan* 26, instead of *chüan* 25 of Buddhabhadra's translation: "Moreover, constructing (*tso*) is the conceptualizing (*nien*) of falsehood in the triple world but is only the construct of the [One] mind" (T.278.9.558c9-10). Cf. Dharmarakṣa's translation from Western Chin, an older redaction than that of Buddhabhadra: "Moreover, evaluative reason (*ssu-wei*) is the triple world, that which is made by the mind" (T.285.10.476b9-10); Kumārajīva's translation (T.286.10.514c25-26) is identical to Buddhabhadra's although none of the manuscripts of Kumārajīva's redaction has the insertion of the character *i* ("one") modifying *hsin* ("mind") as is the case in manuscripts of Buddhabhadra's version. Sikṣananda's translation is the most recent, conducted during the T'ang: "In addition, constructing (*tso*) is conceptualizing the triple world as existent entities (*so-yu*). They are only One Mind" (T.279.10.194a13-14).

88. T.1851.44.527b21-23.

89. For the discussion of the "Empty" and "non-Empty" aspects of the Tathāgatagarbha set forth in the *Śrīmālādevīsiṃhanāda-sūtra* see T.353.12.221c12-23 (Guṇabhadra's recension) and T.310.11.677a19-29 (Bodhiruci's recension). English translations are available in Diana Paul, *The Buddhist Feminine Ideal* (Missoula, 1980), and Alex and Hideko Wayman, *The Lion's Roar of Queen Śrīmālā* (New York, 1974).

90. T.1851.44.530b7-11.

91. T.1851.44.527c1-2.

92. Perhaps these first seven states of mind are what the ŚDS calls "seven [mental] phenomena—the six consciousnesses and the knowl-

edge of [accompanying] mental phenomena that do not continue even momentarily." T.353.12.222b16.

93. See Hui-yüan's quote from ŚDS: T.1851.44.530a25-26. The ŚDS does not use *tsang-shih*, "storehouse consciousness," for the Tathāgatagarbha in either Guṇabhadra's or Bodhiruci's recension. Hui-yüan perhaps had another manuscript of the ŚDS no longer available, or he transposed the more common *ju-lai-tsang* with *tsang-shih*, a practice found in the *Laṅkāvatāra-sūtra*, in order to identify the Tathāgatagarbha with the *ālaya-vijñāna*. See the author's article, "The Concept of Tathāgatagarbha in the *Śrīmālādevī-sūtra*." Chi-tsang in his *Sheng-man ching pao-k'u* (T.1744.37) quotes one unidentified commentator who equates the six consciousnesses with the active consciousnesses and the seventh with mind in general when deluded and with knowledge of the Dharma when enlightened. The eighth consciousness is the storehouse consciousness (*tsang-shih*) or *ālaya-vijñāna*, which suggests that the Tathāgatagarbha is the eighth consciousness (83b25-27). Citing the *Laṅkāvatāra-sūtra*, Chi-tsang gives an example of the fusion of *ālaya* with Tathāgatagarbha that had developed by his generation: "Just as the *Laṅkāvatāra-sūtra* states: 'The sixth and seventh consciousnesses do not receive [the impressions of] suffering nor are they the cause of Nirvāṇa. The storehouse consciousness receives [the impressions of] suffering and is the cause for Nirvāṇa'" (83c18-19). The denial of attributing the cause of defilement to the Tathāgatagarbha, which nevertheless is the basis for both conditioned and unconditioned phenomena, remained a paradox that, in part, contributed to the controversies among the various forms of Chinese Yogācāra.

94. Tokiwa Daijō, *Busshō no kenkyū*, pp. 196-200, compares Hui-yüan's views with the *Ch'i hsin lun*. Tokiwa argues that Hui-yüan combined the theory of One Mind mixed with impurities with his own views on the *ālaya-vijñāna*. He argues that Hui-yüan seems to have been similar, in his interpretation of the *ālaya-vijñāna*, to Hui-ssu of Ch'en who wrote the *Ta-sheng chih-kuan fa-men*, a T'ien-t'ai text (T.1924).

95. See Yoshizu Yoshihide, "Eon no kishinron-shū," pp. 85-86, for a comparison and summary of T'an-yen's and Hui-yüan's views.

96. T.1716.33.744b20-21.

97. T.1716.33.794c29-795a1.

98. This is a paraphrasing of T.1666.32.576b8-9: "What is referred to as 'non-arising and non-ceasing' and 'arising and ceasing' are combined, neither being identical nor different. This is named the *ālaya-vijñāna*." From the English translation by Yoshito Hakeda, *The Awakening of Faith in Mahāyāna* (New York, 1967), p. 36.

99. T.1824.42.104c7-13. Chi-tsang associated the notion of a pure eighth *vijñāna* with Ti-lun, and identified this eighth pure *vijñāna* with both the *ālaya* and Hui-yüan's thought, according to Koseki, "Chi-

tsang's *Ta-ch'eng-hsüan lun,*" pp. 208-9. Chi-tsang either ignored or was unaware of further intellectual developments in Hui-yüan's theories.

100. The basis for this claim is the *Kegon jūjū yuishiki jōkanki* by Gyōnen (1240-1321), composed in 1292, in which he discusses four Mahāyāna theories of consciousness. The second listed is that of Bodhiruci, who established only seven, while Gyōnen goes on to say the fourth theory is that of Paramārtha, who explained nine consciousnesses. See *Nihon daizōkyō, kegon-shū,* 42: 82b (524b). Sakamoto Yukio (*Kegon kyōgaku no kenkyū,* pp. 386-87) is of the opinion that Bodhiruci advocated both seven and eight states of consciousness, depending upon the text translated; he suggests that the *Laṅkāvatāra-sūtra* recension by Bodhiruci vacillates between declaring the *ālaya* the seventh state and the eighth. Gyōnen, however, in his *Kegon kumokushō hotsugoki,* clearly states that Bodhiruci only explained seven conscious states, considering the seventh the *ādāna-vijñāna,* not eight or nine states. See *Dainihon bukkyō zensho,* 122: 70b (388b).

101. See Chan-jan, *Fa-hua hsüan-i shih ch'ien,* T.1717.33.942c19-22.

102. T.1719.34.285a5-6.

103. T.1911.46.54a23-b6.

104. T.1912.46.221c2-9.

Chapter 3

1. Paramārtha's translation of the *Mahāyāna-saṃgraha* has been exhaustively studied by Ui Hakujū in *Shōdaijōron kenkyū* and by Sasaki Gesshō in *Shōdaijōron.* Among the most thorough studies of Yogācāra doctrines found in the *Triṃśikā* and *Viṃśatikā* are: Yūki Reimon, *Seshin yuishiki no kenkyū;* Fukaura Shōbun, *Yuishikigaku kenkyū,* which is a study of Hsüan-tsang's translations contained in the *Ch'eng wei-shih lun;* and Sasaki Gesshō and Yamaguchi Susumu, *Yuishiki nijūron no taiyaku kenkyū.*

2. The Abhidharmist (Vaibhāṣika) position, specifically as recorded in the fifth-century A.D. treatise *Abhidharma-kośa-bhāṣya,* of Vasubandhu, was probably influenced by other contemporary Indian theories of the time, particularly those of the Mīmāṃsakas and Nyāya-Vaiśeṣikas. The Mīmāṃsakas had developed a theory of eternal words and natural meanings. The Nyāya-Vaiśeṣika maintained that the external world corresponds to the categories of language and that universals were actual entities. The Abhidharmists maintain that the name (*nāman*) gives meaning (*artha*) to a word or verbal sound (*vāk*), name being defined as the designation of the nature of a thing (*dharma*). The names are therefore "born with their meanings" (*arthasahaja*) and convey the true nature of the thing. For the Abhidharmist, right knowledge is knowing the particular and clearly defined name that is the conveyor of the

meaning and the nature of the thing. See Stcherbatsky, *Buddhist Logic*, pp. 22-27, and Jaini, "The Vaibhāṣika Theory of Words and Meanings."

3. "The [Mahāyāna] Buddhist, in fact, would like to put all the objects over which our thoughts and other psychological activities may range at the same level; and this will include not only a) things which do exist now (i.e. which are assumed to be existent by the common people or by the realist) but also b) things which do not exist now (i.e. past and future things), c) things which cannot exist (viz. the rabbit's horn), and also d) things of which it would be a logical contradiction to say they exist (viz. the son of a barren woman)." See Matilal, "Reference and Existence in Nyāya and Buddhist Logic," p. 103. The constructive a priori character of knowledge is superimposed on the objects or givens in the world. The Mahāyānists are basically nominalists, claiming that language is merely conceptual and pragmatic with no ontological basis. See Chatterjee, *The Yogācāra Idealism*, pp. 5-8. Though the Mādhyamikan position is that no predicate can be applied to the phenomenal world without leading to semantic paradoxes, the late Yogācārin logicians (beginning with Dignāga) eventually purported that the meanings of words can denote concepts (intension) but not particulars (extension). See Matilal, *Epistemology, Logic, and Grammar in Indian Philosophical Analysis*, pp. 39-49, 159-62.

4. Russell is one example, however, of a philosopher who attempts to avoid an ontology of substances by developing a theory of descriptions that eliminates grammatical subjects in favor of quantifiers. Quine also advocates the development of nonreferential languages that would avoid making any ontological commitments. See Hacking, *Why Does Language Matter to Philosophy?*, chaps. 7 and 13.

5. The *San wu-hsing lun* (Sanskrit: *Tryasvabhāva-prakaraṇa*) (T.1617.-31.867) is an exposition on the three types of insubstantiality of phenomena as counterparts to the three ways of apprehending the nature of phenomena: constructed by conceptualization (*parikalpita*), functional dependency (*paratantra*), and complete knowledge of reality (*pariniṣpanna*). The SWHL is supposed to have been from the same core text as part 7, Ch'eng wu-hsing p'in, from *Hsien-yang sheng-chiao lun* (T.1602.-31.557b4-560b1), translated by Hsüan-tsang in 645, and composed by Asanga. Ui (*Indo tetsugaku kenkyū*, 6: 207-358) gives the parallel texts by Hsüan-tsang and Paramārtha followed by an analysis of Paramārtha's text.

6. The *Chuan shih lun* (T.1587.31.61), supposedly the *Triṃśikā-vijñaptimātratā-siddhi* composed by Vasubandhu, is a general outline of the eight consciousnesses and their specific functions, centering on the theory of the evolution of consciousness (*vijñāna-pariṇāma*). Paramārtha's noteworthy innovation of a ninth consciousness, the *amala-*

vijñāna, is occasionally mentioned in this treatise as the transcendent ground for the other eight functional consciousnesses and will be discussed more fully in the next chapter. See Ui, *Indo tetsugaku*, 6: 405-97, for parallel texts of Hsüan-tsang and Paramārtha followed by an analysis of Paramārtha's text.

7. Cf. *Triṃśikā*, verse XXIV and Sthiramati's commentary. SWHL 1617.867b24-25, c3-5.

8. SWHL 1617.868a2-3.

9. CSL 1588.31.63a15-16.

10. SWHL 1617.869b22-23; cf. *Bodhisattva-bhūmi* (Wogihara ed.), p. 50.

11. The Pūrva Mīmāṃsā believed that there was "an eternal connection between the word and its meaning." Jayatilleke, *Early Buddhist Theory of Knowledge*, pp. 314-15.

12. Early Buddhist texts, specifically the *Nikāyas*, claimed that certain characteristics of things are the foundation and justification for using certain names to denote those things (Jayatilleke, p. 297). In the late Socratic dialogue, *Cratylus*, a similar view is presented in which correct names are considered natural, not conventional. Hermogenes argued that names are conventional and formulated by habitual usage. Socrates claimed that names are instruments for teaching how to distinguish natures of things (388c) but agreed with Hermogenes that "names are conventional and have a meaning to those who agree about them, and who have previous knowledge of the things intended by them" (433d-435d).

13. See the author's article, "An Introductory Note to Paramārtha's Theory of Language," for a more technical study of Paramārtha's use of sense and reference in light of Frege's views.

14. See Mochizuki Shinkō, *Bukkyō Daijiten*, 1: 493b-c, and Morohashi Tetsuji, *Daikanwa jiten*, 9: 75-76, 28504, for the definitions of *i*.

15. *Artha* is the "meaning of what is spoken, namely of words and sentences." In portions of the Pāli *Nikāyas* there is an attempt to differentiate between a word and its meaning: "There is a sense in which the meanings are different as well as the words and a sense in which the meanings are the same, the words alone being different." See Jayatilleke, *Early Buddhist Theory of Knowledge*, pp. 311, 315. The *Aṭṭhasālinī* upholds the position of natural names, i.e. things not named by others but "born with their names" (*opapātikanāma*), and the Vaibhāṣika and Dīpakāra maintain that names are "born with meanings" (*artha-sahaja*), illustrating the fusion of sense and referent. See Jaini, "The Vaibhāṣika Theory of Words," pp. 100-101.

16. CSL 1587.31.62b10-14. Cognition directs its attention outward: it "desires to grasp" an object based upon its sense data, then perception takes place, and sense data are "grasped" as external objects. This passage is a gloss on verse XV from the *Triṃśikā* and is in agreement with

Sthiramati's commentary (Lévi ed., pp. 33-34). The *Chieh-chieh ching* (CCC) (Sanskrit: *Saṃdhinirmocana*) reiterates the same theme in several places; the first occurrence, cited by Sthiramati in his *bhāṣya*, can be found in the first chapter (T.677.16.692b19-c1). There is also an analogy between the magician who conjures up various magical objects and the perceiving consciousness that constructs external objects (T.677.16.-712a12.b16).

17. SWHL 1617.870c3-6; this corresponds to verse VIII (*prabheda-lakṣaṇa* and *paryaya-lakṣaṇa*) in the *Madhyānta-vibhāga: abhūta-parikalpaś ca citta-caittās tridhātukāḥ tatrārtha-dṛṣṭir vijñānaṃ tad-viśeṣe tu caitasāḥ*. See *Madhyānta-vibhāga-bhāṣya*, ed. Nagao Gadjin (Tokyo, 1964), p. 20; *Madhyānta-vibhāga-ṭīka*, ed. Sylvain Lévi and Susumu Yamaguchi (Nagoya, 1934), pp. 30-31. The first line of the *kārikā* also is cited in Sthiramati's exegesis on verse XXI in the *Triṃśikā*.

18. SWHL 1617.31.868b27-c3.

19. SWHL 1617.31.868a10-12.

20. This is a paraphrase of the opponent's argument and the response. For the entire argument see SWHL 1617.31.868a16-26.

21. See chapter 2, *Jñeya-lakṣaṇa*, Paramārtha's translation, T.1593.31.-120b12-19; Hsüan-tsang's translation, T.1594.31.140a14-21. Paramārtha's translation of Vasubandhu's commentary gives a more detailed presentation of the first and second arguments that appears only in a very abbreviated form in the *Saṃgraha* (T.1595.31.191a9-23) and is also found in Hsüan-tsang's edition of the *bhāṣya* (T.1597.31.343a21-b14).

22. SWHL 1617.31.868a21-22.

23. SWHL 1617.31.868a22-23. See note 21 for *Saṃgraha* reference.

24. SWHL 1617.31.868a24-27. See Paramārtha's translation of the *Saṃgraha-bhāṣya*, T.1595.31.191a24-b26. This famous argument is also found in *Nirukta* II.5 and in the Buddhist works, *Abhidharma-kośa* (Pradhan ed.), p. 81, 1-3, composed by Vasubandhu, and in Dharmakirti's *Pramāṇa-vārttika*, II (*pramāṇa-siddhi*), verse XV. The entire passage reads as follows: *gaur ity eṣa śabdo navasv artheṣu kṛtāvidhiḥ: vāg-dig-bhū-raśmi-vajreṣu paśv-akṣi-svarga-vāriṣu nava-svartheṣu medhāvī go-śabdam-upadhārayet iti*. "The sound 'go' can mean voice, place, earth, light, thunderbolt, cow, eye, sky, or water, any of these nine meanings."

25. Paramārtha recognizes that discriminating properties attached to presupposed objects is different from naming those objects. The nature of the intended object is the same although the functions—as discrimination of the object or abstract speculation—are different. See SWHL 1617.31.870a24-29. Since this passage does not occur in Hsüan-tsang's translation, we may presume that it expresses Paramārtha's own views or those of a Yogācārin tradition Paramārtha followed.

26. SWHL 1617.31.868a14-16.

27. SWHL 1617.31.868b4-17. This passage is cited in the *Saṃgraha* and

its *bhāṣya* (see note 24) and in the *Sūtrālaṃkāra*, chapter 13, verse XVI (Lévi ed., p. 88).

28. Similar views of the instrumentality of names are put forth in the *Cratylus*, 387a-391.

29. Paramārtha discusses the connotative qualities of language and how language induces certain behavior and psychological states. Habits condition us to associate certain feelings with certain words. See SWHL 1617.31.868b18-c11, c22-29; 869b24-870a8; CCC 677.16.712c10-25; CSL 1587.31.62c21-63b14.

30. SWHL 1617.31.868b25-c11.

31. T.1617.31.868c12-29.

32. The SWHL divides intentional acts into five categories, presupposing self-existent objects: (1) presupposing the "self-nature" (*tzu-hsing*) of an object intended based upon nominal distinctions (*nāma niśrityārtha-svabhāva-parikalpaḥ*); (2) presupposing the "self-nature" of names based upon perceptually discriminating objects [as necessarily related to their names] (*arthaṃ niśritya nāma-svabhāva-parikalpaḥ*); (3) presupposing the "self-nature" of names based upon other nominal distinctions (*nāma niśritya nāma-svabhāva-parikalpaḥ*); (4) presupposing the "self-nature" of an object intended based upon perceptually discriminating among objects (*arthaṃ niśrityārtha-svabhāva-parikalpaḥ*); and (5) presupposing the "self-nature" of name and object based upon both nominal and perceptual distinctions (*ubhayaṃ niśrityobhaya-svabhāva-parikalpaḥ*). See T.1617.31.869a5-b4. These five kinds of discrimination between names and objects are found in the *Mahāyāna-saṃgraha* (Lamotte ed., II.19, p. 112); Paramārtha's translation, T.1595.31.188c9-189a4; Hsüan-tsang's translation, T.1597.31.342a7-13. Paramārtha's edition of the *Saṃgraha bhāṣya* gives an example and explanation for each of the five types whereas Hsüan-tsang comments briefly through paraphrasing without expansion or example. In the case of the third type, distinctions between names, Paramārtha gives the example of names for things in a foreign language that first one does not understand but, through practice and recognizing the class and definition of a name, will be able to understand. The discrimination between name and intended object, totally absent from the Bodhisattva practice, is found in verse LXXVII, chapter 11, *Mahāyāna-sūtrālaṃkāra* (Lévi ed., p. 76).

33. This group of six types of perceptual discriminations based upon various sorts of nominal and perceptual categories is also found in Hsüan-tsang's text, *Hsien yang sheng-chiao lun* (HYSCL), that corresponds to the SWHL. See Ui, *Indo tetsugaku*, 6: 219-20, for parallel passages from both recensions. These six types of discrimination seem to be related to the four *parikalpa* given in the *Mahāyāna-saṃgraha: svabhāva, viśeṣa, niṣnāta*, and *aniṣnāta* (II.19), to which the HYSCL and SWHL

add the effects from activity (*prayoga*?) and linguistic or nonlinguistic distinctions (*vyavahāra* and *avyavahāra*?). The reason for the addition of these two items is not at all clear to me. They may be another listing as an alternative to that given in the *Saṃgraha* (III.8) as *sanimitta-darśana-dvaya, nānātva, nāma, artha, svabhāva,* and *viśeṣa* or as an alternative to the five types of *parikalpita-svabhāva* given in the *Yogācāra-bhūmi*, T.1579.30.703b13-16, as suggested by Ui, *Indo tetsugaku*, 6: 314. Both Paramārtha and Hsüan-tsang give only the first four types of *parikalpa* in their translations of the *Saṃgraha-bhāṣya* (T.1595.31.188c1-8 and T.1597.31.342a5-7, respectively), eliminating the last two.

34. According to the SWHL, the second stage on the path to wisdom (*darśana-mārga*) through revolving the basis of all conscious activity involves four kinds of reflections (*paryeṣaṇā*): (1) reflection on language (*nāma-paryeṣaṇā*); (2) reflection on classes of intended objects (*artha-* or *vastu-paryeṣaṇā*); (3) reflection on the artificial or superficial character of assumed "self-natures" (*svabhāva-prajñapti-paryeṣaṇā*); and (4) reflection on the artificial or superficial character of distinctions (*viśeṣa-prajñaptiparyeṣaṇā*). See T.1617.31.875b5-876a11; *Bodhisattva-bhūmi* (Wogihara ed.), pp. 53-54; *Sūtrālaṃkāra*, verses 47-48, chapter 19 (Lévi ed., pp. 168-69); *Mahāyāna-saṃgraha*, III.7 and 13 (Lamotte ed., pp. 161-62, 169-70).

35. SWHL 1617.31.869b16-21. This is just one of eight ways in which consciousness discriminates and objectifies its world through the processes of mental construction and language. Other examples are given in this section of the SWHL with a lengthy exegesis by Paramārtha. These eight are found in the *Bodhisattva-bhūmi* (Wogihara ed.), pp. 50-53, and in Hsüan-tsang's recension of the *Yogācāra-bhūmi*, T.1579.30.-489c10-490b1.

36. SWHL 1617.31.869a11-14.

37. SWHL 1617.31.869a29-b2. See Ui, *Indo tetsugaku*, 6: 221-22, for parallel texts corresponding to these two pages.

38. CSL 1587.31.62c8-14; this is Paramārtha's exegesis on verse XVIII of the *Triṃśikā* (Lévi ed., p. 36).

39. Consciousness-only (*wei-shih*), as delineated in the CSL, is the underlying principle by means of which the sense fields are discriminated by a consciousness viewed as other than its object. Cf. T.1587.31.-62b22-28.

40. I have described Paramārtha's epistemology as a "systems oriented" model because of his claim that we cannot differentiate between our sense data and presupposed objects nor can we know of the existence of consciousness except derivatively by means of the activities of conscious states: "Because of its processes (*shih*), we know that this consciousness (*ālaya*) exists. This consciousness can produce all defiled karma and karmic activity. . . . The aspects [sense data] and sensory

objects are not distinguished [from each other] but, because of these processes, one knows that it [*ālaya*] exists." See CSL 1587.31.61c12-13; 62a2-3.

41. This position is argued more fully in my article, "An Introductory Note to Paramārtha's Theory of Language."

Chapter 4

1. Most of the *suttas* in the Pāli Canon describe the training of a monk in terms of these three requirements, beginning with *śīla*, then *samādhi*, and ending with *prajñā*. Buddhaghosa's *Visuddhimagga* (Path of Purity) describes these three practices to Arhatship. Upatissa's *Vimuttimagga* (Path of Freedom) lists five requirements, the above-mentioned three together with freedom (*vimutti*) and the knowledge and discernment of freedom (*vimutti-ñānadassana*) as necessary for eliminating discrimination (see *The Path of Freedom*, trans. N. R. M. Ehara et al., Ceylon, 1961, p. 253). These latter two are usually grouped with *prajñā*.

2. Although *anātman* literally means "non-self," more precisely it is the notion of the nonsubstantial impermanence of an individual composed of a multiplicity of factors (*skandhas*) in continual change. This understanding of the nature of self as a nonabsolute, nonmetaphysical series of psychophysical events could be defined as the true nature of the individual or self.

3. The widest theoretical disparities on this issue were those between the Sarvāstivāda-Vaibhāṣika and the Sautrāntika. These differences in doctrine were the stimulus for the composition of the masterpiece, the *Abhidharmakośa*, by Vasubandhu in the fourth century. See *L'Abhidharmakośa*, trans. Louis de la Vallée Poussin (Paris, 1925).

4. A classic study on the universal Buddhist concern with understanding mental processes and their religious implications is "La Négation de l'âme et la doctrine de l'acte" by Louis de la Vallée Poussin, *Journal Asiatique* (1902-3).

5. Though many of the most significant early Yogācārin treatises written by the brothers Asaṅga and Vasubandhu have been translated, the elaborate account of the system of operations for reinforcing patterns of behavior given in early Yogācāra as opposed to the *Abhidharmakośa*'s systematic treatment has not been so thoroughly discussed. I am primarily concerned with Paramārtha's views; Hsüan-tsang's have been discussed by others, most notably, his *Ch'eng-wei-shih lun*. See Louis de la Vallée Poussin, trans., *Vijñaptimātratāsiddhi: La Siddhi de Hiuan-tsang*, 6 vols. (Paris, 1928-29). Hsüan-tsang represents Dharmapāla's tradition of Yogācāra, however. The most complete treatment of Asaṅga's *Mahāyāna-saṃgraha* is Étienne Lamotte's annotated translation entitled *La Somme du grand véhicule d'Asaṅga* (Louvain, 1938; 2nd ed., 1973), which closely follows Hsüan-tsang's recension rather than Paramārtha's.

6. See *Kokuyaku issaikyō*, 148 (*Yuga-bu*): 1-2. Tzu-en's student, Hui-chao, also cites a text translated by Paramārtha entitled the *Wu-hsiang lun* in his *Ch'eng wei-shih lun liao-i teng* (T.1832.43.729b28-c12). Following the title entry of each of these three texts is the statement that it was extracted from the *Wu-hsiang lun*. See Taishō, vol. 31, nos. 1587, 1617, and 1618. The difficulties involved in identifying these three texts are fully described by Yūki Reimon, *Seshin yuishiki*, pp. 63-164, and will be discussed in chapter 5 below.

7. The question of whether or not human nature was intrinsically spiritual, that is, capable of enlightenment, particularly plagued Chinese Buddhist clergy in the sixth and seventh centuries. The *Ratnagotravibhāga* makes an allusion to an *amala-vijñāna*. One of the names for the *ālaya-vijñāna* of a Tathāgata is *vimala-vijñāna*. See Ruegg, *La Théorie du Tathāgatagarbha et du Gotra*, pp. 443-44. Cf. *Siddhi* (La Vallée Poussin ed.), I, 167. Paramārtha, for purposes of clarity, may have distinguished these two modes of the *ālaya-vijñāna* more systematically by discussing the eighth phase or mode in an ignorant state as the *ālaya-vijñāna* and the ninth state as the *amala-vijñāna*. The term *amala-vijñāna* does not appear in the *Mahāyāna-saṃgraha* but, in my opinion, could have been an accommodation to the controversy between the Northern Ti-lun, who felt the *ālaya-vijñāna* was partly pure in nature yet superficially involved with ignorance, and the Southern Ti-lun, who felt the *ālaya-vijñāna* was intrinsically and entirely pure. For a brief but lucid presentation of "pure consciousness" and the *amala-vijñāna*, see Fukaura Shōbun, *Yuishikigaku kenkyū*, 1: 188-288.

8. The CSL is considered the same text as the *Triṃśikā-kārikās* with the addition of liberal exegetical comments, according to Ui Hakujū, *Indo tetsugaku kenkyū*, 6: 107, 434-35. Fukaura thinks the entire purported trilogy, *Wu-hsiang lun*, was developed from the *Hsien-yang sheng-chiao lun* (HYSCL), T.1602.31, attributed to Asaṅga, whereas Yūki Reimon criticizes both Fukaura and Ui in that the trilogy is not simply a derivation from the HYSCL and is the work of Vasubandhu. See *Seshin yuishiki*, particularly pp. 63-78.

9. There are very few indifferences in listing the mental states. Hsüan-tsang and the Sanskrit text list eleven good mental states, instead of ten. The eleventh is *amoha*, "the absence of delusion." Yūki analyzes the schema of the Abhidharma in Paramārtha's *Hsien-shih lun* and claims that, except for minor discrepancies, Paramārtha follows Vasubandhu whereas Hsüan-tsang follows Asaṅga more closely. See *Seshin yuishiki*, pp. 51-55; also p. 62, n. 5, for differences between Yūki and Ui on authorship of verses and commentary.

10. T.1617.31.867b-878b.

11. T.1602.31.480b-583b; the verses are published separately (T.1603). Ui gives the parallel texts in *Indo tetsugaku*, 6: 207-90.

12. The three natures (*svabhāva*) are well known: *parikalpita*, "the mentally constructed" or "discriminated"; *paratantra*, "the interdependent" or "dependent on another"; and the *parinișpanna*, "absolutely real" or "complete." The *niḥsvabhāva* are related to the *svabhāva* as the emptiness of the latter, namely, the emptiness of aspects that the mind imputes (*alakṣaṇa*), the emptiness of arising or self-causation (*anutpāda*), and the emptiness of any intrinsic nature (*asvabhāva*). See SWHL 1617.-31.867b20-867c28.

13. T.1618.31.878c-882b.

14. See Ui's treatment of the HSL, *Indo tetsugaku*, 6: 379-403.

15. The recursive function of a computer, namely, the potentially infinite acts resulting from a finite set of factors, may be seen as analogous to the operations of consciousness in Paramārtha's system. A recursive function is defined in terms of itself, that is, the definition of the procedure includes the procedure itself. A "loop" or iterative function will indefinitely repeat itself according to a rule or formula involving a finite number of steps unless or until a specified condition is met. We are concerned here with a logical structure presented by Paramārtha that is rather similar to the "loop" or recursive functions employed in computer science. A recursive function will continue to call itself indefinitely unless some condition is specified and then fulfilled at some point in running the program. If that condition is not properly specified or fulfilled, the "loop" becomes an "infinite loop" and the program will run indefinitely. In the case of the mental "programming" of seeds in the "computer," the *ālaya-vijñāna*—the sequence: habit-seeds—is similar to a looping procedure in that each cycle includes the conditions necessary to initiate the succeeding cycle. Only in meditation, whereby one can understand the "loop" mechanism, is the necessary condition met for terminating the "program" of seeds.

16. *Pratītya-samutpāda* has been reinterpreted throughout the history of Buddhist thought. The Chinese Buddhist schools of Yogācāra tended to fall into two categories: (1) those who claimed that Suchness (*tathatā*) or reality is the basis for changes in the world, and (2) those who claimed that it is the mind that, in its eighth mode or function as the *ālaya-vijñāna*, serves as the basis for changes in the world. Paramārtha belongs to the first category; Hsüan-tsang and K'uei-chi belong to the second. Their Indian counterparts are usually considered the Valabhī school represented by Sthiramati and the Nalanda school represented by Dharmapāla, respectively, but this remains controversial. See Ruegg, *La Théorie du Tathāgatagarbha*, pp. 439-44, for a possible Tibetan counterpart to some of Paramārtha's ideas, namely, Jo-nañ-pa. Lai's excellent article, "Chinese Buddhist Causation Theories," summarizes the meaning of *pratītya-samutpāda* in the Chinese Buddhist context, though I would disagree that Fa-tsang was the first to trace *pratītya-samutpāda*

to Suchness. Paramārtha's introduction of the *amala-vijñāna* certainly maintains the same principle.

17. The threefold structure of consciousness is said to be continually evolving or transforming (*vijñāna-pariṇāma*). See *Triṃśikā-kārikā*, verse 1. The subjective side of this evolutionary process grasps (*grāhaka*) the objective side of the process (*grāhya*) as animate beings and inanimate things.

18. T.1587.31.61c1-3.

19. T.1587.31.61c3-4. See *Triṃśikā*, verse 2, in which the second level is called *manana*, that is, *manas*. The *Ch'eng wei-shih lun* consistently uses the terms *ālaya-vijñāna* and *ādāna-vijñāna* for the first level or structure, corresponding to the eighth function of consciousness. See *Shindō jōyuishikiron*, ed. Saeki Join, pp. 14-15. The term *ādāna-vijñāna*, for Hsüan-tsang, refers to the "collecting of the seeds." For Paramārtha, *ādāna* appropriates an ego, performing the functions usually attributed to the *manas*. The *Ta-sheng i chang* uses the term *ādāna-vijñāna* for the seventh consciousness, attributing this usage to the *Laṅkāvatāra-sūtra*. See Fukaura, *Yuishikigaku kenkyū*, 1: 194-95. Paramārtha sometimes uses the term *ādāna-vijñāna* to refer to the eighth consciousness as well as the seventh although the reason for this remains unclear to me; see *Yuishikigaku kenkyū*, 1: 332-33.

20. An excellent study of the Sarvāstivāda-Vaibhāṣika/Sautrāntika controversy over the causal connections between virtuous acts and ignorant acts is Jaini, "The Sautrāntika Theory of Bīja." In brief, the Theravādins claim that a neutral, intervening factor (*avyākṛta-citta*) between ignorance and wisdom allows for changes in one's mental states. The Sarvāstivāda-Vaibhāṣika exerted a force of attraction (*prāpti*) or repulsion (*aprāpti*) that either enhances or interferes with the production of a good or bad mental state. The Sautrāntika, objecting to both the Theravādin and Vaibhāṣikan theses, offer a seed theory in which latent good, bad, and neutral mental energy or dispositions succeed each other, accounting for the change in mental states.

21. The terms *bīja* and *vāsanā* are usually interpreted as synonyms for the power (*vaśa*) or energy (*śakti*) of the mind, and Paramārtha sometimes uses *hsi-ch'i* and *hsün-hsi* interchangeably for *vāsanā*. In itself, *bīja* or *vāsanā* is only nominally existent—that is, it is a term used as a metaphor to describe the process of conceptual and attitudinal changes. See Jaini, "The Sautrāntika Theory," pp. 242-44. Anacker, "Vasubandhu: Three Aspects," makes the distinction between *bīja* and *vāsanā*, the latter being "the process of everything in past experience entering the consciousness-stream to help in its transformation" (p. 246), following Asaṅga's *Mahāyāna-saṃgraha*, I, 18. Also see the *Triṃśikā*, verse XVIII, and Sthiramati's *bhāṣya*, which glosses *sarva-bījam* as *sarva-dharmotpadāna-śakty anugamāt*, "following the power to produce all phenom-

ena." Paramārtha also makes a similar temporal distinction between the result of the *bīja* and the act of implanting the *bīja*, namely, the *vāsanā*. The latent habits or influences (*hsün-hsi*) from past *karma* are the act or process of planting the seeds of *karma* (CSL 62c22), the act itself of influencing the consciousness-stream in some future deed. The energy from these habits (*hsi-ch'i*) results from the influence or implantation of the latent habit (*hsün-hsi*). The distinctions are fairly precise: past habits or influences (*hsün-hsi; vāsanā*) are the planting of seeds (*bīja*) for future *karma*. The energy (*hsi-ch'i; śakti*) from these habits, that is, the energy of these seeds (*bīja*), in actuality is the ignorant act (or act of wisdom), CSL 63a8. The relationship may have had its prototype in the relationship between latent dispositions (*anuśaya*) and active defilements (*paryavasthāna* or *upaklesa*), corresponding to *vāsanā* and the effect or *śakti* of the *bīja*, respectively. See the *Śrīmālādevī-sūtra* for a striking parallel, cited in Paramārtha's CSL 63c13. The first *chuan* of the SWHL is devoted to the different types of habits and their perpetuation.

22. See CSL 61c9-62a2. One infers that the *ālaya-vijñāna* exists because we can observe its effects, namely, the behavior produced because of past experiences. The backlog or clearinghouse of one's past that influences present responses is assumed to exist in order for there to be "conditioning" between past and present actions. Paramārtha, in his exegesis, gives ignorance as an example, but admittedly an unclear one. He makes the claim that one can only infer that there is ignorance because of its effects on one's behavior.

23. The distinction between the first and second structure of consciousness is primarily based upon the more specialized nature of the second or *ādāna-vijñāna*. Though all normal states of consciousness function in a dualistic manner, as subjective and objective constituents, the *ādāna-vijñāna* is the structure of dominant, narcissistic subconscious and conscious energy, viewing the nature of self as a substrate. The *ādāna-vijnana* is left undeveloped in both the CSL and SWHL; a definition of the *ādāna-vijñāna* (or the more common term *manas*, in Hsüan-tsang's translations) is given in the HSL as the attachment that then makes the *ālaya-vijñāna* the seat of the ego. Attachment is the *ādāna-vijnana*, and its nature is the belief in the ego (T.1618.31.879b10-11, 15-16). In addition, the *ādāna-vijñāna* accepts or appropriates (analogous to *upādi*?) the body, and does not retain any seeds (HSL 879b5), in agreement with the usage of the term *ādāna* in the *Saṃdhinirmocana*. Hsüan-tsang and Bodhiruci, however, identify the *ādāna* with the *ālaya* in their translations of the *Saṃdhinirmocana* (T.676.16.692b15-c14 and T.675.669a23-b16, respectively). See Weinstein, "The *Ālaya-vijñāna* in Early Yogācāra Buddhism," pp. 56-57. Also see note 19 above. Unfortunately, Paramārtha and Guṇabhadra's translations of the *Saṃdhinir-*

mocana do not have the sections corresponding to these descriptions of the *ālaya* and *ādāna*.

24. CSL 1587.31.62a6. See Stcherbatsky, *The Central Conception of Buddhism*, pp. 46-47: "The element of consciousness according to the same laws [*pratītya-samutpāda*] never appears alone, but always supported by an object (*viṣaya*) and a receptive faculty (*indriya*)." See *Abhidharma-kośa*, 3: 143, on the *saṃprayuktas*, definition of sensory contact (*sparśa*): "Concours des trois, *trika-saṃnipāta*. La triade est l'organe, l'objet, le Vijñāna (*indriya, viṣaya, vijñāna*). . . . Ces trois préexistent à l'état de Bījas." Examples of this threefold interaction are given on pp. 143-45.

25. The CSL (62a8-11) gives the following metaphor for these cognitive states: "Attention is like a galloping horse and volition is like the rider. A horse only gallops straight ahead but cannot avoid the wrong or head toward the right place. Because of the rider, a horse can avoid the wrong and head toward the right place. Volition [like a rider] thus can enable one's attention to avoid reckless actions." The implications of attention (*manasikāra, manaskāra*) have not been fully appreciated by Buddhologists. Attention is the primitive function of the mind to be prepared to turn toward an object. For the early Yogācāra such as Paramārtha, this primitive state of mind already starts the process of mental construction, or "intending an object." Cf. *Abhidharma-kośa*, 3: 146-47, for sectarian differences in interpretation of *manasikāra*. See Edgerton, *Buddhist Hybrid Sanskrit Dictionary*, *ābhujati, ābhoga* [glosses for *manasikāra* (*manaskāra*)], p. 99, for difficulties in defining this state. The most interesting equivalent is "assumed," "effort directed towards something concretely existing" or what I should prefer to call "preparation for assuming an external object," "intending," or "getting ready for sensation." Sthiramati supports this claim: *ābhujanam ābhogaḥ / ālambane yena cittam abhimukhīkriyate*. Cited by Poussin in the *Kośa*, p. 147.

26. T.1587.31.62a11-12.

27. CSL 62b17-19: "On what occasions does this intellect (*manovijñāna*) not arise? Except for these six states—[cessation] meditation without conceptualization (*asamjñika-samāpatti* and *nirodha-samāpatti*), [meditation associated with the third level or *dhyāna* in] heavens without conceptualization (*asamjñika-sattva*), dreamless sleep, drunken stupor, unconsciousness, or a coma (*acittakā mūrchā*)—the others always have it [intellect or ideation]." This is a paraphrasing of verse XVI in the *Triṃśikā*.

28. T.62c13-14, 17-19. Compare Sthiramati's commentary on verse XXII: *yadi hi pariniṣpannaḥ paratantrād anyaḥ syād evaṃ na parikalpitena paratantraḥ śūnyaḥ syāt*. "If the absolute nature were other than the dependent nature, then the dependent nature would not be empty of the discriminated nature." A discussion of the differences between Para-

mārtha and Sthiramati on the *trisvabhāva* theory will be presented in chapter 5.

29. See Streng, "The Process of Ultimate Transformation in Nāgārjuna's Mādhyamika," for an interpretation of Nāgārjuna's dialectical method as a therapeutic device for liberation from mental suffering. Note especially pp. 19-21 and verses 18: 4, 5, and 7 cited on p. 12.

30. McDermott succinctly pleads the case that Mādhyamika and at least certain theories in Yogācāra have a close affinity. The major similarity she brings out is the identity between the *ālaya-vijñāna* and reality (*tathatā*) when ignorance no longer is operative, that is, when the influences (*vāsanā*) from past ignorance have dissolved. See "Asaṅga's Defense of Ālaya-Vijñāna." This identity is given the name *amala-vijñāna* by Paramārtha.

31. See Matilal, "A Critique of Buddhist Idealism," in *Buddhist Studies in Honour of I. B. Horner,* p. 139: "Just as the 'Emptiness' doctrine (*śūnyavāda*) supplies the philosophic basis for the therapeutics of Nirvāṇa so also idealism or *vijñaptimātratā* doctrine provides the metaphysical rationale for pursuing the religious programme to realise Nirvāṇa in the form of pure, translucent consciousness, the 'absolute.'"

32. The Bodhisattva states of knowledge are equated with the seven kinds of reality (*tathatā*), SWHL 1617.31.873a23-29. This revolution of the basic structure of consciousness (*āśraya-parāvṛtti*) has two stages and five subdivisions: (1) partial revolution for the Two Vehicles and beginning Bodhisattvas, (2) active revolution for the seventh-stage Bodhisattva through the ninth stage, the tenth stage of practice, and the ultimate stage of Buddhahood (SWHL 874c3-12). The Bodhisattva's use of language and discrimination is described at length in SWHL 875b5-876c1. See *Mahāyāna-sūtrālaṃkāra* for a discussion of the seven kinds of *tathatā*, XIX, verse 44 (Lévi, pp. 167-68).

33. Mental construction is inherent in all nonmeditative states in the early Yogācārin system as contrasted to the views of Digñāga. The first of the three types of insubstantiality of phenomena is *parikalpita-svabhāva*, that is, construction by conceptualization. Mental construction begins to dissipate in meditation but is not totally eliminated until the highest stage, *nirodha-samāpatti,* when both conceptualization and feelings cease. See Anacker, "Vasubandhu: Three Aspects," pp. 157-65.

34. The discussion, together with figures 1 and 2, is based on the following passages from the SWHL: 867b27-c1; 867c29-868b24.

35. The Chinese characters for object (*ching* or *ching-chieh*) have a variety of possible meanings, depending upon their Sanskrit equivalents. Nagao Gadjin, *Madhyāntavibhāga-bhāṣya*, gives the Sanskrit equivalents *artha, gocara,* and *viṣaya* for *ching; ālambana, gocara*(*tva*), and *jñeya* for *ching-chieh.* Since the CSL is an exegesis of the *Triṃśikā,* we find that in verses II and VIII where *viṣaya* occurs in the Sanskrit, Paramārtha has

translated the term by the less ambiguous character, *ch'en*, literally, "dust." The *viṣaya* is the sense-object, the sense data with which the sense organs come into contact. The *ālambana*, appearing in verses V and XXVIII, is translated by *yüan* and *yüan* (*tz'u*) *ching*, respectively. Cf. Nagao, *Madhyāntavibhāga*, p. 186, *enkyōgai: ālambane*. The *ālambana* is, strictly speaking, an object of consciousness, which may or may not have a referent. In other words, it can be the idea conditioned by an object, suggested by the Chinese term *yüan*, "to have an affinity to," "be affected by (an object)," or "to affect (an object)." *Ching-chieh* may simply be used as a gloss for *so fen-pieh*, "that which is *discriminated*," *yad vikalpyate* of verse XVII, that is, an object of a discriminating consciousness. In this respect, *ching-chieh* is closer in meaning to an *ālambana*, that is, the objectified content of mind, the perceived object. See La Vallée Poussin, *Siddhi*, I, 42.

36. That is, "what is discriminated" or "that which is discriminable." Sanskrit: *parikalpita*. Chinese: *fen-pieh hsing*. Usually this term is translated as the "nature of discrimination" or "the discriminative nature," but the focus of this principle is weighted toward the objectification of the world, toward the purported self-existence of the object, imputing characteristics constructed by the discriminating subject on to the objects discriminated.

37. Sanskrit: *paratantra*, literally, "dependent on another," which Paramārtha carefully translated as *i-t'a hsing*.

38. Many specialists on Yogācāra view the entire tradition as adhering to the idealist's position that external objects do not exist in any way whatsoever. Though some later Yogācārans such as Hsüan-tsang certainly may lead one to that conclusion, the writings of Vasubandhu in particular do not necessarily do so. For philosophical argumentation, Vasubandhu challenges the opponent's complacent belief that he knows the external world and can articulate its reality. He does not necessarily make the logical error of assuming that simply because the mind cannot know anything except its own states, it follows that what is not knowable to the mind simply does not exist. Anacker, "Vasubandhu's *Karmasiddhiprakaraṇa*," and McDermott, "Asaṅga's Defense," are in agreement with the interpretation I give of the philosophical force of early Yogācāra. The labeling of Vasubandhu's view as "subjective idealism" seems to me to bear the same sort of unjustifiable attack as the label "nihilism" does to Nāgārjuna's views. Although Vasubandhu claims that sense objects are dependent upon mind, he also makes the corollary that the mind is dependent upon objects in normal cognitive states. Asaṅga, his older brother, can be more appropriately labeled "idealist" because of his flights into the meditative vision of a world devoid of objects. Nonetheless, in their works the discussion of "objects" always refers to objects of consciousness (*ālambana*).

39. The cumulative influences (*vāsanā*) from past experiences determine the way in which an individual develops a highly personal style of constructing his world yet at the same time views this world as if it were independent of individual interpretation. These *vāsanā* are the source for wrong notions that objects have autonomous powers over one's existence. See Matilal, "A Critique of Buddhist Idealism," pp. 146, 154.

40. CSL 62b22-23.

41. In Paramārtha's description of the "seed" structure, a parallel may be seen with *sva-saṃvitti* or self-awareness, the underlying unity for projection of a subject over and against an object. See Matilal, "Buddhist Idealism," for a brief summary of *sva-saṃvitti*; also Hattori Masaaki, *Dignāga: On Perception*, pp. 101-6. The *Triṃśikā* and Sthiramati's *bhāṣya* have no theory of *sva-saṃvitti* although it is implicit in Paramārtha's exegesis on the verses.

42. The entire argument is given in CSL 62b25-c20. The question is raised in that passage concerning the name "Consciousness-Only." If both sense object *and* sensory ideational consciousness are eliminated, how can one say there is "Consciousness-Only"? The answer has two parts. (1) The functioning of consciousness is the only type of world we know; when this system of how consciousness functions is understood, this is "Consciousness-Only." (2) When the interdependency of consciousness and its objects is completely understood, this is knowledge of Emptiness. This interdependency is expressed by Paramārtha as both the absolute nature (*pariniṣpanna*), the real, and Pure Consciousness (*amala-vijñāna*). In other words, knowledge of reality is called "Consciousness-Only" or "Pure Consciousness."

43. The Chinese equivalent for this conscious energy is *hsi-ch'i, ch'i* connoting "energy" and *hsi*, "habit." The Sanskrit equivalent is *vāsanā*, according to Lamotte, "Passions and Impregnations of the Passions in Buddhism," p. 91, whereas *hsün-hsi*, "latent habits," corresponds to *vāṣanā* according to Nagao, *Madhyāntavibhāga*, p. 130. *Hsün* literally means "scent," "vapor," or "perfume," derived from the meaning of *vāsanā* as "perfuming" or "infusing" as well as from the metaphor found in the *Kośa*, namely, that lingering effects of past *karma* remain in the mind just as a sesame seed perfumed by a flower retains the scent. See *Abhidharmakośa* (La Vallée Poussin ed.), chap. 4, p. 249 (Hsüan-tsang xviii, fol. 17a-b). Compare HSL 1618.31.880c11-15. This metaphor is repeated in the *Siddhi*, I, 122. Both *hsi-ch'i* and *hsün-hsi* have usually been translated as equivalents, but there seems to be a temporal relationship between them. *Hsi-ch'i* is the energy produced by *hsün-hsi*, via a seed. The *hsi-ch'i* is, properly speaking, the *vāsanā* or energy from past habits that have efficacy (*bīja*), lingering in the mind (*hsün-hsi*) as an act of impregnation (*hsün-hsi* is probably *bhāvanā*), responsible for

producing defilement, which in turn has a habit energy (*hsi-ch'i*) or resulting effect that begins the cycle again. See *Siddhi*, II, 475, and note 21 above.

44. "Seed-consciousness" is my abbreviated translation for *vipakāḥ sarvabījakam*, from verse II of *Triṃśikā*, "the retributive result [consciousness], consisting of all seeds." See CSL 61c6-7.

45. That is, delusions about selfhood (*ātma-moha*), and theoretical views about selfhood (*ātma-dṛṣṭi*) (CSL 62a15).

46. *Hsiang hsi-ch'i*, "influential force of aspects," and *ts'u chung hsi-ch'i*, "gross influential forces," are tentative translations for an obscure concept appearing in both CSL and SWHL. The object discriminated is the gross form of latent habits that generates potential situations for defilement (*kleśa*). The subject who does the discriminating manufactures the content of the delusion, that is, the aspects or appearances of objects in a world. See CSL 62c26-63a17. The SWHL reverses the terms, using *hsiang huo lei* for the discriminated object and *ts'u-chung* for the discriminating subject. See SWHL 870c10-16, 871a14-19. In the CSL, Paramārtha notes this reversal in terminology but does not explain the inconsistency.

47. CSL 62c21-25. This is Paramārtha's exegesis on verse XIX of the *Triṃśikā*. Sthiramati's commentary on this verse for the twofold latent impressions of perceiving (*grāha*) is as follows: *pūrvotpanna-grāhya-grāhaka-grāhākṣiptam anāgata-tajjātīya-grāhya-grāhaka-grāhotpatti-bījaṃ grāha-dvaya-vāsanā*. "The twofold latent impressions of perceiving are brought about by the previously occurring perceiver/perceived act which is the seed for the generation of a perceiver/perceived act of a similar kind some time in the future."

48. *Hsi-ch'i*, the latent energy from past habits or *vāsāna*, is usually not considered defilement (*kleśa*) but the accumulation of patterns of reflexive responses. Lamotte gives some humorous examples of *vāsanās* monks have retained even though they no longer engage in acts of an unethical nature. For example, there was a handsome monk, Nanda, who still habitually gazed upon women whom he taught even though he no longer had passion for them. See Lamotte, "Passions and Impregnations," p. 93.

49. Emptiness is not always defined in negative terms, traced back to the correlation between Emptiness and interdependent existence (*pratītya-samutpāda*) by Nāgārjuna and the *Prajñāpāramitā* tradition. See the articles by Obermiller, "A Study of the Twenty Aspects of Śūnyatā," and Nagao Gadjin, "What Remains in Śūnyatā: A Yogācāra Interpretation of Emptiness." Also see Ruegg, *La Théorie du Tathāgatagarbha*, pp. 319-57, for an excellent and detailed description of the absolute knowledge of the Buddha as a definition of Emptiness in Tathāgatagarbha literature.

50. See La Vallée Poussin, *Kośa*, II, 185; *Triṃśikā*, verse I and the *bhāṣya*.

51. The elimination of discriminating what actually has only imputed characteristics is the elimination of the constructing function of the *ālaya-vijñāna*. This type of wisdom is technically called nondiscriminative wisdom (*nirvikalpa-jñāna*), that is, wisdom defined in terms of what it lacks. A positive definition of this same knowledge is knowledge of reality, the Suchness (*tathatā*) of all things. This Suchness can also be called the Pure Consciousness (*amala-vijñāna*), according to Paramārtha's own interpretation, or the revolution of the basis for discrimination (*āśraya-parāvṛtti*). CSL 1588.31.63c4-5; SWHL 1617.31.871c22-24, 873c23-24; *Triṃśikā*, verse XXIX.

52. CSL 63b21-24. Compare Sthiramati's commentary on verse XXV: *Sa yasmāt pariniṣpannaḥ svabhāvaḥ sarva-dharmāṇām paratantrātmakānāṃ paramārthaḥ tad-dharmateti kṛtvā tasmāt pariniṣpanna eva svabhāvaḥ paramārtha-niḥsvabhāvatā pariniṣpannasyābhāva-svabhāvatvāt.* "Because the absolute nature is the truth of all phenomena that are interdependent themselves, it is the Dharma Nature of those [phenomena]; therefore, the absolute nature has no nature of the truth for the absolute nature has no existence [as some sort of substantial entity]."

53. The seed-sprout metaphor is used to suggest the uninterrupted series of conscious moments and the changes that take place in successive moments of consciousness. See La Vallée Poussin, *Kośa*, IX, 296; *Triṃśikā-bhāṣya*, commentary on verse XIX.

54. The major part of the *San wu-hsing lun* is devoted to an analysis of the types of discriminations based on mental constructs (868c12-871b15), namely, the obstacles of defilement (*kleśāvaraṇa*) and obstacles to knowledge (*jñeyāvaraṇa*). The corresponding knowledge of Suchness devoid of these obstacles is then explained (871b15-873a17). The description of the path toward the final elimination of discrimination and the understanding of dependence between subject and object is described in detail (874a29-878b25).

55. Both the Bodhisattva stages and the Buddha stages are the attainment of nondiscriminative wisdom (SWHL 876c9-10), but the causal realm of the Bodhisattva is that of skill-in-means whereas that of the Buddha is the result of having benefited both self and other without being attached to either *saṃsāra* or *nirvāṇa* (878a10-b25).

56. *Kośa*, IV, 1-2.

57. See, for example, the *Śrīmālādevī-sūtra*, in its discussion of *anuśaya*, or mind-disassociated defilement. This doctrine was also held by the Vibhajyavādins.

58. Jaini, "The Sautrāntika Theory of Bīja," pp. 248-49.

59. See my discussion of Mahāsāṃghika, Sautrāntika, and Tathāgatagarbha thought in chapter 2 of *The Buddhist Feminine Ideal*.

Chapter 5

1. The *Ta-chou k'an ting chung-ching mu-lu*, abbreviated as *Ta-chou lu* (TCL), was compiled by Ming-ch'uan of T'ang in 695. Entries for CSL, SWHL, and HSL: T.2153.55.408a1, 406c13, and 407b2. The HSL has been misidentified by the TCL as a translation by Hsüan-tsang, but three manuscripts footnoted in the Taishō correctly identify Paramārtha as the translator.

2. T.2154.55.545c4.

3. NTL 2149.55.273b8; KYL 2154.55.545b24.

4. Ui Hakujū, *Indo tetsugaku kenkyū*, 6: 94, 105-9, 291-99, et passim; Sasaki Gesshō, *Shōdaijōron*, pp. 8-9; Katsumata Shunkyō, *Bukkyō ni okeru shinshikisetsu no kenkyū*, pp. 750-65 et passim.

5. See T.1537.31.61 note 36, and Ui, pp. 105-6. The Kao-li manuscript of the HSL, according to Ui, does not give the *p'in* title for the text, but the three manuscripts from Sung, Yüan, and Ming insert *p'in* before the character *lun*.

6. T.1846.44.262c5-6.

7. T.1587.31.61c8-9. Fa-tsang uses *ching-chieh* in his commentary where Paramārtha's text has *ching*.

8. T.1666.32.577a8-10.

9. Hui-chao uses *chai-she*, whereas Paramārtha uses *so ch'i ch'u*. T.1832.43.729c1-2.

10. T.1586.31.61c8-9.

11. T.2319.369a71.22-25.

12. T.1587.31.61c5-6; 62c18-20. The CSL has the additional character *chung* and the transliteration for *ādāna* instead of that for *manas*. The CSL has "true nature" (*chen hsing*), instead of "the nature of Emptiness" (*k'ung hsing*) in both instances. I could not locate a line corresponding to "Only the *amala-vijnāna* is Suchness."

13. The relationship between the *ādāna-vijñāna* and the *ālaya-vijñāna* is given its fullest treatment in the HSL, T.1618.31.878-882, in which the *ādāna* is described as grasping on to the *ālaya* as its object, viewing it as selfhood. The *ādāna* is therefore the foundation for notions of self. This seventh state is usually termed *manas* or *kliṣṭa-manas*, reserving the term *ādāna* as a synonym for the *ālaya*. At other times, Paramārtha does use *ādāna* synonymously with *ālaya*—for example, in his translation of the *Mahāyāna-saṃgraha*, T.1593.32.114a10-17, in which a verse from the *Saṃdhinirmocana-sūtra* is cited. See Fukaura Shōbun, *Yuishikigaku kenkyū*, 1: 332-33. Later adherents to the She-lun system such as Hui-yüan used the term *ādāna* for the seventh mode of consciousness. The *Daśabhūmika* (*Shih-ti ching lun*), by Bodhiruci of Northern Wei, uses the term *ādāna* once, as the unenlightened consciousness (*wu-chieh shih*), but it is not clear whether the *ādāna* is a seventh state. *Ādāna* is mentioned

as being a distinct cognitive state, separate from the *ālaya*, however (T.1522.26.170c). Professor Takasaki has pointed out to me that the Tibetan parallel passage does not have the term *ādāna*, but *pravṛtti-vijñāna*. See vol. 104 of the Peking ed., Bstan-hgyur, p. 105, third block, lines 2-3 of block 258. The term *ādāna* deserves more detailed discussion. In the glosses of both the *Triṃśikā* and the *Saṃgraha* on a quote from the *Saṃdhinirmocana*, *ādāna* is closely related to *upādi* and *upādāna*, meaning something that appropriates a physical body that conceals the *ālaya-vijñāna*, and also the conscious faculty that appropriates physical organs and their support as well as *vāsanā* of characteristics imputed on to sense data and the like. In other words, in the earliest Yogācāra material, *ādāna* is closely associated with the continuation of mind and body from one rebirth to the next. Compare Paramārtha's translation (T.1595.31.157b10-158a17) and Hsüan-tsang's (T.1597.31.324b24-325-b4). Weinstein discusses the relationship between *ādāna* and *upādāna* in two articles, "The *Ālaya-vijñāna* in Early Yogācāra Buddhism" and "The Concept of *Ālaya-vijnāna* in pre-T'ang Chinese Buddhism." Though *ādāna* is always a defiled state of consciousness (*āsrava*) and cannot be present in Buddhahood, for both Paramārtha and Sthiramati view the seventh or *manas* similarly, the seventh state may become purified in Hsüan-tsang's CWSL. At least in this matter Sthiramati and Paramārtha share the same doctrinal views. See Sasaki, *Shōdaijōron*, pp. 49-50.

14. HKSC 2060.50.501c19.

15. T.2154.55.609a18-21.

16. *Ta-sheng wei-shih lun* (T.1589.31), attributed to Vasubandhu.

17. Ui, *Indo tetsugaku*, 6: 113.

18. *Ibid.*, p. 109.

19. T.1602.31 and T.1603.31 [verses]. The original Sanskrit title of the work is unknown. The two translations by Hsüan-tsang discuss the most important tenets from the *Yogācāra-bhūmi*, analogous to the overall structure of the *Abhidharma-samuccaya*, also composed by Asaṅga. There is not a single commentary on the HYSCL that is extant, but at least five commentaries did exist at one time, including one by K'uei-chi. See Kamimura Shinjō, "Ken'yō-shōgyōron-naiyō no tokui ten," p. 32.

20. Wŏnch'ŭk, *Chieh shen-mi ching shu*, ZZ 34.382b15-383a3.

21. Ui gives a very convenient arrangement of parallel texts by Hsüan-tsang and Paramārtha. For the SWHL see *Indo tetsugaku*, 6: 207-90.

22. Ui Hakujū, *Kokuyaku issaikyō*, 148: 2 (Yūga-bu). Sasaki (*Shōdaijōron*, p. 9) also considers the commentary to be Paramārtha's.

23. Yūki Reimon, *Seshin Yuishiki no kenkyū*, pp. 63-78.

24. *Ibid.*, p. 50.

25. T.1828.42.318a13-15.

26. T.1587.31.63a25-62.

27. T.1617.31.872a5-15.

28. T.2807.85.

29. T.2807.85.1016c19-21.

30. Katsumata, *Bukkyō ni okeru shinshikisetsu*, pp. 758-59. Katsumata does not give the Taishō reference to the SWHL (T.1617.31.872a5-6; a14-15), nor does he indicate the ellipsis in the material from the SWHL. The Tunhuang manuscript also does not indicate the ellipsis. A similar passage may be found in the CSL 1587.31.63a25-b2.

31. Katsumata, p. 759. *Shih-pa k'ung lun*, T.1616.31.864b12. The text identifies *amala-vijnāna* with *prabhāsvaram cittam*, suggesting a Tathagatagarbha influence (864a28).

32. See chapter 2, *Jñeya-lakṣaṇa* (The Characteristics of the Object Known), in Lamotte, trans., *La Somme du grand véhicule d'Asañga*, pp. 88-89; Paramārtha's translation, T.1593.32.118a21-b1. Ui points out the similarity between the HSL and the *Saṃgraha* but does not consider the HSL to be exegesis on the *Saṃgraha*.

33. Yūki, *Seshin yuishiki*, pp. 108-9; Fukaura, *Yuishikigaku kenkyū*, 2: 267.

34. All references to the Sanskrit verses in the *Triṃśikā* are taken from the edition by Sylvain Lévi, *Vijnaptimātratā-siddhi* (Paris, 1925). Verses are found grouped together on pages 13-14 for easy reference and interspersed in Sthiramati's commentary on pages 15-45. CSL 1587.31.61c1. Fukaura, *Yuishikigaku kenkyū*, 1: 294-310, gives parallel texts for Hsüan-tsang's and Paramārtha's recension, and Yūki, *Seshin Yuishiki*, 1: 198-206, gives parallel texts for the Sanskrit and Hsüan-tsang's recension. On pages 79-100, Yūki gives more precise markings for the parallel texts for Hsüan-tsang and Paramārtha than does Fukaura, who is incorrect in several places.

35. T.1587.31.61c2-3.

36. Lévi, p. 14; Sthiramati's commentary, pp. 18-19.

37. T.1587.31.61c5-8. Sthiramati's commentary is similar.

38. Lévi, p. 14; Sthiramati's commentary, pp. 19-21.

39. T.1587.31.61c8-62a4. Sthiramati's commentary differs here. It is because of discrimination of selfhood (*ātman*) and substantial things such as form that the *ālaya* is known. Of course, the intent of both the CSL and Sthiramati is similar here since Sthiramati's examples are based upon interpreting the principle of ignorance.

40. T.1587.31.62a4-11. Conceptualization (*samjñā*) is not discussed as part of the metaphor. Since this mental state is the primary concern of the text, it is discussed in considerable detail as discriminative thinking (*vikalpa*) later on. (The reference to the horse metaphor is 62a8-10.)

41. Lévi, p. 14; Sthiramati's commentary, pp. 21-22. T.1587.31.62a-11-14.

42. Lévi, p. 14; Sthiramati's commentary, pp. 22-23. Actually, the verse says *mananā* as does verse II, but Sthiramati glosses this term in his commentary on verse V as *kliṣṭaṃ manas*.

43. T.1587.31.62a14.

44. Lévi, p. 14; Sthiramati's commentary, p. 23: *nivṛtāḥ kliṣṭatvāt*. T.1587.31.62a14-17.

45. Lévi, p. 14; Sthiramati's commentary, pp. 23-24.

46. T.1587.31.62a17-20.

47. Lévi, p. 14; Sthiramati's commentary, pp. 24-25. T.1587.31.62a-20-23.

48. Lévi, p. 14; Sthiramati's commentary, pp. 25-33. T.1587.31.62a-27-29. The passage in the CSL corresponding to verses IX through XIV: T.1587.31.62a27-29.

49. Lévi, p. 15; Sthiramati's commentary, pp. 33-34.

50. T.1587.31.62b8-17.

51. Lévi, p. 15; Sthiramati's commentary, pp. 34-35.

52. T.1587.31.62b17-19.

53. T.1587.31.62b19-20.

54. T.1587.31.62b21-22. Sthiramati's commentary, pp. 35-36.

55. T.1587.31.62b22-24.

56. Lévi, p. 15; T.1587.31.62b25-28.

57. T.1587.31.62b29-c2. Ui thinks that *shih yüeh* indicates that these are Paramārtha's own ideas, but it could suggest that a more detailed line-by-line commentary follows. The material following this notation (*shih yüeh*) is substantially different from the *Triṃśikā* and does introduce the theme of the *amala-vijnāna*.

58. T.1587.31.62c15-19.

59. T.1587.31.62c20-21.

60. Lévi, p. 15; Sthiramati's commentary, pp. 36-37.

61. T.1587.31.62c20-23.

62. T.1587.31.62c23-2. Sthiramati's commentary: *grāhadvayaṃ: grāhya-grāho grāhakagrāhaś ca* (p. 36).

63. T.1587.31.62c26-63a2.

64. T.1587.31.63a2-10.

65. T.1587.31.63a10-17.

66. T.1587.31.63a17-21.

67. Lévi, p. 15; Sthiramati's commentary, pp. 39-41.

68. T.1587.31.63a21-23.

69. Paramārtha's CSL seems to be most compatible with the type of Yogācāra philosophy that Ratnākaraśānti called *nirākāravādin Yogācāra*, in contrast to *sākāravādin Yogācāra*. The former holds that the highest form of knowledge, wisdom of the absolutely real, is devoid of subject-object relationships and their images, whereas that same consciousness engaged in subject-object relationships is only conventionally real. See Kajiyama Yuichi, *An Introduction to Buddhist Philosophy*, pp. 148-49, 154-55, and Hattori Masaaki and Ueyama Shunbei, *Bukkyō no shisō*, vol. 4, *Ninshiki to chōetsu Yuishiki*, pp. 106-7, for excellent summaries of these two types of Yogācāra. Sthiramati has often been characterized as a *nirākāravādin Yogācārin*, but Nagao disagrees with that view. See *Chū-kan to Yuishiki*, note 40 to chapter 20, "Yuishikigi no kiban to shite no

sanshō-setsu," p. 498, discussion on p. 479. According to Nagao, since Sthiramati in his *Triṃśikā-vijñapti-bhāṣya* says that consciousness produces the aspects (*ākāra*) of the object, Sthiramati cannot be called a *nirākāra-vijñanāvādin* as Mokṣākāragupta has traditionally labeled him.

70. Sthiramati, p. 40; T.1587.31.63a25-b14.

71. Lévi, p. 15; Sthiramati's commentary, pp. 41-42; T.1587.31.63b15-16.

72. T.1587.31.63b19-21.

73. T.1587.31.63b25-26.

74. T.1587.31.63b26-27.

75. Gloss on *vijñaptimātratā* of verse XXV: *ati viśuddha-lakṣaṇāvabodhād yatho'ktam*, p. 42.

76. Lévi, p. 15; Sthiramati's commentary, p. 42; T.1587.31.63b27-29.

77. Lévi, p. 15; Sthiramati, pp. 42-43; T.1587.31.63b29-c2.

78. T.1587.31.63c4-5; Lévi, p. 15; Sthiramati's commentary, pp. 43-45; T.1587.31.63c4-5, 8-10.

79. T.1587.31.63c10-19.

80. T.1585.31.1-59. This work is based upon the teachings of Hsüan-tsang's teacher, Śīlabhadra, who transmitted Dharmapāla's ideas on Yogācāra. In this discussion, I omit the four-*bhāga* theory which, though entirely absent in Paramārtha's CSL, is central in Hsüan-tsang's tract; the three issues that I discuss are central themes in the *Triṃśikā-kārikā*, and they will serve to highlight some of Paramārtha's innovations.

81. *Parāvṛtti* means to reverse directions, to go in the opposite direction; *āśraya-parāvṛtti* is "the fundamental change in mental attitude which is taught as necessary to knowledge of the true doctrine." See Edgerton, *Buddhist Hybrid Sanskrit Dictionary*, p. 320: *paravṛtta*. In Monier-Williams, *Sanskrit-English Dictionary*, p. 591, *paravṛtti* is defined as "turning back or round, returning, revolving, change, interchange, exchange."

82. Sthiramati, p. 44.

83. T.1585.31.51a3-16.

84. Paramārtha discusses the twofold *paratantra-svabhāva* in his translation of Asaṅga's *Mahāyāna-saṃgraha* (T.1593.31.118b6-8; 119c14-25), but in his translation of Vasubandhu's commentary on the *Saṃgraha* he states that since *paratantra-svabhāva* is the cause for the appearance of objects that really do not exist, *paratantra* itself does not truly exist (T.1595.31.182a23-b1). Hsüan-tsang's translation of the *Mahāyāna-saṃgraha-bhāṣya* merely says that the appearances of objects caused by *paratantra-svabhāva* do not exist (T.1597.31.338b11-13).

85. Sthiramati, p. 44: *āśrayo 'tra sarvabījakam ālayavijñānam*. Sthiramati, in his gloss on *āśraya-parāvṛtti* (Lévi, p. 44), says *tasya parāvṛttir*, making *tasya* a referent for the *ālaya* or *āśraya*. Therefore, *āśrayasya parāvṛttir* or *ālayasya parāvṛttir* must refer to something other than the *ālaya*.

86. In the *Mahāyāna-saṃgraha,* however, Paramārtha does give due recognition to a pure and impure *paratantra* in his translation. Cf. T.1595.31.188a12-17, b6-21, but *parinispanna* also has two meanings, pure Suchness (*nirmalā tathatā*) and impure Suchness (*samalā tathatā*) (188b27-29).

87. A discussion of the use of *parīṇāma* in the *Abhidharma-kośa* is given by Suguro Shinjō, "Seshin yuishiki sanjū-shō no kaishaku," in which he lists the occurrences of the term to describe the continuity of *karma* and as the power of the seeds or *bīja* to produce consecutive moments of variations in perceptions. The term *pariṇāma* occurs in verses VI and IX of the *Viṃśatikā*: "If you assert in this way that the existence of beings there [in hell] is due to their *karma,* why not acknowledge that the evolution of consciousness is also [due to *karma*]?" (*yadi tat-karmabhis tatra bhūtānāṃ saṃbhavas tathā / iṣyate pariṇāmas ca kiṃ vijñānasya neṣyate*). "Since cognition having some appearance arises from the same seed [as the object], the sage said that these two are the two kinds of states of the sensory processes [the appearance of perceiver and perceived, of sense organ and sense field] for that cognition" (*yataḥ svabījād vijñaptir yadābhāsā pravartate / dvividhāyatanatvena te tasyā munir abravīt*). (Lévi ed., p. 5.) For the Sāṃkhyan theory of *pariṇāma* see Hattori and Ueyama, *Ninshiki to chōetsu,* pp. 20-22, 110-13.

88. Conze, *Materials for a Dictionary of the Prajñāpāramitā Literature,* p. 246; Edgerton, *Buddhist Hybrid Sanskrit Dictionary,* p. 323: *pariṇāma:* "development, ripening, maturing," hence my translation of *vijñāna-pariṇāma* as evolution of consciousness.

89. Verdu, *Dialectical Aspects in Buddhist Thought,* pp. 34-39, gives an excellent summary of Paramārtha's analysis of *pariṇāma.* Although he cites Ueda as his source for the presentation of Paramārtha's ideas, Verdu clearly and accurately analyzes the threefold movement of consciousness in subject-object correlatives without the intrusion of any of Ueda's errors in analyzing Paramārtha's works (T.1585.31.1a15). Ueda Yoshifumi, in his essay "Pariṇāma ni tsuite" from *Yuishiki shisō nyūmon,* pp. 109-68, discusses different definitions of *pariṇāma* in Mahāyāna literature. In his analysis of Hsüan-tsang's usage, he claims that the CWSL joins *pratibhāsa* or phenomenal appearances with *pariṇāma* whereas Paramārtha does not. But in interpreting Vasubandhu's use of *pariṇāma* from the *Triṃśikā,* Ueda misconstrues *pariṇāma,* stating that it is twofold: *vikalpa* and *vikalpyate,* which do not correspond to the two *bhāga, nimitta,* and *darśana.* Though Vasubandhu never used the latter terms, the text clearly indicates that the perceiver and perceived are the principles being discussed. Ueda apparently minimizes the primary meaning of *pariṇāma* as the activity of consciousness in consecutive moments. Further, Ueda claims (p. 156) that Paramārtha's translation of *pariṇāma* as *pien-i* and *chuan-i* is a more accurate translation, closer to Sthiramati,

than Hsüan-tsang's. But in the CSL Paramārtha does not use these translation equivalents.

90. T.1585.31.1a15. Nagao, *Chūkan to Yuishiki*, p. 343, discusses Hsüan-tsang's translation style in the CWSL. Nagao correctly describes the use of *chuan* to translate *pravartate* but misidentifies the Chinese equivalent for *pariṇāma* as also being *chuan* in verse I when in fact *pariṇāma* is translated as *neng pien* and *vijñāna-pariṇāma* as *i shih so pien*.

91. T.1585.31.46b5-9: "The verse [XXI] that says 'discrimination that arises from conditions' should be understood as meaning the impure part of *paratantra*, since the pure part of *paratantra* is *pariniṣpanna*. Some consider all pure and impure states of mind as denoting discrimination because they all can condition deliberative thought." The Sanskrit is: *paratantra-svabhāvas tu vikalpaḥ pratyayodbhavaḥ* ("The nature of dependence is discrimination that arises from conditions"). Also see K'uei-chi's commentary, *Ch'eng wei-shih lun shu-chi*, T.1830.43.243b20-c1.

92. T.1830.43.243c2-5. For K'uei-chi and Hsüan-tsang, because consciousness is the foundation for phenomenal appearances, it is real.

93. See Nagao, *Chūkan to Yuishiki*, pp. 341-72, for a discussion of Sthiramati's notion of *pariṇāma* in which Nagao argues that *vijñāna-pariṇāma* and *vikalpa* are interchangeable. In addition, *vijñapti-mātratā* means *vijñāna-pariṇāma-mātratā*. Nagao suggests that Sthiramati placed more emphasis on the generation of the seven consciousnesses from the *ālaya* whereas Hsüan-tsang and Dharmapāla placed more emphasis on the dual aspects of perception (*nimitta* and *darśana-bhāga*); he thinks these two divisions, equated with *paratantra*, were Dharmapāla's invention (pp. 457-64).

94. In Sthiramati's *bhāṣya* (p. 16) an ambiguity occurs with the genitive *vijñānasya* in the line: *pratītya-samutpannatvam punar vijñānasya pariṇāma-śabdena jñāpitaṃ*. Grammatically, the genitive could modify either *pratītya-samutpanna* (the more common reading by Buddhologists) or *pariṇāma*. Because the preceding sentence in the *bhāṣya* links *vijñāna* with *pratītya-samutpāda*, the context would indicate that the two are related; on the other hand, the genitive usually precedes the noun it modifies, which would link *vijñānasya* with *pariṇāma*.

95. See Bodhiruci of Northern Wei's translation of the *Saṃdhinirmocana*, completed in A.D. 514 (T.675.16.669c14-22).

96. Lévi, p. 39: *yena yena vikalpena yad yad vastu vikalpyate / parikalpita evāsau svabhāvo na sa vidyate*. Katsumata (*Bukkyō ni okeru shinshikisetsu*, pp. 254-71) discusses verses XX-XXII of the *Triṃśikā*, comparing Paramārtha and Hsüan-tsang's translations. His analysis of the affinity between Paramārtha and Sthiramati is not clear to me, however.

97. Lévi, p. 39: *paratantra-svabhāvas tu vikalpaḥ pratyayodbhavaḥ*.

98. The dispute between Sthiramati and Dharmapāla on whether the introduction of dualistic perceptions resides in the *paratantra-svabhāva*

or in the *parikalpita-svabhāva* is discussed in the *Siddhi*, p. 9, and in O'Brien, "A Chapter on Reality," p. 288, note 32. Nagao states, in his *Chūkan to Yuishiki* (p. 479 and note 38), that in the *Madhyānta-vibhāga-ṭīkā*, Sthiramati associates this dualism with *paratantra-svabhāva*. Hsüan-tsang, on the other hand, asserts that the perceiver and perceived are *parikalpita* but consciousness itself is *paratantra*. Nagao goes on to demonstrate (p. 483) that the dualism in perception can be either *parikalpita* or *paratantra* for both Dharmapāla and Sthiramati. O'Brien implies that Hsüan-tsang held one side and Sthiramati the other but does not specify who says it is *parikalpita* and who says it is *paratantra*. Wŏnch'ŭk, in his commentary on the *Mādhyānta-vibhāga* entitled *Pien chung-pien lun*, states that Dharmapāla viewed the dualism as *paratantra* whereas Sthiramati viewed it as *parikalpita* (T.1835.44.16b26-28).

99. Lévi, p. 40, commentary on verse XXI: . . . *tasmin vikalpe grāhya-grāhaka-bhāvah parikalpitaḥ / tathā hi tasmin vikalpe grāhya-grāhakatvam avidyamānam eva parikalpyata iti parikalpitam ucyate*. T.1587.31.62c11-12.

100. T.1587.31.63a19-23.

101. *Madhyānta-vibhāga-ṭīkā*, p. 217 (chapter 5, verse XV): *dvayena grāhya-grāhakatvena pratibhāsate / kaḥ / paratantra-svabhāvah*. Cited in Nagao, *Chūkan to Yuishiki*, pp. 479 and 498, note 38. Nagao does not speculate on the differences in Sthiramati's thought on this issue between the *Madhyānta-vibhāga-ṭīkā* and his *Triṃśikā-vijñapti-bhāṣya*.

102. Lévi, p. 40, commentary on verse XXI: *tena grāhya-grāhakeṇa paratantrasya sadā sarva-kālaṃ atyanta-rahitatā yā sa parinişpanna-svabhāvaḥ*.

103. *Bukkyō shisōshi kenkyū*, pp. 45-60.

104. Fukaura, *Yuishikigaku kenkyū*, 2: 248-49.

105. Yūki, "Shina yuishiki gakushijō ni okeru Ryōgashi," especially pp. 26-42.

106. T.681.16.734.a24; T.682.16.759c29.

107. T.1587.31.62c18-19. It is important to note that the CSL uses *shih-hsing* or "true nature" here in two different places: "When both subject and object dissolve, this is *shih-hsing*. *Shih-hsing* is identical to the *amala-vijñāna*." This is clearly not a scribe's error for *chen-shih hsing*, the translation Paramārtha consistently gives for *parinişpanna*. *Shih-hsing* may indicate some other technical term, perhaps *tattva* or *tathatā* (usually translated *chen-ju* or *ju-ju*), but the reading is difficult to establish.

108. T.1587.31.63b26-27.

109. Ui believes that this text is the same work as the *chiu shih chang* (Chapter on Nine Consciousnesses), which Wŏnch'ŭk cites in his *Jen wang ching shu* as being a basis for Paramārtha's nine-consciousness theory, crowned by the *amala-vijñāna*. Since neither the *chiu shih i-p'in* nor the *chiu shih chang* exists, it is impossible to determine whether that text—referred to only by Wŏnch'ŭk—had any reference to an *amala*. See *Indo tetsugaku*, 6: 77-79.

110. See Ching-sung's biography, KSC 2060.50.502a2-3, which only indicates a commentary written on Paramārtha's *chiu shih* without furnishing a complete title for either the *chiu shih i p'in* or *chiu shih chang*; T'an-ch'ien's biography, KSC 2060.50.574b4, also lists a commentary on the *chiu shih*, but the complete title of the work is not given.

111. Paramārtha was in Fu-ch'un at this time and did not move to Hsin-wu until 554. The translation date in the LTSPC must therefore be incorrect. See Katsumata, *Bukkyō ni okeru shinshikisetsu*, p. 691. LTSPC 2034.49.99a12.

112. T.2149.55.266b6.

113. ZZ 34.360a-b. We do not know if the *chiu shih p'in* was part of a larger work, although *p'in* suggests that it was. The Chinese can be read alternatively as "the *chiu shih p'in* of the *Chüeh ting tsang lun*"; however, no section with that title is found in the extant text. The text in its present form is two *chüan*, but the KYL (538b5) lists it as three *chüan*. Also, some catalogues had lost the name of the translator but the KYL attributes the work to Paramārtha.

114. Lévi, p. 43, commentary on verse XXVIII: *evaṃ hi samam-anālambyālambakaṃ nirvikalpaṃ lokottaraṃ jñānam utpadyate / grāhya-grāhakābhiniveśānuśayā prahīyante sva-citta-dharmatāyāṃ ca cittam eva sthitaṃ bhavati.*

115. T.670.16.565b23-24.

116. T.1604.31.623a3-9c (*Sūtrālaṃkāra*). The verse by Asaṅga reads as follows: "Having explained the intrinsic purity of mind, covered by extraneous defilement, it still is not separate from the Suchness of mind nor other than the intrinsic purity of mind." Vasubhandhu's commentary states: "The character (*hsiang*) of dependency (*paratantra-lakṣaṇasya*) is the intrinsically pure mind or Suchness of mind. That mind is the *amala-vijñāna*." The words *amala-vijñāna* are not found in the Sanskrit. See Katsumata, *Bukkyō ni okeru shinshikisetsu*, pp. 707-9, for a detailed comparison between the Sanskrit and the Chinese. Though the commentary equating the intrinsically pure mind with the *amala-vijñāna* is not extant in Sanskrit, it represents a view identical to that in Paramārtha's translations. The Tibetan also seems to indicate a term that could be reconstructed as *amala-vijñāna*, according to Iwata, "Shindai no amara-shiki setsu ni tsuite," p. 48. The *Ratnagotra*, verse XXVI, mentions *amala-jñāna* (Iwata, pp. 53-54).

117. T.1617.31.873c23-24.

118. See Ui, *Indo tetsugaku*, 6: 257, for a convenient presentation of parallel passages.

119. T.1587.31.63c4-5.

120. T.1579.30.579-601. Ui gives a convenient presentation of the parallel text, *Indo tetsugaku*, 6: 543-707. He attempts to reconstruct the Sanskrit title in defense of Paramārtha's translation of the title, claiming

that the compound *chüeh ting* means *nirṇaya* ("demonstration" or "conclusive argument") not *niyama*, as the *Yü-chia lu-tsuan* claims. Hsüan-tsang's translation for *viniścaya* ("philosophical disquisition") is cited in the *Yü-chia lu-tsuan* (6: 104-5). See Iwata Ryōzō's study of three recensions—Hsüan-tsang, Paramārtha, and the Tibetan—"Shindai no amara-shiki ni tsuite." The Tibetan agrees with Hsüan-tsang's translation. Katsumata, *Bukkyō ni okeru shinshikisetsu*, pp. 699-700, also compares *āśraya-parāvṛtti* with *amala-vijñāna*.

121. Ui, *Indo tetsugaku*, 6: 563; T.1584.30.1020b10-12.

122. Ui, 6: 564-65; T.1584.30.1020b12-19; 23-24.

123. See, for example, Iwata's study, "Shindai no amara-shiki," pp. 46-56, in which he asserts that Paramārtha reserves the term Tathāgatagarbha for stages of defilement and *amala-vijñāna* for stages without defilement (p. 54). See T.1595.31.191c20-24: "The first kind of pure Dharma is the intrinsic and original purity, namely Suchness, Emptiness, the limit of reality, the aspectless, the absolutely real, and the Dharma-dhātu. The commentary states: The intrinsic and original purity of this [absolute nature]—this purity is called Suchness, which is equally possessed by all sentient beings. Because of this universal characteristic and because the Dharma exists, we say all phenomena are the Tathāgatagarbha." Hsüan-tsang also mentions the Tathāgatagarbha in his translation (T.1597.31.344a3-7) but total separation from impurity is identified with Buddhahood. See Ota Hisanori, "Shindai sanzō soyaku ronten ni mirareru nyoraizō." The basis for all phenomena is identified with the *ālaya* by Hsüan-tsang and with the Tathāgatagarbha by Paramārtha, glossing *dhātu* with the famous passage from the *Mahāyānābhidharma-sūtra*. Ota concludes that the Tathāgatagarbha and the *amala-vijñāna* are the same (the opposite of Iwata's position). Because Tathāgatagarbha literature is inconsistent in relating Tathāgatagarbha to defilement, it is possible that *amala-vijñāna* is also inconsistently used with regard to this same relationship. Ōgawa Kōkan discusses some of Paramārtha's interpolations of Tathāgatagarbha in his translation of the *Saṃgraha-bhāṣya* in "Shindai soyaku shōron ni okeru shiki."

124. Ui, 6: 565; T.1584.30.1020b27-28.

125. Ui, 6: 582-83; T.1584.30.1022a15-17.

126. Ui, 6: 619; T.1584.30.1025c23-26.

127. Ui, 6: 664; T.1584.30.1031a3-4. See Iwata, "Shindai no amara-shiki," pp. 47-55, in which he lists the Sanskrit equivalents *āśraya-parāvṛtti*, *āśraya-parāvṛtti-balādhāna*, and *viśuddha-vijñāna* in places where Paramārtha uses the term *amala-vijñāna*. Iwata agrees that *amala-jñāna*, the wisdom of Tathāgatahood described in the *Bodhisattva-bhūmi*, is the same notion as *amala-vijñāna*, since Paramārtha translates both *jñāna* and *vijñāna* in the same way. Iwata also maintains that *āśraya-parāvṛtti*, *amala-vijñāna* (or *amala-jñāna*), and Tathāgatagarbha are interchangeable

terms in Paramārtha's corpus. There are some fine comparisons made between *amala-vijñāna* and Tathāgatagarbha, but Iwata's contention that there is an identity between the two seems to be an overstatement. In addition, *vijñāna* implies an object to be known by consciousness, yet *amala-vijñāna* has no object. Iwata's claim is not substantiated, because the use of *amala-vijñāna* as an alternative term for *prabhāsvaram cittam* does not mean they are identical. Historically, the theory of *prabhāsvaram cittam* precedes the notion of *amala-vijñāna*.

128. This information on the Tibetan tradition is based upon Nagao's essay in chapter 16 of *Chūkan to Yuishiki*, pp. 413-25. Tsoṅ-kha-pa's writings being discussed are in the Peking edition, 6149, pp. 173-95. Chos-grub's translation of Wŏnch'ŭk's commentary is entitled *Dgons-'grel-gyi 'grel-chen* (Tōhoku 4016; Peking 5517). Wŏnch'ŭk was generally regarded as unorthodox, though he was a disciple of Hsüan-tsang, but his writings from the Hsi-ming monastery were, it is thought, introduced to the region surrounding Tunhuang by T'an-k'uang (d. 788). Chos-grub (Chinese: Fo-ch'eng) is believed to have translated the commentary into Tibetan at the Hsiu-to monastery in Kanchou, and the dates 842 and 846 inscribed on his translations from this monastery would seem to indicate that Wŏnch'ŭk's views were imported to Tibet via Tunhuang. See *Tonkō koshaku-gyō*, vol. 2, ed. Nogami Shunjō (Kyoto, 1972), pp. 6, 113-19.

129. Tsoṅ-kha-pa refers to Paramārtha as Yaṅ-dag-bden-pa or Don-dam-pa and to the CTTL as *Rnam-par ṅes-pa'i mdzod*. Nagao summarizes Tsoṅ-kha-pa's refutation of the nine-consciousness teaching in *Chūkan to Yuishiki*, pp. 419-21.

130. See Ui, *Indo tetsugaku*, 6: 133-74, for parallel texts. Paramārtha's other translation is the *Chung-pien fen-pieh lun*, T.1599.31.451, which may have been written earlier than the *Shih pa k'ung lun* (wrongly attributed to Nāgārjuna). There may be some doubt about assigning a translator's name to the *Shih pa k'ung lun*. Ui thinks it is a fragment of the longer work, *Chung-pien fen-pieh lun* (*Indo tetsugaku*, 6: 101).

131. Ui, p. 148; T.1616.31.863b18-21.

132. Nagao Gadjin, *Madhyānta-vibhāga-bhāṣya* (Tokyo: Suzuki Research Foundation, 1964), p. 27.

133. Ui, p. 156; T.1616.31.864a28.

134. Yūki, for example, does not believe that Paramārtha invented the *amala-vijñāna* as a ninth consciousness.

135. T.1851.44.524c7-525a1.

136. T.1851.44.530b7-8; c9-15. See *Laṅkāvatāra*, T.670.16.565b23-24.

137. See chapter 2 above for direct quote from the *She ta-sheng lun* and for the reference.

138. See chapter 2 above for direct quote from the *Chieh shen-mi ching shu* and for the reference.

139. T.1783.39.4a.
140. ZZ 66.43b.
141. T.1830.43.344c9-13; T.1828.42.605b22-23.

Translation

Throughout the *Chuan shih lun*, Paramārtha does not closely follow the Sanskrit verses of the *Triṃśikā* but paraphrases them in prose form, and freely interprets them according to his own doctrinal orientation. For this reason it is often difficult to break the CSL into lines exactly corresponding to the verses in the *Triṃśikā-kārikās*. Frequently, Paramārtha will omit a term that is in the original and then insert it elsewhere in the text. He also weaves the commentary and verses closely together and supplies the missing referents for pronouns to aid the reader. I have attempted to indicate, without unnecessary awkwardness, the portions of the CSL that are renditions of the *kārikās*. (Roman numerals indicate verse numbers.) The Japanese Buddhologists Ui Hakujū and Yūki Reimon, among others, have put together parallel Sanskrit and Chinese texts, but their verse references are often inclusive of exegetical material. Occasionally, in the case of Yūki, the verses are misnumbered. Paramārtha's breaks in verse often correspond to places where Sthiramati breaks the verses to interpolate. This is a provocative similarity, but we cannot be certain whether or not Paramārtha knew of Sthiramati's commentary—although it is highly unlikely, since he probably left India before Sthiramati wrote his commentary. Possibly, Paramārtha used as a model some other commentary that is now lost. The consistent breaks in the verses suggest some standard text preceding Paramārtha, but his exegesis diverges considerably from Sthiramati. In addition, it is important to note that there are instances when the line breaks differ markedly.

Chuan shih, as verbal adjective-noun, should be translated as "evolved (or revolving) consciousnesses." *Chuan* has the same range of meanings as *pravartate* in Sanskrit (see note 1 below) and denotes the revolution of a wheel, hence the evolved process of mental states engaged in cyclic activity. *Chuan shih* could be translated freely as "cycles of conscious activity." In general (as I show in chapter 3), Paramārtha's interpretation of Vasubandhu's *Triṃśikā-kārikās* is one that analyzes conscious activity as a series of circular developments "churning out" notions of persons and things, in which one rotation develops into another to complete a finished "product" or concept.

Pariṇāma has the meaning of "change, alteration, transformation into, development, evolution" (Monier-Williams, p. 594), which the Chinese character *chuan* also connotes. The best English equivalent is "evolution" or "unrolling" in a certain direction toward change and development. *Pariṇāma* refers to the transformations or changes in the consciousness-series (*saṃtāna*) whereas in Saṃkhyā it is a technical term for the causal process from which the world appears as its effects. Here, in Yogācāra, *pariṇāma* does not refer to the material world but describes only consciousness. *The Awakening of Faith in Mahāyāna* (AFM) (*Ta-sheng ch'i hsin lun*) uses the phrase *chuan shih* to denote the [*kliṣṭa-*] *manas* (*i*) or defiled consciousness (T.1666.577b7-8). Sthiramati defines *pariṇāma* as "the state of becoming other" (*anyathātvam*). "*Pariṇāma*" is "the coming into of a self[-existence] of the effect, dissimilar from ('the moment of') the cause but simultaneous with the termination of ('the moment of') the cause" (*kāraṇa-kṣaṇa-nirodha-samakālaḥ kāraṇa-kṣaṇa-vilakṣaṇah kāryasyātma-lābhaḥ pariṇāmaḥ*, Lévi ed., p. 16). Compare *Abhidharma-kośa*, Pradhan ed., p. 64, ll.5-6; *ch.* 4, T.1558.29.22c14-15: "What is *pariṇāma*? It is the continually changing sequence of different consecutive moments"—that is, the characteristics of conditioned things, changing from one moment to the next in succession.

The system of *pariṇāma* becomes more elaborate in Sthiramati's *bhāṣya*. Nagao gives a detailed description of two kinds of *pariṇāma* as interpreted by Sthiramati. *Hetu-pariṇāma* is the process of the generative cause or impure thoughts in the *ālaya-vijñāna* that increases both the *niḥṣyanda-vāsanā* and the *vipāka-vāsanā*. *Niḥṣyanda-vāsanā* causes the generation of the six consciousnesses and *manas*, both of which arise at the same moment out of the *ālaya-vijñāna* when the *vāsanā* ceases. *Niḥṣyanda-vāsanā* supplies the content of present experience, both good and bad. *Phala-pariṇāma* is due to the functioning of the *vipāka-vāsanā*. When previous *karma* has been completed, the compensatory effect of what species one will be reborn in (*nikāya-sabhāga*) is brought about, and this is also due to *niḥṣyanda-vāsanā*. *Vipāka-vāsanā* maintains the cycle of successive rebirths. The six consciousnesses are based upon both *niḥṣyanda* and *vipāka-vāsanā* for their functioning, but the seventh consciousness is dependent only upon *niḥṣyanda-vāsanā*. See *Chūkan to Yuishiki*, pp. 348-57. In other words, the *ālaya-vijñāna*, according to Sthiramati, is dependent upon the evolution of the first seven consciousnesses yet is their *vāsanā* or latent force. The first seven consciousnesses also rely upon the *ālaya* as a continuity of conscious activity, introducing the notion or sense of time.

1. *Chuan* may stand for *pravartate* found in verse I of the *Triṃśikā*. *Pravartate* can be translated as "occur" or "arise" and also has the meaning of rolling or revolving as a wheel on its axle (Monier-Williams, p. 693), as does the Chinese character *chuan*. Verse I closely associates *vijñāna-pariṇāma* or "evolution of consciousness" with *pravartate* or revolving in a metaphorical sense: *ātmadharmopacāro hi vividho yaḥ pravartate / vijñānapariṇāme 'sau / pariṇāmaḥ sa ca tridhā*. "The various mistaken apprehensions of things and selves *occur in the evolution of consciousness*, this evolution being threefold."

2. *So-yüan* is literally translated as "what is conditioned" or "the conditioned object." It is a translation of *ālambana*, or objective support for consciousness, i.e., an epistemological object that is one's impression of a purported object external to consciousness. *Ālambana* are impressions of "externality," the intended object of any cognition. *Yüan* or "conditioned" expresses the notion of "dependent origination" (*pratītya-samutpāda*), the process of ongoing change without positing independent or "noncontingent" entities. The Chinese character *yüan* means "connection" or "affinity," the interconnected process of the subjective side of consciousness (*neng-yüan*) and the objective side. Everything, being impermanent and changing, is either a sentient being, i.e., conscious, or an object, i.e., an object of consciousness. The relationship is a contingent one, between the subjective and objective sides of conscious activity.

3. The subjective side of consciousness (*neng-yüan*) affects or produces the object while the objective side (*so-yüan*) is affected by the subjective side (consciousness) as the object perceived. This causal relationship expressed as a subject-object dichotomy is a chain of events. The phenomenal world is evolved or projected externally from the subjective activities of the sense consciousnesses. An "inward" causality between the three sets of cognitive faculties (*ālaya*, *ādāna*, and *pravṛtti-vijñāna*) is generated by their own productive force. This passage is cited by Shinkō (934-1004) in his work, *Yuishikigi shiki*, T.2319.71.-369a22-24, and attributed by him to the *chuan shih p'in* from the WHL. The *ālaya* brings forth the other seven cognitive states and logically precedes any other subjective process. It is simply the locus for the seeds that gradually evolve into all cognitive experiences in a series of conscious and subconscious moments.

4. The seventh consciousness is usually denoted as *manas* or *kliṣṭamanas*, but Paramārtha prefers *ādāna*. The Sanskrit equivalent, found in verse II, reads *manana: vipāko mananākhyaś ca / vijñaptir viṣayasya ca / tatrālayākhyaṃ vijñānaṃ vipākaḥ sarvabījakam*. "[The threefold evolution of consciousness] is known as retribution, intellect (*manana*), and the cognition of sense objects. Here, retribution is the consciousness containing all seeds known as the *ālaya*." "Appropriating" (*ādāna-manas*) is Paramārtha's designation for what in Sanskrit is simply *mananā*, ideation, intellect, or the conceptualizing faculty. Paramārtha may be interpreting *manana* as a type of "pride" or "attachment" from *māna*, stemming from the same verbal root (*man*) as *manas*. See Edgerton, *Buddhist Hybrid Sanskrit Dictionary*, *māna* and *mananā*, p. 417; Conze, *manana*: "conceitedness," *mananā*: "mental attitude," p. 312. Certainly Paramārtha's interpretation can be defended, given that the *manas* is the source for the ego and therefore is "defiled" (*kliṣṭa*). The *Ta-sheng i chang* uses the term *ādāna-vijñāna* for the seventh consciousness, attributing this

usage to the *Laṅkāvatāra-sūtra*, presumably Bodhiruci's translation. See Fukaura Shōbun, *Yuishikigaku kenkyū*, 1: 194-95; no citation is given from Bodhiruci's work, however. Also, Bodhiruci's translation of the *Laṅkāvatāra-sūtra* does not list the *ādāna-vijñāna* and *ālaya-vijñāna* as separate cognitive states. See his translation of the *Daśabhūmika* (*Shih-ti ching lun*, T.1522.26.170c) for one occurrence of the term *ādāna* as "the unenlightened consciousness" (*wu-chieh shih*). It is not clear in that text whether the *ādāna* is a seventh state, but it is definitely separate from the *ālaya*. Bodhiruci in his translation of the *Saṃdhinirmocana* (T.675.16.-692) uses the terms *ādāna-vijñāna* and *ālaya-vijñāna* interchangeably. Paramārtha sometimes uses the term *ādāna-vijñāna* as a synonym for the eighth consciousness (*ālaya-vijñāna*)—for example, in his translations of the *Saṃdhinirmocana-sūtra* and *Mahāyāna-saṃgraha-bhāṣya*. See Hakamaya Noriaki, "*Mahāyāna-saṃgraha* ni okeru shinshikisetsu." The reason for this inconsistency remains unclear to me. Katsumata (*Bukkyō ni okeru shinshikisetsu no kenkyū*, pp. 720-21) thinks Paramārtha uses the term *ādāna-vijñāna* for the *ālaya-vijñāna* in the *Saṃdhinirmocana* because this was one of his early translations and his technical vocabulary had not yet been standardized. But Paramārtha uses these two terms interchangeably in his translation of the *Mahāyāna-saṃgraha* and its *bhāṣya* (T.1593.31.114a; T.1595.31.157b), which were among his last translations. See Fukaura, 1: 332-33. The *ādāna-vijñāna* is ordinarily a term for the *ālaya-vijñāna*. For example, a verse cited by Sthiramati in his *Triṃśikā-vijñapti-bhāṣya* (Lévi ed., p. 44) says: "The appropriating consciousness should be known as being characterized by two obstacles: it contains all seeds and the seeds of defilement. . . ." (*jñeyam ādāna-vijñānaṃ dvayāvaraṇa-lakṣaṇaṃ / sarva-bījam kleśa-bījam*). I intend to write a monograph on the notion of *ādāna-vijñāna* in North-South Dynastic Buddhism, with reference to Bodhiruci and Paramārtha.

5. *Ch'en-shih* literally means "dust consciousness," but it is more clearly rendered as the "consciousness of sense data," "dust" referring to the objects of the senses or sense data, i.e., form (*rūpa*) and the like. See Sthiramati's *bhāṣya*, Lévi ed., p. 18. The AFM lists five sorts of sense objects (T.1666.577b10) and sometimes six (T.1666.578a17), the sixth being ideas or concepts, the "objects" of the conceptualizing mind or *mano-vijñāna*. In verses II and VIII, Paramārtha has translated the term *viṣaya* as *ch'en*. The *viṣaya* is the sense object, the sense data with which the sense organs come into contact. In his translation of the *Madhyānta-vibhāga* Paramārtha translates both *artha* and *viṣaya* by the character *ch'en*. According to his biography in the *Hsü kao seng chuan* (T.2060.50.-430b5-6), his teaching of world-negating theories of consciousness—"there is no dust," i.e., no sense objects, "only consciousness" (*wu ch'en wei-shih*)—was criticized by other influential monks as damaging to government policy and national morale.

6. *Pen-shih* may refer to the *mūla-vijñāna*, the antecedent prototype for the Yogācārin innovation of the *ālaya-vijñāna* and a common synonym for the *ālaya*. See Demiéville, "Sur l'authenticité du *Ta Tch'eng K'i Sin Louen*," p. 48; Ruegg, *La Théorie du Tathāgatagarbha et du Gotra*, p. 440; Lamotte, *La Somme du grand véhicule*, p. 27. The *Triṃśikā* sometimes uses these two terms interchangeably.

7. *Chung-tzu*, literally "seeds," is a translation of the Sanskrit *bīja*. The *bīja* are only nominally existent; the term is used metaphorically for the power or energy (*śakti*) of the mind to undergo conceptual and attitudinal changes. Sthiramati gives the following description of *sarva-bīja*: ". . . because it has the power that produces all things" (*tatra sarvadharmotpadāna-śakty-anugamāt sarva-bījaṃ*), Lévi, p. 36. The *ālaya-vijñāna* is defined functionally as the system of conscious activity that reinforces certain modes of behavior and conceptions. It is a repository or "storehouse" for *karma*, "seeds" or stimuli that emerge in the future as conscious acts of an ethical nature similar to that of the preceding acts. A deluded act or thought, in this system of analysis, has a preparatory stage in which a latent impression stored in the *ālaya-vijñāna* becomes active, influencing the present deluded act. Retribution or the compensatory effects of one's actions is the system of operations called the *ālaya-vijñāna*, a mechanism that activates past habits or "seeds," on the one hand, while in turn being a "clearinghouse" for the collection of latent habit-impressions (*vāsanā*) on the other. The "seeds" are a more general term for the power of the *ālaya-vijñāna* to produce phenomenal appearances. The "habit-impressions" (*vāsanā*) are retributive (*vipāka*) or defiled (*niḥṣyanda*) in nature, being the ethical consequence or retribution from specific past acts. The functional, sense consciousnesses (*pravṛtti-vijñāna*) are based upon both *vipāka* and *niḥṣyanda-vāsanā* whereas the *ādāna* (*kliṣṭa-manas*) is based only upon *niḥṣyanda-vāsanā*; see Sthiramti, p. 18 of Lévi edition. Hui-chao, in his *Wei-shih liao-i teng* (T.1832.43.729b28-29), cites the WHL as indicating that the place where all seeds are concealed is called *wu-mo* and the "abode" consciousness.

8. A pun on *wu-ming*, "devoid of knowledge" or "ignorance," is lost in translation. The argument put forth by the opponent can be paraphrased as follows: If one can distinguish between appearance and reality, this is not ignorance as we commonly define it; if one cannot distinguish between the two [appearance and reality], then one should deny the existence of knowledge. Yet we do affirm that there is knowledge and ignorance and deny their nonexistence.

9. Sthiramati explains the relationship between the *ālaya* and its objects as inseparable or indistinguishable from each other: "Cognition of conditions is cognition that is attachment to a world or place. And it is also said to be not well known because it is the functioning of an object and aspect [or form] that are inseparable [or indistinguishable from the

ālaya]. How could consciousness be distinguished from its object and aspect?" Lévi ed., p. 19. (*sthāna-vijñaptir-bhājana-loka-saṃniveśa-vijñaptiḥ / sāpy aparicchinnālambanākāra-pravṛttatvād asaṃviditety ucyate / kathaṃ vijñānam aparicchinnālambanākāraṃ bhaviṣyatīti*.) This passage from the CSL is cited by Fa-tsang in his *Ch'i hsin lun i-chi*, T.44.262c5-6.

10. These eight categories are glossed in Hui-yüan's *Ta-sheng i-chang* and listed by Demiéville, "Sur l'authenticité," p. 50, n. 3. See T.1851.44.-524c7-525a1 for Hui-yüan's descriptions of the *ādāna* and *ālaya*.

11. This first category is not listed in Demiéville but must be an equivalent of the Sanskrit term *āśraya*.

12. The Sanskrit is tentatively reconstructed *a-laya*, "nondissolution," in what appears to be a folk etymology for *ālaya*. Chinese: *wu-mo*. This is glossed by Hui-yüan as "existing in *saṃsāra* but not submerged or lost in it," identified with *ju-lai-tsang*, the Tathāgatagarbha, which is the foundation for ordinary conscious activity and for a religious state of perfection, namely, Buddhahood, based upon the interpretation given in the *Śrīmālādevī-sūtra*.

13. Chinese: *tsang*. Sanskrit would probably be *garbha*, standing for the Tathāgatagarbha, "storehouse of the Buddha-dharmas."

14. Chinese: *sheng*. A Sanskrit equivalent is difficult to reconstruct, although the "sagely" consciousness refers to the Great Sages (*muni*), the Buddhas.

15. Chinese: *ti-i-i*. Sanskrit equivalent is probably *paramārtha*, the "supreme truth."

16. Chinese: *ching*. Sanskrit equivalent is probably *amala*, the "pure" or *vimala*, Lévi, trans., *Siddhi de Hiuan-tsang*, 1: 167.

17. Chinese: *chen*. A Sanskrit equivalent is difficult to reconstruct, perhaps *tattva*, "truth" or "reality."

18. Chinese: *chen-ju*. Usually an equivalent for the Sanskrit *tathatā*, Suchness or the reality of things as they are.

19. This chapter is no longer extant although it is often cited by Buddhologists to support the claim that Paramārtha expounded a system of *nine* modes of consciousness rather than the more conventional eight. The ninth consciousness is termed the *amala-vijñāna* or Pure Consciousness, that is, the religious state of mind of transcendent, nondiscriminative wisdom, realized through meditation. Paramārtha, for purposes of clarity, may have distinguished two modes of the *ālaya-vijñāna* by discussing the eighth phase or mode in an ignorant state as the *ālaya-vijñāna* and the ninth as the *amala-vijñana*. The term *amala-vijñāna* does not appear in the *Mahāyāna-saṃgraha*, but, in my opinion, this theory of nine consciousnesses could have been an accommodation to the controversy between the Northern Ti-lun, who felt the *ālaya-vijñāna* was partly pure in nature yet superficially involved with ignorance, and the Southern Ti-lun, who felt the *ālaya-vijñāna* was intrinsically and entirely

pure. For a brief but lucid presentation of the *amala-vijñāna* see Fukaura, *Yuishikigaku kenkyū*, 1: 188-228. There is also some evidence in the late addition to the Sanskrit text of the *Laṅkāvatāra* (*Sagāthakam*, verse 13) of a ninth mode of consciousness as well as in a Tibetan commentary by Tsoṅ-kha-pa. See Ruegg, *La Théorie du Tathāgatagarbha*, p. 439, n. 1; Nagao, chap. 16 of *Chūkan to Yuishiki*, pp. 413-25.

20. There are five kinds of mental states that accompany all thought, called the *mahābhūmikās* in Sanskrit, literally, "great elements" or the "universals" (*sarvaga* or *sarvatraga*). Vasubandhu, in his *Pañca-skandha-prakaraṇa*, distinguishes between the five universal (*sarvaga*) mental states mentioned here and the five restricted (*pratiniyata-viṣaya*) states mentioned in the list of ten states as being more subtle: desire (*chanda*), understanding (*adhimokṣa*), mindfulness (or memory) (*smṛti*), meditation (*samādhi*), and wisdom (*dhī, prajñā*, or *mati*). Cf. *Kośa*, II.24, 153; *Siddhi*, III, fol. 1, 143-51; Sthiramati's commentary on verses IX and X, pp. 25-26.

21. See *Kośa*, III, pp. 146-47 for sectarian differences in interpretation of *manaskāra*. The most interesting equivalent given in Edgerton, p. 99, is "assumed," "effort directed towards something concretely existing" or what I should prefer to call "preparation for assuming an external object," "intending," or "getting ready for sensation." Sthiramati supports my claim: *ābhujanam ābhogaḥ / ālambane yena cittam abhimukhīkriyate manaskāraś cetasa ābhogaḥ*; Lévi, p. 20. Cited by La Vallée Poussin in *Kośa*, III, p. 147.

22. See Stcherbatsky, *The Central Conception of Buddhism*, pp. 46-47: "The element of consciousness according to the same laws [*pratītya-samutpāda*] never appears alone, but always supported by an object (*viṣaya*) and a receptive faculty (*indriya*)." This threefold interaction (*trika-saṃnipāta*) exists in a *bīja* or latent state prior to the moment of sensation. Examples of this threefold interaction are given in the *Siddhi*, La Vallée Poussin, III, pp. 143-45.

23. In other words, the *ālaya-vijñāna* experiences no pleasure or pain but is indifferent or neutral to such sensations. Verse IV reads: *Upekṣā vedanā tatrānivṛtāvyākṛtaṃ ca tat / tathā sparśādayas tac ca vartate srotas-aughavat.* "There are neutral sensations and it [*ālaya-vijñāna*] is indeterminate and not hidden [by defilement] (*anivṛtāvyākṛtam*). Sensory contact, etc., are likewise [indeterminate]. It moves (*vartate*) like the current in a river." Paramārtha omits the term *anivṛta*. According to Conze, *Materials*, *avyākṛta* means "unpredicted, indeterminate" (p. 87). Edgerton gives "indeterminate, indistinct, neutral" (p. 79). Lévi gives "une chose neutre" (p. 76). Morohashi gives "something that cannot be retained or remembered" for the Chinese equivalent, *wu-chi*. This may be an attempt to allude to the subconscious, which is morally indeterminate. Sthiramati (p. 21) defines *avyākṛta* as "the opposite of good and evil" (*kuśalākuśala-vyavacchedārtham*).

24. The Sanskrit text may have been playing with the words *srotas*, "river," and the Arhat who begins his saintly career as a "stream-winner" (*srotāpatti*). The Arhat is capable of totally eliminating the fundamental consciousness ("river") and the five mental states of sensory contact and others ("current").

25. Paramārtha qualifies this statement later on in this treatise (T.1587.31.62a16-20) when he states that the Arhat eliminates only the coarse, not the subtle, forms of mental states characteristic of the *ālaya-vijñāna*.

26. Verse V reads: "Based upon that, there is the consciousness named *manas*, consisting of mentation, having for its object that (*ālaya*)." (*tasya vyāvṛttir arhatve*) *tad āśritya pravartate* / *tad-ālambanaṃ mano-nāma vijñānaṃ mananātmakam*.

27. *Huo*, literally "delusion," refers to *kleśa* in verse VI.

28. *Ātma-moha* is glossed as *ajñānam* in Sthiramati's commentary, p. 23.

29. The Sanskrit verses claim that the *manas* is hidden and neutral (in verse VI), but the *ālaya*, in contrast, is indeterminate and not hidden (in verse IV). *Nivṛta* is defined as defiled (*kliṣṭatva*) by Sthiramati (p. 23). CSL describes both the *ālaya* and *ādāna* as being neutral (*avyākrta*) and says that the ādana is hidden (*nivṛta*) by defilement. The *ālaya-vijñāna*, however, is not described as hidden by defilement in verse IV. This leaves open the question of whether or not the *ālaya-vijñāna* itself is defiled. In Paramārtha's subsequent passages the implication is that the *ālaya* is defiled.

30. The Sanskrit equivalent in verse VII is *nirodha-samāpatti*, "attainment of [the meditation of] cessation."

31. What Paramārtha means here by "the defiled consciousness" is perhaps *kliṣṭa-manas*, that is, the *ādāna-vijñāna*. Compare Sthiramati's commentary on verse VII: "It (*kliṣṭa-manas*) is not able to occur in the transcendent path because the doctrine of the insubstantiality of self is the counteracting principle to views of selfhood." The Tunhuang manuscript, *She ta-sheng i-chang*, paraphrases this passage, citing the WHL, and stresses the fact that the *ādāna-vijñāna* is the repository for these defilements of "the flesh" or body and the Arhat alone can eliminate them (T.2809.85.1041c23-24; 1042a3-4; a11-12; a12-14; a15-16). Katsumata (*Bukkyō ni okeru shinshikisetsu*, p. 759) hypothesizes that Tao-chi (577-637), a She-lun disciple, may be the author of this Tunhuang commentary. This passage is also cited by K'uei-chi, in his *Ta-sheng fa-yüan i-lin chang* (T.1861.45.285a14-15).

32. *Kośa*, II: 41-42, for the extinction of forms of delusion in the *lokottara-mārga*.

33. This refers to *viṣayasya upalabdhiḥ*, "the apprehending of sense objects." The act of apprehending here implies grasping a thing as if it existed as a material entity outside of the mind. Compare Sthiramati's

usage of *upalabhate* in his comments on verse 28, Lévi, p. 43. See the verse given in Paramārtha's translation of the *Madhyānta-vibhāga* (T.1599.31.451b7-8); Yamaguchi ed., p. 16.

34. This refers to verse IX: *sarvatragair viniyataiḥ kuśalaiś caitasair asau / samprayuktā tathā kleśair upakleśais trivedanā.* Paramārtha here does not describe these mental states as "restricted" (*viniyata*) or "universal" (*sarvatraga* or *sarvaga*), as they are described in the Sanskrit, although later in the text he does describe them that way (62b8).

35. *Ta hsiao huo,* "major and minor forms of defilement," refers to *kleśa* and *upakleśa*. Their definitions occur in the *Kośa,* 2: 24, n. 4.

36. These are listed in verse X. *Hui* corresponds to *dhī* in verse X. *Dhī* is also glossed as *prajñā* in Sthiramati's commentary, Lévi ed., p. 26, and in Vasubandhu's *Pañca-skandha-prakaraṇa*. See Lévi, p. 85, n. 3.

37. *Wu-liu hsin* is a peculiarity of Paramārtha's translation style. It does *not* appear in the AFM, which has the more conventional *wu-lou* for *anāsrava* or the religious state of mind unhampered by delusions of any kind. Specifically, this is the mind without the impure mental impressions of the *ālaya-vijñāna* or the "current" described in the metaphor above.

38. In the *Triṃśika,* illusion (*śāṭhya*) is listed in verse XIII, preceding the vice of intoxication (*mada*), rather than in verse XII.

39. The universal mental states are the five most primitive or basic states of cognitive activity, the above-mentioned sensory contact, attention, sensation (or feeling), volition, and conceptualization. The five restricted mental states are desire, understanding, mindfulness (or memory), meditation, and wisdom. See note 20 above for textual references to these mental states.

40. The Sanskrit reads *mūla-vijñāne*. Verse XV only mentions the five sense consciousnesses and the *ālaya-vijñāna*, but Sthiramati's commentary adds: "the consciousness of vision, etc. are supported by the *mano-vijñāna* as their attendant" (*cakṣur-ādi-vijñānāṃ tad-anucara-mano-vijñāna-sahitānāṃ*), p. 33.

41. The Sanskrit verse does not mention the *kliṣṭa-manas* or *ādāna-vijñāna*, but Sthiramati cites the following verse from the *Saṃdhinir-mocana-sūtra* in his commentary: "Profound and subtle is the *ādāna-vijñāna*, having all seeds, moving like a river. Fools would falsely imagine it is a self because of their delusion; therefore, it is not revealed to them." (*ādāna-vijñāna-gabhīra-sukṣmo ogho yathā vartati sarvabījo / bālāna eṣo mayi na prakāśito mā haiva ātmā parikalpayeyuḥ*, Lévi ed., p. 34; corrected by Lamotte, *La Somme du grand véhicule*, p. 14.) Paramārtha cites this verse in his *Mahāyāna-saṃgraha-bhāṣya*, T.1595.31.157b10-11. This verse makes it clear that the *ādāna-vijñāna* is the same as the *ālaya-vijñāna* since it serves the function of being the repository for all seeds of experience. This is quite different from Paramārtha's interpretation of verse XV.

42. Paramārtha's interpretation of verse XVII deserves attention, for it is an explicit denial of the existence of both consciousness and the object. The verse itself simply states: "Evolution of consciousness is discrimination that is falsely discriminated (*vikalpyate*); therefore, it does not exist. Thus, all is Consciousness-Only." (*vijñāna-pariṇāmo 'yaṃ vikalpo yad vikalpyate / tena tan nāsti tenedaṃ sarvaṃ vijñapti-mātrakam.*) Vasubandhu states explicitly that *vijñāna-pariṇāma* and *vikalpa* are the same. What does not exist [ultimately] is ambiguous from the verse itself. The verse concludes that everything is only an act of cognition. From Sthiramati's commentary, it is evident that he interprets what does not exist as simply the thing discriminated. In other words, the verse is translated as "Evolution of consciousness is discrimination. That which is discriminated by it [by false discrimination or *vijñāna-pariṇāma*] does not exist. Therefore, all is Consciousness-Only." On first reading, Paramārtha's translation agrees with Sthiramati's interpretation, but in his exegesis Paramārtha adds that "the discriminator also does not exist." In other words, the referent for *tan* is interpreted by Paramārtha as *vijñāna-pariṇāmo* and *vikalpa*, not *yad vikalpyate* as in Sthiramati's commentary. For Sthiramati, only what is discriminated as objects does not exist: "What is discriminated by the three kinds of discrimination, the *ālaya*, *kliṣṭa-manas*, and sense consciousnesses, as a world, self, aggregate, element, sense field, form, sound, etc., does not exist. For that reason, *vijñāna-pariṇāma* is called *vikalpa* because the object [of consciousness] does not exist." (*tena trividhena vikalpenālaya-vijñāna-kliṣṭamanaḥ-pravṛtti-vijñāna-svabhāvena sasaṃprayogeṇa yad vikalpyate bhājanam-ātmā skandha-dhātv-āyatana-rūpa-śabdādikaṃ vastu tan nāstīty ataḥ sa vijñāna-pariṇāmo vikalpa ucyate / asad-ālambanatvāt*), p. 35. See Nagao, chapter 12 of *Chūkan to Yuishiki*, pp. 341-46, for his analysis of Sthiramati's definition of *vijñaptimātratā* as an equivalent for *vijñāna-pariṇāma-mātratā* and for *vikalpa-mātra*. Paramārtha is denying that *vijñāna-pariṇāma* exists [ultimately] since both discriminator and discriminated are nonexistent. Consciousness-Only is not equivalent to *vijñāna-pariṇāma* since only by dispensing with the latter altogether [both the discriminator and its objects] is Consciousness-Only established. No other world is ours to *experience*. Sthiramati, on the other hand, retains the subjective side of consciousness as existent: "however, consciousness, because it is conditioned, is a real ['substantial'] state." (. . . *vijñānaṃ punaḥ pratītya-samutpannatvād dravyato 'stīty abhyupeyam*), Lévi ed., p. 16.

43. The use of the term *shih*, which occurs here for the first time in the CSL, indicates a line-by-line exegesis of verse XVIII, rather than the paraphrasing of the entire content of the verse as in the exegesis preceding this passage. *Shih* also occurs two more times in the CSL for exegesis on specific quotes from a given verse. It does not seem to indicate a given commentary as Ui claims (*Indo tetsugaku*, 6: 107). Throughout

my translation, the exegeses, distinct from the verses, have been indicated by brackets for convenience, and I have usually discussed the exegeses as if they were Paramārtha's; but there is still a problem about the true authorship of exegeses attributed to Paramārtha. Further research on some of Paramārtha's more original works will help to resolve this question.

44. Compare Sthiramati's commentary, which presents a substantial sort of consciousness as possessor of all seeds and as an origin of reality: "It [the verse] says 'consciousness' because some imagine that some sort of Primary Source (*pradhāna*) other than consciousness is the seed of everything." (*vijñānād anyad api kaiścit pradhānādi sarva-bījaṃ kalpyata iti vijñānam ity āha*, Lévi, p. 36.)

45. This interpretation is similar to Sthiramati's: "'*Tathā tathā*' [from verse XVIII] means that it [evolution] provides a situation for each potentiality to generate, without interruption, a variety of discriminations, each according to its type." (*tathā tatheti tasya tasya vikalpasyānantarotpādana-samarthāvasthāṃ prāpnotīty arthaḥ*, Lévi, p. 36.)

46. Sthiramati gives the following gloss for "mutual interaction": "'Because of the mutual interaction' means, for example, when the cognitive act of vision, etc., is present, nurtured by its own power, it becomes a cause for the evolution of the *ālaya-vijñāna* that has a special power. The evolution of the *ālaya-vijñāna* also becomes a cause for the act of vision, etc. Thus, because of the mutual interaction, the two occur together." (*anyonya-vaśād iti / tathā hi cakṣur-ādi-vijñānaṃ sva-śakti-paripoṣe vartamānaṃ śakti-viśiṣṭasyālaya-vijñāna-pariṇāmasya nimittaṃ so 'pi ālaya-vijñāna-pariṇāmaḥ cakṣur-ādi-vijñānasya nimittaṃ bhavati / evam anyonya-vaśād yasmād ubhayaṃ pravartate*, Lévi, p. 36.) Paramārtha's interpretation of verse XVIII stresses the various forms of discrimination that evolve into one's self and into other selves. This is the mutual interaction that occurs. There is no mention of the reciprocal causation between the *ālaya-vijñāna* and the other seven *vijñāna*.

47. Whereas the Sanskrit verse simply states that discrimination (*vikalpa*) is produced, Paramārtha interpolates "discrimination and discriminated objects" for *vikalpa*. Paramārtha's usage of *fen-pieh* to translate *vikalpa* and *parikalpita* (*fen-pieh hsing*) may incorrectly lead the reader to conclude that *vikalpa* and *parikalpita-svabhāva* are the same.

48. Here is the first occurrence of the term *amala-vijñāna* as the supreme truth behind all cognitive experience. It is important to note that the commentary by Sthiramati stresses the supremacy of the *ālaya*: "Therefore, various kinds of false discriminations are produced from the *ālaya-vijñāna*, which is not governed by anything else." (*tasmād ālaya-vijñānād anyenānadhiṣṭhitād aneka-prakāro vikalpaḥ sa sa jāyate*, p. 36.) It is not clear (in Sthiramati's system) whether the *ālaya* no longer functions when cognition apprehends the true reality or whether it ceases. The Tunhuang manuscript, *She ta-sheng lun chang*, attributes the follow-

ing to the WHL: "The characterless and unproduced state is the *amala* [-*vijñāna*], the ultimately pure consciousness" (T.2807.85.1013c20-21). "The nature of discrimination (*parikalpita-svabhāva*) is forever nonexistent. The nature of dependence (*paratantra-svabhāva*) also does not exist. As for these two, they have no existence and this is identical to the *amala-vijñāna*. Thus, it is ultimately the only pure consciousness. Furthermore, it is a foreign tradition that states in the *Shih-ch'i ti-lun*, 'Chapter on the Bodhisattva,' that the *amala-vijñāna* is explained as the ninth consciousness." (T.2807.85.1016c19-22.) Compare CSL 63a25-b2.

49. The CSL has the character *chi*, which perhaps signals that the verse is adapted somewhat more distinctively from the Sanskrit original. This character occurs one other time in the text, again for a passage substantially different from the Sanskrit original. Though Ui considers this to be commentarial material, I think it would be better to interpret the use of the character *chi* as an indication to the reader that the verse is substantially and intentionally altered by Paramārtha.

50. Verse XIX lists *karmaṇo vāsanā* and *grāha-dvaya-vāsanayā*. Neither the *kārikās* nor Sthiramati gives two forms of *vāsanā* of *karma*. I have interpreted the latter part of the lines in the CSL in correspondence with verse XIX, because otherwise the meaning is not clear. The Sanskrit verse reads: "The latent impressions from past *karma* together with the latent impressions of a twofold perception ['attachment' or 'grasping'] produce another consequence [or retribution] when the previous consequence has been ended." (*karmaṇo vāsanā grāha-dvaya-vāsanayā saha / kṣīṇe pūrva-vipāke 'nyad vipākaṃ janayanti tat*, p. 36.)

51. See SWHL 870c10-16 and 871a14-19 for the reversal of terminology. In that text "the categories for aspects" is the discriminated object whereas in the CSL the discriminated object is the gross form of latent impressions that generate potential situations for defilement. The "gross" or primitive [delusions] in the SWHL are the sphere of the discriminating subject, whereas in the CSL the discriminator manufactures the content of the delusion, constructs the aspects or appearances of objects in the world, and is termed "the latent force of aspects." Though the CSL notes the difference in terminology, Paramārtha does not explain the inconsistency.

52. The use of the character *chi* to introduce these lines may, as I have suggested, indicate to the reader a substantial revision in the verse. Here, the corresponding verse (XX) reads as follows: "Whatever thing is falsely discriminated by various discriminations is only imaginatively constructed in nature and does not exist" (*yena yena vikalpena yad yad vastu vikalpyate / parikalpita evāsau svabhāvo na sa vidyate*). The *She ta-sheng i-chang* (T.2809.85.1045a2-3) cites the WHL: "As for the nature of discrimination, the nature of all phenomena, denoted through naming and language, is only appearance." Compare the SWHL: "If one explains discrimination per se, one means the mind and mental phenomena of

the triple world. Its support and object then are not separate [from the discriminating mind] because the support [for discrimination] is the intended object that appears as if it were matter and the object of discrimination is the name of that intended object that appears as if it were matter." (T.1617.31.870c3-6.)

53. Verse XXI: "The nature of being dependent on another is discrimination that arises from conditions. The state of being always separate from the previous state is the completion of that." (*paratantra-svabhāvas tu vikalpaḥ pratyayodbhavaḥ / niṣpannas tasya pūrveṇa sadā rahitatā tu yā,* p. 39.) Here, Sthiramati interprets the verse as meaning that separation of *paratantra-svabhāva* from *parikalpita-svabhāva* renders *paratantra-svabhāva* equivalent to *parinispanna-svabhāva*, or the perfect nature (*tena grāhya-grāhakeṇa paratantrasya sadā sarva-kālaṃ atyanta-rahitatā yā sa pariniṣpanna-svabhāvaḥ,* p. 40). Paramārtha is interpreting the nature of dependence quite differently, as I mentioned in chapter 5. The CSL denies the separation between the nature of discrimination and that of dependence, thus contradicting the position of Sthiramati and all other major proponents of Yogācāra.

54. According to the SWHL, the nature of discrimination does *not* include the five ways in which phenomena can exist: "The nature of discrimination has no characteristics that are substantial. Why? Because this nature is not included within the five sets [of phenomenal existence]. If phenomena exist, then they are nothing but these five sets. The five sets are: (1) characteristics, (2) names, (3) discrimination, (4) Suchness, (5) nondiscriminative wisdom" (T.1617.31.867c29-868a2). However, the *Madhyānta-vibhāga* disagrees with the SWHL and agrees with the CSL; T.1599.31.456b24-25 (Paramārtha's translation).

55. Compare Sthiramati's argument in his gloss on verse XXII for the mutual dependency ("neither identity nor difference") between the nature of dependence and the nature of the absolute. "If the absolute nature were other than the dependent nature, then the dependent nature would not be empty of the imaginatively discriminated. But if the absolute is the same [as the dependent nature], its objects (*ālambanaḥ*) would not be pure because it would be in a defiled state like the dependent nature. Likewise, the dependent nature would not be a defiled state [since, being identical to the absolute, it would be pure]. Because it [the dependent nature] is not other than the absolute, it is like the absolute." (*yadi hi pariniṣpannaḥ paratantrād anyaḥ syād evaṃ na parikalpitena paratantraḥ śūnyaḥ syāt / athānanya evam api pariniṣpanno na viśuddhālambanaḥ syāt paratantravat saṃkleśātmakatvāt / evaṃ paratantraś ca na kleśātmakaḥ syāt / pariniṣpannāt ananyatvāt pariniṣpannavat,* p. 40.)

56. Again, Sthiramati is arguing for the reciprocal relation between the nature of dependence and the nature of the absolute, interpreting "when one is not seen, then the other is not seen" (*nādṛṣṭe 'smin sa dṛśyate*) as "when the absolute is not seen [or understood], the dependent

nature is [also] not seen" (*ataḥ pariniṣpanne adṛṣṭe paratantro na dṛśyate*, p. 40).

57. Verse XXIII: "The state of being devoid of a substantial nature that applies to all phenomena is taught by positing three types of states devoid of substantial natures for the three natures." (*trividhasya svabhāvasya trividhāṃ niḥsvabhāvatāṃ / saṃdhāya sarva-dharmāṇāṃ deśitā nihsvabhāvatā*, p. 40.)

58. Sthiramati: *lakṣaṇa-niḥsvabhāvatā* (commenting on verse XXIII), defined in his gloss on verse XXIV as: "The first is the nature [of a thing] that is imaginatively constructed. And that [nature] is devoid of a substantial nature by virtue of its characteristics since those characteristics [assigned to the nature of a thing] are imputed. For example, [the nature called] form is characterized by form, feeling by experience, etc. Thus, because it [the nature of a thing] has no form per se like a flower in the sky, it is devoid of a substantial nature on the grounds of that form itself [since that form does not exist]." (*prathamaḥ parikalpitaḥ svabhāvaḥ ayaṃ ca lakṣaṇenaiva niḥsvabhāvaḥ tal-lakṣaṇasyotprekṣitatvāt / rūpa-lakṣaṇaṃ rūpaṃ anubhava-laksaṇā vedanety ādi / ataś ca svarūpābhāvāt khapuṣpavat svarūpeṇaiva niḥsvabhāvaḥ*, p. 41.)

59. Sthiramati: *utpatti-niḥsvabhāvatā* (commenting on verse XXIII), defined in his gloss on verse XXIV as: "'The second' means the dependent nature. Certainly, this does not exist by itself because, like an illusion, it is produced dependent upon some other [conditions]. Thus, accordingly it can be demonstrated that as there is no production [by itself but only in conjunction with other factors] so it is said [in the verse]: 'the state devoid of a substantial nature that is produced.'" (*aparaḥ punar iti paratantra-svabhāvaḥ / na svayaṃbhāva etasya māyāvat parapratyayenotpatteḥ / ataś ca yathā prakhyāti tathāsyotpattir nāstīti ato 'sya utpatti-niḥsvabhāvatety ucyate*, p. 41.)

60. The SWHL gives a further description of this relationship between matter and names [or essences]: "If one explains discrimination per se one means the mind and mental phenomena of the triple world. Its support and object then are not separate [from the discriminating mind] because the support [for discrimination] is the intended object that appears as if it were matter, and the object of discrimination is the name of the intended object that appears as if it were matter." SWHL 870c3-6.

61. Compare Sthiramati's use of the seed-sprout metaphor in his discussion of *vāsanā*, commenting on verse XIX, pp. 36-37.

62. Sthiramati: *paramārtha-niḥsvabhāvatā* (commenting on verse XXIII) defined this state in his gloss on verse XXV: "Because the absolute nature is the absolute truth of all phenomena, which are dependent [by nature], it is their 'Dharma Nature.' Therefore, the absolute nature is the state devoid of any substantial nature from the perspective of the absolute truth because the nature of the absolute is not to have any sub-

stantial existence." (*sa yasmāt pariniṣpannaḥ svabhāvaḥ sarva-dharmāṇāṃ paratantrātmakānāṃ paramārthaḥ tad-dharmateti kṛtvā tasmāt pariniṣpanna eva svabhāvaḥ paramārtha-niḥsvabhāvatā pariniṣpannasyābhāva-svabhāvatvāt*, p. 41.)

63. Verse XXV has the term *dharmāṇāṃ paramārthaḥ*.

64. Verse XXVI does not have this phrase.

65. Sanskrit: *grāha-dvayasyānuśayaḥ*.

66. The Sanskrit verse (XXVII) is somewhat different: "Someone who posits in front of him something, saying 'This is Consciousness-Only' on the basis of the apprehension [of an object] cannot possibly be established in its true nature." (*vijñapti-mātram evedam ity api hy upalambhataḥ / sthāpayann agrataḥ kim çit tan-mātre nāvatiṣṭhate*, p. 42.) The CSL uses the term *chih* for *upalambhataḥ*, perhaps linking it closely with the latent impressions of dualistic perceptions (*grāhya-grāhaka*). The implication is that when there is no perception of an object, one has understood Consciousness-Only, according to Sthiramati, whereas the CSL interprets *upalambhataḥ* to mean that both perceiver and perceived object are no longer apprehended. Sthiramati does define *upalambhataḥ* as grasping (*grahaṇataḥ*) and making manifold [through logic] (*citrī-karaṇataḥ*), but the emphasis is on the elimination of the perceived object as existing outside the mind, not on the perceiver as equally unreal. Verse XXVIII, discussed below, demonstrates Sthiramati's position as, in fact, also eliminating the perceiver. In this respect, the two Yogācārins are compatible.

67. Verse XXVIII: "When consciousness does not apprehend any object [of consciousness], then one stands in Consciousness-Only, where there is nothing to be perceived because there is no perception of that [thing]." (*yadā tvālambanaṃ [vi]jñānaṃ naivopalabhate tadā / sthitaṃ vijñāna-mātratve grāhyābhāve tad-agrahāt*, p. 43.) The verse here suggests that when there is no perception of an object, the *act* of perception cannot take place. Paramārtha's interpretation of the verse, however, clearly states that *the two* are not manifested, that is, neither the object nor the perceiver, not simply the act of perception involved with objects. Paramārtha intentionally uses *yüan* for *upalabhate* to suggest the dualistic relationship (*so yüan* and *neng yüan*) between the object perceived and the perceiver in a similar fashion to his use of *chih* to indicate dualistic "grasping." Compare Sthiramati's interpretation of this verse: "Only when there is something to be perceived can there be a perceiver and not when there is nothing to be perceived. 'When there is nothing to be perceived' means that there also is no perceiver and it is not simply the absence of the act of perceiving. Of course, this is equivalent to the production of the transcendent knowledge devoid of false discrimination, having neither the object nor what supports the object [namely, consciousness]. Then, there is only mind abiding in the Dharma-Nature of itself since the subtle propensities of attachment to something per-

ceived and to the perceiver are eliminated." (*grāhye sati grāhako bhavati na tu grāhyābhāva iti / grahyābhāve grāhakābhāvam api pratipadyate / na kevalaṃ grāhābhāvaṃ / evaṃ hi samamanālambyālambakaṃ nirvikalpaṃ lokottaraṃ jñānaṃ utpadyate / grāhya-grāhakābhiniveśānuśayā[ḥ] prahīyante svacitta-dharmatāyāṃ ca cittam eva sthitaṃ bhavati*, p. 43.)

68. Sanskrit: *anupalambha*.

69. Sanskrit: *acitta*.

70. Sanskrit: *jñānaṃ lokottaram*.

71. Sanskrit: *acintya*.

72. Sanskrit: *kuśala*.

73. Sanskrit: *dhruva*.

74. Sanskrit: *sukha*.

75. Sanskrit: *vimukti-kāya*.

76. Compare Sthiramati's commentary on verse XXVI, p. 42. A similar passage is cited in a Tunhuang commentary, *She ta-sheng lun chang* (T.2807.85.1021a15-16): "The virulent *kleśa* and *anuśaya* ('latent, subtle propensities') are cut off by seeing the truth [in the path of Insight]. *Vāsanā* and *kleśa* are cut off when one has attained the wisdom of Suchness." This Tunhuang manuscript attributes this quote to the WHL.

77. There is no passage in the ŚDS that corresponds exactly to this quote. In Guṇabhadra's translation, however (T.353.12.220b12-14), the passage occurs: "If the stage of ignorance is not absolutely eliminated, then the phenomena more numerous than the sands of the Ganges which should be eliminated will not be absolutely eliminated." The phrase "the phenomena more numerous than the sands of the Ganges"—used where the CSL has "the limitless four stages of abiding" [in time, desire, form, and existence]—refers to the strongest, latent types of defilement—by implication, the four stages of abiding that accompany ignorance: false views of monism, desiring sensuous pleasures, desiring forms, and desiring existence. The ŚDS goes on to say that the knowledge (*chih*) of enlightenment (*bodhi*) that the Tathāgata possesses is capable of eliminating ignorance and all defilement. Paramārtha seems to be interpreting the *ālaya-vijñāna* as equivalent to the stage of ignorance; the propensities for dualism as the four abiding stages of defilement. The *Ta-sheng ch'i hsin lun*, almost certainly a composition after Paramārtha's time, does fuse the stage of ignorance with the *ālaya-vijñāna* as its base: "The causes and conditions for life and death refer to living beings who depend upon the evolutions (*chuan*) of the mind, *manas*, and *mano-vijñāna*. It is said that there is ignorance based upon the *ālaya-vijñāna*" (T.1666.32.577b3-4).

78. The meaning of this last sentence is apparently twofold: (1) as the conclusion of the text by the name *Chuan shih lun* (although here it is called *Shih chuan p'in*); and (2) as a referent for the ultimate state of transforming from a deluded consciousness to the transcendent wisdom of Consciousness-Only. This is Ui's interpretation (*Indo tetsugaku*, 6: 485).

Selected Bibliography

Primary Sources

I. SANSKRIT

Abhidharma-kośa, by Vasubandhu. Translated by Louis de La Vallée Poussin as *L'Abhidharmakośa de Vasubandhu*. Paris, 1925.

Abhidharma-samuccaya, by Asaṅga. Translated by Walpola Rahula as *Le compendium de la super-doctrine*. Paris, 1971.

Bodhisattva-bhūmi, by Asaṅga. Edited by Unrai Wogihara as *Bodhisattva-bhūmi: A Statement of Whole Course of the Bodhisattva*. Tokyo, 1938-39; reprint, 1971.

Daśabhūmika-sūtra. Edited by J. Rahder. Paris, 1926.

Laṅkāvatāra-sūtra. Edited by Bunyiu Nanjio. Tokyo, 1923. Translated by Daisetz T. Suzuki. London, 1932; reprint, 1968.

Madhyānta-vibhāga-bhāṣya, by Vasubandhu; verses by Asaṅga. Edited by Nagao Gadjin. Tokyo, 1964.

Madhyānta-vibhāga-ṭīkā, by Sthiramati. Edited by Susumu Yamaguchi. Tokyo, 1934; 2nd ed., 1966.

Mahāyāna-saṃgraha, by Asaṅga. Translated by Étienne Lamotte as *La Somme du grand véhicule d'Asaṅga*. Louvain, 1938; 2nd ed., 1973.

Mahāyāna-sūtrālaṃkāra, attributed to Asaṅga. Translated and edited by Sylvain Lévi. *Bibliotheque de l'École des Hautes Études*, vols. 159 and 190. Paris, 1907, 1911.

Ratnagotra-vibhāga. Edited by E. Johnston. Patna, 1950. Also translated by Jikidō Takasaki as *A Study on the Ratnagotra-vibhāga*. Rome, 1966.

Saddharmapuṇḍarīka-sūtra. Translated by Leon Hurvitz as *Scripture of the Lotus Blossom of the Fine Dharma*. New York, 1976.

Saṃdhinirmocana-sūtra. Translated by Étienne Lamotte as *Samdhinirmocana Sūtra: L'explication des mystères*. Louvain, 1935.

Śrīmālādevī-sūtra (ŚDS). Translated by Diana Y. Paul as *The Buddhist Fem-*

inine Ideal: Queen Śrīmālā and the Tathāgathagarbha. Missoula, Mont., 1980. Translated by Alex and Hideko Wayman as *The Lion's Roar of Queen Srimala*. New York, 1974.

Vijñaptimātratā-siddhi, by Hsüan-tsang. Edited and translated by Louis de La Vallée Poussin as *Vijñaptimātratāsiddhi: La Siddhi de Hiuang-tsang*. 6 vols. Paris, 1925-28.

Yogācārabhūmi-śāstra, by Asaṅga. Edited by V. Bhattacharya as *The Yogācāra-bhūmi of Ācarya Asaṅga: Part I*. Calcutta, 1957.

II. CHINESE AND JAPANESE

Ch'en shu, compiled by Yao Ssu-lien (557-637). Peking, 1972, 2 vols.

Chen yüan hsin ting shih chiao mu-lu, compiled by Yüan-chao of T'ang in 800. T.2157.55.

Ch'eng wei-shih lun shu-chi, by K'uei-chi (632-82) of T'ang, 20 *ch.* T.1830.43.

Chieh-shen-mi-ching shu, by Wŏnch'ŭk (613-95) of T'ang, 7 *ch.* ZZ 34.

Chou shu, compiled by Ling-hu Te-fen (583-666), 50 *ch.* Peking, 1971, 3 vols.

Chüeh ting tsang lun (CTTL), part of the *Yogācāra-bhūmi*, attributed to Asaṅga, translated by Paramārtha. T.1584.30.

Chung ching mu-lu (FC), compiled by Fa-ching in 594, 7 *ch.* T.2146.55. A Sui dynasty catalogue of 2,250 Buddhist texts.

Fa-hua hsüan-i shih-ch'ien, by Chan-jan (711-82) of T'ang, 20 *ch.* T.1717.33.

Hsü kao seng chuan (HKSC), compiled by Tao-hsüan (596-667), in 645, 30 *ch.* T.2060.50. A record of approximately 340 eminent monks and 60 of their assistants or disciples who lived A.D. 520-641.

Jen wang ching shu, by Wŏnch'ŭk (613-95), 6 *ch.* ZZ 40.

Ju leng-chia ching (*Laṅkāvatāra-sūtra*), translated by Bodhiruci of Northern Wei, 10 *ch.* T.671.16.

K'ai-yüan shih chiao mu-lu (KYL), compiled by Chih-sheng (668-740) of T'ang in 730, 20 *ch.* T.2154.55.

Kao seng chuan (KSC), compiled by Hui-chiao (497-554) in 530, 14 *ch.* T.2059.50. A record of approximately 257 eminent monks and 243 of their assistants or disciples who lived A.D. 67-519.

Kegon jūjū yuishiki jōkanki, by Gyōnen (1240-1321) in 1292. *Nihon daizōkyō, Kegon-shū*, vol. 42.

Kegon kumokushō hotsugoki, by Gyōnen. *Dainihon bukkyō zensho*, vol. 122.

Ku-chin i ching t'u chi (KC), compiled by Ching-man between 648 and 664, 4 *ch.* T.2151.55. A catalogue of Buddhist texts dated through the time of Hsüan-tsang, listing 1,518 texts and 298 lost works.

Leng-chia a-pa-to-lo pao ching (*Laṅkāvatāra-sūtra*) in 4 *ch.*, translated by Gunabhadra in 443. T.670.16.

Liang shu, compiled by Yao Ssu-lien (557-637). Peking, 1972, 3 vols.

Li-tai san-pao chi (LTSPC), compiled by Fei-chang of Sui in 597, 15 *ch.*

T.2034.49. A catalogue of Buddhist texts from late Han through Sui.

Nan shih, compiled by Li Yen-shou (7th century). Peking, 1975, 6 vols.

She ta-sheng i-chang, unknown authorship, 4 *ch*. T.2809.85.

She ta-sheng lun (*Mahāyāna-saṃgraha*), by Asaṅga, translated by Paramārtha, 3 *ch*. T.1593.31.

Sheng-man pao-k'u, by Chi-tsang (549-623), 6 *ch*., T.1744.37.

Shih-pa k'ung lun (SPKL), part of the *Madhyānta-vibhāga*, by Vasubandhu, 1 *ch*. T.1616.31.

Ta-chou k'an ting chung ching mu-lu (TCL), compiled by Ming-ch'uan in 695, 15 *ch*. T.2153.55. A catalogue of 3,616 Buddhist texts, sponsored during the reign of Empress Wu Tse-t'ien.

Ta-sheng ch'i-hsin lun, composition attributed to Aśvaghoṣa and translation attributed to Paramārtha, 1 *ch*. T.1666.32. Translated by Yoshito Hakeda as *The Awakening of Faith in Mahāyāna* (AFM). New York, 1967.

Ta-sheng ch'i hsin lun i-shu, attributed to Hui-yüan (523-92), 4 *ch*. T.1843.44.

Ta-sheng chih-kuan fa-men, by Hui-ssu (515-77), 4 *ch*. T.1924.46.

Ta-sheng fa-yüan i-lin chang, by K'uei-chi (632-82), 7 *ch*. T.1861.45.

Ta-sheng i-chang, by Hui-yüan (523-92), 26 *ch*. T.1851.44.

Ta-t'ang nei-tien lu (NTL), compiled in 664 by Tao-hsüan (596-667), 10 *ch*. T.2149.55. A catalogue of Buddhist texts from Han through the beginning of the T'ang dynasty.

Ta-tz'u-en ssu san-tsang fa-shih chuan, biography of Hsüan-tsang by K'uei-chi (632-82), 10 *ch*. T.2053.50.

Yü-chia lun chi, by Tun-lun of T'ang, based upon K'uei-chi's *Yü-chia lun liao tsuan*; 48 *ch*. T.1828.42.

Yuishikigi shiki (alternate title: *Yuishiki gishō*), by Shinkō (934-1004), based upon part of K'uei-chi's *Fa-yüan i lin chang*; 12 *ch*. T.2319.71.

Secondary Sources

Akanuma Chizen. *Indo Bukkyō koyū meishi jiten*. Kyoto, 1967 reprint.

Anacker, Stephan. "Vasubandhu: Three Aspects." Unpublished Ph.D. dissertation, University of Wisconsin, 1970.

———. "Vasubandhu's *Karmasiddhiprakaraṇa* and the Problem of the Highest Meditations." *Philosophy East and West*, 23, no. 3 (January 1972): 247-58.

Chatterjee, Ashok Kumar. *The Yogācāra Idealism*. New Delhi, 1962.

Chattopadhyaya, Sudhakar. *Early History of North India: From the Fall of the Mauryas to the Death of Harśa (c. 200 B.C.-A.D. 650)*. Calcutta, 1968.

Ch'en, Kenneth. *Buddhism in China: A Historical Survey*. Princeton, N.J., 1964.

Coedès, George. *Les États Hindouisés d'Indochine*. Paris, 1948; 2nd ed., 1964.

Conze, Edward. *Materials for a Dictionary of the Prajñāpāramitā Literature*. Tokyo, 1973.

Dai nihon zokuzōkyō (*Hsü tsang ching*). Hong Kong, 1967.
Demiéville, Paul. "Sur l'authenticité du *Ta Tch'eng K'i Sin Louen*," in *Choix d'Études Bouddhiques (1929-1970)*, pp. 1-79. Leiden, 1973.
Dien, Albert E. *Pei ch'i shu 45: Biography of Yen chih-t'ui*. Wurzburger Sino-Japonica, no. 6. Frankfurt, 1976.
Edgerton, Franklin. *Buddhist Hybrid Sanskrit Dictionary*. New Haven, 1970.
Filliozat, Jean. *Political History of India*. Translated by Philip Spratt. Calcutta, 1957.
Fleet, John Faithfull. *Corpus Inscriptionum Indicarum*. Calcutta, 1888.
Fuji Ryūshō. "Shōron gakuha ni okeru Amara (*amala*)-shiki no mondai." *Ryūkoku Daigaku bukkyō bunka kenkyūsho kiyō*, no. 4 (May 1965): 113-17.
Fukaura Shōbun. "Genjō sanzō zehiron," *Bukkyōgaku kenkyū*, vol. 1, *Ryūkoku Daigaku bukkyō gakkai* (January 1949): 1-18.
———. *Yuishikigaku kenkyū*. 2 vols. Kyoto, 1954; 2nd ed., 1977.
Goyal, S. R. *A History of the Imperial Guptas*. Allahabad, 1967.
Hacking, Ian. *Why Does Language Matter to Philosophy?* Cambridge, Eng., 1975.
Hakamaya Noriaki. "*Mahāyāna-samgraha* ni okeru shinshikisetsu." *Tōyō bunka kenkyūjo kiyō*, no. 76 (March 1978): 197-309.
Hattori Masaaki. *Dignāga: On Perception*. Cambridge, Mass., 1968.
Hattori Masaaki and Ueyama Shunbei. *Bukkyo no shisho*, vol. 4: *Ninshiki to chōetsu yuishiki*. Tokyo, 1970.
Hirakawa Akira. *Daijō kishinron*. Tokyo, 1973.
Iwata Ryōzō. "Shindai no amara-shiki ni tsuite." *Suzuki Gakujutsu Zaidan Kenkyū nempō*, 8 (1971): 46-56.
———. "Shindai no sanshōsetsu ni tsuite." *Indo bukkyōgaku kenkyū*, 21, no. 1 (December 1972): 355-58.
Jaini, Padmanabh S. "The Sautrāntika Theory of Bīja." *BSOAS*, 22, pt. II (1959): 236-49.
———. "The Vaibhāṣika Theory of Words and Meanings." *BSOAS*, 22, pt. I (1959): 95-107.
Jayatilleke, K. N. *Early Buddhist Theory of Knowledge*. London, 1963.
Kajiyama Yuichi. *An Introduction to Buddhist Philosophy*. Kyoto University Memoirs of the Faculty of Letters, no. 10. Kyoto, 1966.
Kamata Shigeo. *Chūgoku kegon shisōshi no kenkyū*. Tokyo, 1965.
Kamimura Shinjō. "Ken'yō-shōgyōron-naiyō no tokui ten." *Taishō Daigaku gakuhō*, 12 (May 1932): 130-65.
Katsumata Shunkyō. *Bukkyō ni okeru shinshikisetsu no kenkyū*. 3rd ed. Tokyo, 1969.
Kawakatsu Yoshio. "Kōkei no ran to Nanchō no kahei keizai." *Tōhō gakuho*, 32 (1962): 69-118.
———. "La décadence de l'aristocratie chinoise sous les Dynasties du Sud." *Acta Asiatica*, 21 (1971): 13-38.

Kokuyaku issaikyō. Edited by Ono Masao. Tokyo, 1958.

Koseki, Aaron. "Chi-tsang's *Ta-ch'eng-hsüan lun*: The Two Truths and the Buddha-Nature." Unpublished Ph.D. dissertation, University of Wisconsin, 1977.

Lai, Whalen. "Chinese Buddhist Causation Theories: An Analysis of a Sinitic Mahāyāna Understanding of *pratītya-samutpāda*." *Philosophy East and West*, 27, no. 3 (July 1977): 241-64.

Lamotte, Étienne. "Passions and Impregnations of the Passions in Buddhism." In *Buddhist Studies in Honour of I. B. Horner*, edited by L. Cousins. Dordrecht, 1974.

La Vallée Poussin, Louis de. "La Négation de l'âme et la doctrine de l'acte." *Journal Asiatique*, 1902-3, pp. 237-450.

McDermott, A. Charlene. "Asaṅga's Defense of Ālaya-Vijñāna." *Journal of Indian Philosophy*, 2 (1973): 167-74.

Majumdar, Ramesh Chandra. *Kambuja-deśa: An Ancient Hindu Colony in Cambodia*. Madras, 1944.

Malasekera, G. P. *Dictionary of Pali Proper Names*. London, 1960.

Malleret, Louis. *L'Archéologie du Delta du Mekong*, vol. 3: *La Culture du Fou-nan*. Paris, 1962.

Matilal, Bimal Krishna. "A Critique of Buddhist Idealism." In *Buddhist Studies in Honour of I. B. Horner*, edited by L. Cousins. Dordrecht, 1974.

———. *Epistemology, Logic, and Grammar in Indian Philosophical Analysis*. The Hague, 1971.

———. "Reference and Existence in Nyāya and Buddhist Logic." *Journal of Indian Philosophy*, 1, no. 1 (1970): 83-110.

Miyakawa Hisayuki. *Rikuchōshi kenkyū*. Tokyo, 1956.

Mochizuki Shinko. *Bukkyo Daijiten*. 10 vols. Kyoto, 1957.

———. "Daijō kishinron." *Nihon shūkyō kōza* (also titled *Nouveaux Cours des Religions Japonaises*), 2 (1934): 1-88.

Monier-Williams, M. *Sanskrit-English Dictionary*. Oxford, Eng., 1899; 2nd ed., 1970.

Mori Mikisaburō. *Ryō no butei*. Kyoto, 1956.

Morohashi Tetsuji. *Daikanwa jiten*. 11 vols. Tokyo, 1964.

Nagao Gadjin. *Chūkan to Yuishiki*. Tokyo, 1978.

———. "What Remains in Śūnyatā: A Yogācāra Interpretation of Emptiness." In *Mahāyāna Buddhist Meditation*, edited by Minoru Kiyota. Honolulu, 1978.

Nath, Jagan. "Early History of the Maitrakas of Valabhi." *Indian Culture*, April 1939, pp. 407-14.

Obermiller, E. "A Study of the Twenty Aspects of Śūnyatā." *Indian Historical Quarterly*, March 1933, pp. 170-87.

O'Brien, Paul Wilfred. "A Chapter on Reality from the *Madhyānta-vibhāga-śāstra*." *Monumenta Nipponica*, 9, no. 1-2 (1953): 277-303.

Ogawa Kōkan. *Chūgoku nyoraizō shisō kenkyū*. Tokyo, 1976.
———. "Shindai soyaku shōron ni okeru shiki." *Komazawa Daigaku Bukkyō gakubu kenkyū kiyō*, 23 (1965): 43-58.
Ota Hisanori. "Shindai sanzō soyaku ronten ni mirareru nyoraizō." *Indo bukkyōgaku kenkyū*, 14, no. 1 (December 1965): 189-92.
Paul, Diana Y. *The Buddhist Feminine Ideal: Queen Śrīmālā and the Tathāgatagarbha*. Missoula, Mont., 1980.
———. "The Concept of Tathāgatagarbha in the *Śrīmālādevī-sūtra* (Sheng-man ching)." *JAOS*, 99, no. 2 (April-June 1979): 191-203.
———. "An Introductory Note to Paramārtha's Theory of Language." *Journal of Indian Philosophy*, 7, no. 3 (September 1979): 231-55.
Reynolds, Frank E., and Capps, Donald, eds. *The Biographical Process: Studies in the History and Psychology of Religion*. The Hague, 1976.
Ruegg, David Seyfort. *La Théorie du Tathāgatagarbha et du Gotra*. Paris, 1969.
Saeki Join, ed. *Shindō jōyuishikiron*. Nara, 1940.
Sakaino Kōyō. *Shina bukkyō seishi*. Tokyo, 1935; 2nd ed., 1972.
Sakamoto Yukio. *Kegon kyōgaku no kenkyū*. Tokyo, 1956; 2nd ed., 1964.
Sasaki Gesshō. *Shōdaijōron*. Tokyo, 1931; 2nd ed., 1935.
Sasaki Gesshō and Yamaguchi Susumu. *Yuishiki nijuron no taiyaku kenkyū*. Tokyo, 1923; 2nd ed., 1977.
Sircar, Dines Chandra, ed. *Select Inscriptions Bearing on Indian History and Civilization*. Calcutta, 1965.
Stcherbatsky, Th. *Buddhist Logic*. Leningrad, 1930.
———. *The Central Conception of Buddhism*. London, 1923; reprint, Calcutta, 1961.
Streng, Frederick. "The Process of Ultimate Transformation in Nāgārjuna's Mādhyamika." *Eastern Buddhist*, 9, no. 2 (October 1978): 12-32.
Strickmann, Michel. "On the Alchemy of T'ao Hung-ching." In *Facets of Taoism: Essays in Chinese Religion*, edited by Holmes Welch and Anna Seidel. New Haven, 1979.
Suguro Shinjō. "Seshin Yuishiki sanjū-ju no kaishaku." *Osakigakuhō*, no. 103 (June 1955): 31-46.
Taishō shinshū daizōkyō. Edited by Takakusu Junjirō. 85 vols. Tokyo, 1914-22.
Takakusu Junjirō. "La Sāṃkhya-kārikā." *Bulletin de L'École Francaise d'Extrême Orient*, no. 4 (1904): 60-65.
Takasaki, Jikidō. "Shindaiyaku Shōdaijōron seshinshaku ni okeru nyoraizō setsu." *Bukkyō shisōshi ronshū*, 1963, pp. 241-63.
———. "Shōmangyō to Yuishiki shisō." *Shōtoku Taishi ronshū*, November 1971.
Takemura Makio. "Jiron-shū Shōron-shū Hossō-shū." In *Kōza Daijō Bukkyō*, edited by Takasaki Jikidō, vol. 8. Tokyo, 1982.

Takeuchi Shōkō. "Shindaiyaku ni okeru *manas* no yakugo ni tsuite." *Ryūkoku Daigaku ronshū*, no. 400-401 (March 1973): 234-42.

T'ang Yung-t'ung. *Han Wei Liang-chin Nan-pei-ch'ao Fo-chiao shih*. Shanghai, 1938.

Taranatha. *History of Buddhism in India*. Edited by Debiprasad Chattopradhyaya. Simla, 1970.

Tokiwa Daijō. *Busshō no kenkyū*. Tokyo, 1972.

———. *Shina bukkyō no kenkyū*. 3 vols. Tokyo, 1941; 2nd ed., 1978.

Tonkō koshakugyō. Edited by Nogami Shunjō. Vol. 2. Kyoto, 1972.

Tsurumi Ryōdō. "Shōman hōkutsu no senjō eji-setsu." *Komazawa daigaku bukkyō gakubu ronshū*, 6 (October 1975): 134-40.

Ueda Yoshifumi. *Bukkyō shisōshi kenkyū*. Kyoto, 1967.

———. *Yuishiki shisō nyūmon*. Kyoto, 1964.

Ui Hakujū. *Indo tetsugaku kenkyū*. 6 vols. Tokyo, 1930.

———. *Shōdaijōron kenkyū*. 2 vols. Tokyo, 1966.

Verdu, Alfonso. *Dialectical Aspects in Buddhist Thought: Studies in Sino-Japanese Mahāyāna Idealism*. Lawrence, Kans., 1974.

Watters, Thomas, trans. *On Yuan Chwang's Travels in India (629-645 A.D.)*. London, 1904.

Weinstein, Stanley. "The *Ālaya-vijñāna* in Early Yogācāra Buddhism." *Transactions of the International Conference of Orientalists in Japan*, 1958, pp. 46-58.

———. "The Concept of *Ālaya-vijñāna* in pre-T'ang Chinese Buddhism." In *Bukkyō shisōshi ronshū*, pp. 33-50. Tokyo, 1964.

Yamada Ryōsen. "Yuishiki kyogaku ni okeru manashiki no tokusei." *Ōtani gakuhō*, 22 (March 1941): 14-31.

Yoshida Dōkō. "Chūgoku nambokuchō Zui-Tō-sho no Jiron-Shōron no kenkyū shatatsu." *Komazawa Daigaku bukkyō gakubu ronshū*, 5 (December 1974): 91-101.

Yoshizu Yoshihide. "Eon no Kishinron-shū o meguru shomondai." *Komazawa daigaku bukkyō gakubu ronshū*, 3 (December, 1972): 82-97.

Yūki Reimon. *Seshin yuishiki no kenkyū*. Tokyo, 1955.

———. "Shina Yuishikigaku shijō ni okeru Ryōga-shi no chii." *Shina bukkyō shigaku*, 1 (May 1937): 21-44.

———. "Tenjikiron to Yuishiki Sanjū-ju to no dōhon iyaku kankei o utagau." *Tohō gakuhō*, no. 11, pt. 1 (March 1940): 384-93.

Character List

An-le
安樂

A-yü-wang ching
阿育王經

chai
宅

Ch'an-ting
禪定

Chang Fan
長凡

Chang Szu (Chang Fan)
張記(張氾)

Chao-t'ai
紹泰

Ch'ao-ting
潮亭

chen-ju
真如

Ch'en shu
陳書

Chen-ti
真諦

Chen-ti i
真諦訳

Chen yüan hsin ting shih chiao mu lu
貞元新定釈教目録

Cheng-kuan temple
正觀

Ch'eng k'ung pin
成空品

Cheng lun shih i
正論釈義

Ch'eng-sheng
承聖

Ch'eng wei-shih lun (CWSL)
成唯識論

Ch'eng wei-shih lun liao-i teng
成唯識論了義燈

Ch'eng wei-shih lun shu-chi
成唯識論疏記

ch'eng wu-hsing p'in
成無性品

Ch'i-hsin lun
起信論

Chi-tsang
吉藏

chia
家

Chiang-ling
江陵
Chieh-chieh ching (CCC)
解節経
Chieh shen-mi ching shu
解深密経疏
Chien-hsing
建興
Chien-k'ang
建康
Chien pei i-ch'ieh chih te ching
漸備一切智徳経
Chien-tsao
建造
Chien-wen
簡文
Chien-yüan
建元
chih
止
Chih-chi
智敫
Chih-chih
制旨
Chih-hsiu
智休
Chih-i
智顗
Chih-k'ai
智愷
Chih-ning
智凝
Chih-shou
智首
Chih-tse
智則
Chih-wen
智文
Chih-yen
智厳
Chin-an
晋安
ching-chieh
境界
Ching-shao
警韶
Ching-t'ai
靜泰
ching-t'u
清土
Ching-ying
浄影
Chiu shih i p'in
九識義品
Chiu shih p'in
九識品
Chou shu
周書
ch'u
麁
chuan
転
chuan-i
転依
Chuan shih lun (CSL)
転識論
Chüeh ting tsang lun (CTTL)
決定藏論
Chung ching mu-lu (FC)
衆経目録
Chung-kuan lun shu
中観論疏
Chung-pien fen-pieh lun
中辺分別論
Chung-yün tien
重雲殿
Fa-ch'ang
法常
Fa-chieh t'i hsing wu fen-pieh ching
法界体性無分別経
Fa-ching
法経
Fa-chun
法准
Fa-hsiang
法相
Fa-hu
法護
Fa-hua hsüan-i shih ch'ien
法華玄義釈籤

Fa-jen
法忍
Fa-k'an
法兄
Fa-shang
法上
Fa-t'ai
法泰
Fa-tsang
法藏
Fa wu-tzu-hsing p'in
法無自性品
fen-pieh hsing
分別性
Fo-li temple
仏力
Fu-ch'un
富春
Funan
扶南
Gyōnen
凝然
han-jen
寒人
han-men
寒民
Hou Ching
侯景
hsi-ch'i
習氣
hsiang
相
hsiang hsi-ch'i
相習氣
hsiang huo lei
相感類
Hsiang-tung
湘東
Hsiao Ch'a
蕭察
Hsiao Chi
蕭紀
Hsiao Fang-chih
蕭方智
Hsiao I
蕭繹
Hsiao Kang
蕭綱
Hsiao Po
蕭勃
Hsiao Tung
蕭棟
Hsiao Wu
孝武
Hsiao Yü
蕭譽
Hsiao Yüan-ming
蕭淵明
Hsien-ming
顯明
Hsien shih lun (HSL)
顯識論
Hsien-yang sheng-chiao lun (HYSCL)
顯揚聖教論
hsin
心
Hsin-ho chin kuang-ming ching
新合金光明経
Hsü kao seng chuan (HKSC)
續高僧伝
Hsüan-tsang
玄奘
hsün-hsi
熏習
Hua-yen
華嚴
Hui-chao
慧沼
Hui-hsien
慧顯
Hui-jen
慧忍
Hui-k'ai
慧愷
Hui-k'uang
慧曠
Hui-ming
慧明
Hui-yüan
慧遠
Hui-yün
慧雲
Hung-shih
弘始

i
義

i (manas)
意

i-t'a-hsing
依他性

Jen wang ching shu
仁王経疏

Jen wang pan-jo ching
仁王般若経

Jih-yen
日厳

ju-lai-tsang
如来藏

K'ai-huang
開皇

K'ai-yüan shih chiao mu-lu (KYL)
開元釈教目録

Kao Ch'eng
高澄

Kao Huan
高歡

Kao seng chuan (KSC)
高僧伝

Kao Yang
高洋

Kegon jūjū yuishiki jōkanki
華厳十重唯識瑺鑑記

Kegon kumokushō hotsugoki
華厳孔目章發悟記

Ku-chin i ching t'u chi (KC)
古今訳経図紀

Kuang-i fa-men ching
廣義法門経

Kuang-ta
光大

Kuang-t'ai
光太

K'uei-chi
窺基

Leng-chia-a-pa-to-lo pao ching
楞伽阿跋多羅宝経

Li-k'ung p'in
立空品

Li-tai san-pao chi (LTSPC)
歷代三宝紀

Liang-an
梁安

Liang-shu
梁書

Lin-ch'uan
臨川

Liu Wen-t'o
劉文陀

Lu Yüan-che
陸元哲

Lung-an
隆安

Mei-yeh
美業

Mi-lo hsia sheng ching
彌勒下生経

Miao-fa lien-hua ching hsüan-i
妙法蓮華経玄義

Ming-yung
明勇

Mo-ho chih kuan
摩訶止観

Nan-k'ang
南康

Nan-ling
南嶺

Nan shih
南史

nan-yüeh
南越

neng-pien
能変

neng-yüan
能縁

Ouyang Ho
歐陽紇

Ouyang Wei
歐陽頠

Pai-t'a
白塔
Pao-ch'iung
宝瓊
Pao-kuei
宝貴
Pao-t'ien
宝田
Pao-yün
宝雲
Peng-ch'eng
彭城
p'u-sa t'ien-tzu
菩薩天子
P'u-sa tsang ching
菩薩蔵経
San wu-hsing lun (SWHL)
三無性論
Seng-jung
僧榮
Seng-ming
僧明
Seng-pien
僧辯
Seng-ta
僧達
Seng-tsung
僧宗
Shan-hui
善慧
She chüeh tse fen
摂決擇分
She-lun
摂論
she-shen
捨身
She ta-sheng lun
摂大乗論
She ta-sheng lun chang
摂大乗論章
shen-hsien
神仙
shen-wu
深悟
Sheng-man ching
勝鬘経
shih
事
Shih-ch'i ti-lun
十七地論
Shih chu ching
十住経
shih chuan
識転
Shih-hsing
始興
Shih-pa k'ung lun (SPKL)
十八空論
shih so-pien
識所変
shih-tsang
識蔵
shih yüeh
釈曰
so fen-pieh
所分別
so-yüan
所縁
Ssu-fen-lü shu shih-tsung i-chi
四分律疏飾宗義記
Ssu-t'ien-wang
四天王
ssu-wei
思惟
Sui-hsiang lun shih-liu ti shu
随相論十六諦疏
Ta-chou k'an ting chung-ching mu-lu (TCL)
大周刊定衆経目録
Ta fa ku ching
大法鼓経
Ta-pao
大宝
Ta-sheng ch'i-hsin lun
大乗起信論
Ta-sheng ch'i hsin lun i-chi
大乗起信論義記
Ta-sheng chuang-yen ching lun
大乗荘厳経論

Ta-sheng i chang 大乘義章

Ta-sheng pao-yün ching 大乘宝雲経

Ta-sheng wei-shih lun 大乘唯識論

Ta t'ang nei tien lu (NTL) 大唐内典録

Ta-tsung-chih 大總持

Ta-t'ung 大同

Ta-yen 大衍

T'ai-chien 太建

T'ai-ch'ing 太清

T'ai-pao 太宝

T'an-ch'ien 曇遷

T'an-luan 曇鸞

T'an-tsun 曇遵

T'an-yen 曇延

T'an-yin 曇隠

Tao-an 道安

Tao-chi 道基

Tao-hsüan 道宣

Tao-ni 道尼

Tao-yüeh 道岳

t'i 体

Ti-lun 地論

T'ien-chia 天嘉

T'ien-kuan 天観

T'ien-pao 天宝

T'ien-t'ai 天泰

Ting-pin 定賓

Ts'ao P'i 曹毗

ts'u chung hsi-ch'i 麁重習氣

Tun-lun 遁倫

T'ung-t'ai 同泰

Tzu-en (K'uei-chi) 慈恩

tzu-hsing 自性

Wang Chung-hsüan 王仲宣

Wang Fang-she 王方奢

wang nien 妄念

Wang Seng-pien 王僧辯

wei-shih 唯識

Wei-shih lun 唯識論

Wei-shih lun wen-i ho ○文義合

wei shun 違順

Wen-hsüan 文宣

Wen-shu-shih-li so shuo pan-jo po-lo-mi ching 文殊師利所説般若波羅密経

Wŏnch'ŭk 圓測

Wu 武

wu-ch'en wei-shih 無塵唯識

wu chieh-t'o
無解脱

wu ch'ü-shou
無取授

Wu-hsiang lun (WHL)
無相論

wu-hsing
無性

wu-kou
無垢

Wu-shang i ching
無上依経

Yang Hsiung
楊雄

Yen Chih-t'ui
顔之推

yin-yüan
因縁

you ch'ü-shou
有取授

yu
有

Yü-chia lun-chi
瑜伽論記

Yü-chia shih ti lun
瑜伽師地論

Yü-wen T'ai
宇文泰

yüan
縁

Yüan-ch'an
願禪

Yüan-chao
圓照

Yüan-chia
元嘉

Yüan-k'ang
元康

yung
用

Yung-ting
永定

Index